MENTAL RETARDATION IN SOCIAL CONTEXT

Duane F. Stroman

UNIVERSITY
PRESS OF
AMERICA

Copyright © 1989 by

University Press of America,® Inc.

4720 Boston Way
Lanham, MD 20706

All rights reserved

Printed in the United States of America

Library of Congress Cataloging-in-Publication Data

Stroman, Duane F.
Mental retardation in social context / by Duane F. Stroman.
p.   cm.
Bibliography: p.
Includes index.
1. Mentally handicapped– –United States. 2. Mentally handicapped–
–Care– –United States– –History. 3. Mentally handicapped– –Government
policy– –United States. 4. Mentally handicapped– –Services for–
–United States. 5. Mental retardation. I. Title.
HV3006.A4S77   1989   89–5455 CIP
362.3'0973– –dc19
ISBN 0–8191–7392–4 (alk. paper)
ISBN 0–8191–7393–2 (pbk. : alk. paper)

All University Press of America books are produced on acid-free paper.
The paper used in this publication meets the minimum requirements of American
National Standard for Information Sciences—Permanence of Paper for Printed Library
Materials, ANSI Z39.48–1984.   ∞

Acknowledgements

In writing a book such as this, a writer draws on the thinking and research of many individuals. In addition to those recognized in the citations and bibliography, I want to extend my deep appreciation to the following authors, editors and/or publishing firms that have given me permission to quote more extended passages from their published works:

To Jane R. Mercer(author) and Richard Koch(editor) for quotations found on pages 29 and 33 in this work found on pages 28 and 45 of Jane R. Mercer, "The Meaning of Mental Retardation"(1976) in R. Koch & J. Dobson(Eds.). *The Mentally Retarded Child and His Family*(2nd Ed.). New York: Brunner/Mazel.

To Haworth Press Inc. for Figure 5.1 found on page 134 of this work from the figure found on page 15 of R. Perlman and J.Z. Giele, "An Unstable Triad: Dependents' Demands, Family Resources, Community Supports"(1983) in R. Perlman(Ed.). *Family Home Care.* New York: Haworth Press.

To Richard C. Scheerenberger and the Paul H. Brookes Publishing Co. for quotations found on pages 97, 98, 115, 124-25 in this work from passages found on pages 175, 250, and 254 in Scheerenberger, Richard C. *A History of Mental Retardation.* Baltimore: Paul H. Brookes Publishing Co.(PO Box 10624, Baltimore, MD 21285-0624), c. 1983.

To the American Association on Mental Retardation(formerly AAMD) for quotations found in this book on pages 17-18, 19-20, and 21-22 from passages found on pages 1, 25, and 204-5 in H.J. Grossman. *Classification in Mental Retardation.* Washington: American Association of Mental Deficiency, 1983; and for the table found on page 214 of this work taken from page 243 of F.A. Hauber, R. H. Bruininks, B.K. Hill, H.C. Lakin, R.L. Scheerenberger, and C.C. White. "National Census of Residential Facilities: A 1982 Profile of Facilities and Residents," *American Journal of Mental Deficiency* 83, 3, 234-45, 1984.

To Houghton Mifflin Co. for the right to quote the fourteen principles to facilitate learning found on pages 281-82 of this work and located on pages 156-58 of S.A. Kirk and J.J. Gallagher. *Educating Exceptional Children*(4th Ed.). New York: Houghton Mifflin, 1983.

To Pro-Ed Inc. (8700 Shoal Creek Blvd., Austin, TX 78758) who owns the rights to the following two works, for the permission to quote passages found on pages 204-5, 207-8 of this book found on pages 139, 143-44 and 148 in G. Patterson, "Basic Principles and Philosophies for Developing Residential Services in the Community," in P. Roos, B. McCann and M.R. Addison(Eds.). *Shaping the Future.* Baltimore: University Park Press, 137-49, 1980; and for the right to quote the passage found on pages 127-28 of this work from pages 32-33 of Bengt Nirje, "The Normalization Principle," in R. Flynn and K. Nitsch(Eds.). *Normalization, Social Integration and Community Services.* Baltimore: University Park Press, 31-50, 1980.

To Aubrey Milunsky for the permission to use the table found on pages 65-66 of this work located on page 16 of A. Milunsky, "Genetic Aspects of Mental Retardation: From Prevention to Cure," in F.J. Menolascino, R. Newman and J.A. Stark(Eds.). *Curative Aspects of Mental Retardation.* Baltimore: Paul H. Brookes, 15-26, 1983.

To Jack A. Stark for permission to use the table found on page 88 of this work taken from page 5 of J.A. Stark, "The Search for Cures of Mental Retardation," in F.J. Menolascino, R. Newman and J.A. Stark(Eds.). *Curative Aspective of Mental Retardation.* Baltimore: Paul H. Brookes, 1-8, 1983.

To Bonnie Shoultz and Paul Williams for the permission to quote the passages found on pages 191-192, 194-195, and 196 of this work as found originally in pages 51, 223-224, 29-30, 54 and 56 of Paul Williams and Bonnie Shoultz. *We Can Speak for Ourselves.* Bloomington: Indiana University Press, 1982.

I would also like to publicly thank Sylvia Kurtz for doing an excellent job of word-processing the manuscript into clear print, for imaginatively compressing large tables into sizes allowed by the publisher, and for assisting in the construction of the index.

And I also want to thank my wife, June, for understanding my long absences from home while I worked on this book about persons and issues about which I feel strongly.

Table of Contents

List of Tables and Figures

Preface

The content of this book originates from three sources. The first is my experience as a teacher in a course entitled, Mental and Physical Handicaps. I found no single book that pulled together both the academic material dealing with mental retardation and the many practical aspects of providing services to those who are mentally retarded. I wanted to write a useful book that looked at the nature of intelligence and its origins while at the same time it described the wide and growing range of services provided to the mentally retarded. I wanted students to be aware of the historical evolution of the treatment of the retarded so that the policy issues in the treatment of the retarded could be understood within the social, political and economic context of the times in which they were created.

The second origin of this book arose from my experience as an administrator of a for-profit company that provides residential and behavior shaping services to the mentally retarded. I wanted to write a book that would be of some assistance to direct service staff who work with the mentally retarded on a daily basis. I did not want to write a "how to" book but rather one that would give service providers an overview of the complex origin and nature of the normalization movement, and the need for and range of health, educational, residential, advocacy and social services that would enhance the development of handicapped persons. I wanted to write a book that describes not only the goals of normalization but fleshed out those goals with substantial illustrations of social science research findings.

The third origin of this book is what I perceived as a need to deal with some of the policy issues in mental retardation. What kind of services are needed by the mentally retarded, who should provide them and how should they be paid for? These questions are indirectly raised in many chapters and finally deal with what kind of a society we are and want to be. Sometimes these issues are dealt with only in specialized monographs rather than in more eclectic textbooks. Of the four books I have written this book turned out to be the most difficult. Perhaps this is so because of the diversity of the literature dealing with the many aspects of retardation. In this book one will find ideas ranging from the genetic inheritance of intelligence to the social factors which precipitated the self-advocacy movement, from the cost of operating group homes to the legal aspects of the right of mentally retarded to bear children, and from the problems of operating rehabilitation workshops to the educational politics of integrating handicapped students into the least restrictive environment. It is my hope that I have dealt with these issues in an interesting and informative and objective way so that the reader comes away with a better understanding of mental retardation and how our society has changed in its treatment of the mentally impaired.

Duane Stroman
Huntingdon, Pennsylvania
December 1, 1988

Chapter 1

Issues in Mental Retardation

This book is about people with impaired intelligence who often face a variety of problems in coping with life. The purpose of this very brief chapter is to identify the major questions that will be addressed in the remainder of the book. By first raising the questions and indicating their importance I hope to stimulate the reader by getting him or her into the issues I have raised and attempted to answer in each chapter.

In Chapter 2, the Nature, Prevalence and Variations of Mental Retardation, I raise a number of questions. The first of these has to do with the meaning of intelligence. How would you describe an intelligent or unintelligent person? What mental, verbal, social or physical characteristics would you expect of such persons? Is intelligence a series of traits or is it qualities of the mind involved in processing information and making judgments? Is intelligence something that is inherited, or is it a product of a person's environment or is it a product of both genetic endowment and environmental opportunities and constraints in interaction?

Once you have defined intelligence how do you measure it? Can it be done by observation and if so what is to be observed? Can it be measured by paper and pencil tests and put into test score results that will be reliable over time? Many issues exist over how to measure the many facets of intelligence.

Since mental retardation is at the low end of the continuum we call intelligence, how do we define the cutoff point? What are the gradations of low intelligence and how many persons are in each of the gradations? How has the terminology relating to degrees of retardation changed

1

over time? And is mental retardation related to other handicapping conditions such as epilepsy, Down Syndrome, mental illness, poor health, and a variety of physical disabilities?

In Chapter 3, The Causes and Prevention of Mental Retardation, I look at two central questions the answers to which are very complex and not unanimously agreed upon. The first question concerns the causes of retardation. The answer is that there is strong evidence for both the biological and environmental origins of retardation. However, the biological origins can be subdivided into a complex variety of genetic and nongenetic factors while the environmental origins are difficult to conceptualize and measure. A related question here is how to develop models that will aid in our understanding of the hereditability and environmental origins of mental retardation. The second major question has to do with the prevention and "cure" of retardation. How much retardation by what steps and at what costs can be prevented? Is it realistic to assume we can reduce the prevalence of retardation by 50% as one President's Committee on Mental Retardation did? How would this be done? What social issues are involved in some forms of prevention such as abortion? Or if retardation is detected, can the severity of it be reduced by some biological and/or "educational" intervention? These are important questions for the answers will determine incidence and prevalence rates in the future and the kinds of human, economic, and social costs that will be borne by handicapped individuals, their parents and society at large.

In Chapter 4, The Treatment of the Mentally Retarded in Historical Perspective, I start off with an analytical scheme of different models of perception. These seven models of how the mentally retarded have been perceived are (1)as sick persons, (2)as subhuman, (3)as a menace, (4)as objects of pity, (5)as a burden of charity, (6)as a holy innocent, and (7)as capable of development. In various periods of American history some of these models were predominant while others were subthemes or relatively dormant. Why is this the case? What social forces were at work that emphasized optimistic models of growth around the civil war period only to turn into pessimistic models of the retarded around the turn of the century and then back to optimistic growth models in the 1960s. How did these models of perception affect social policy toward

2

them as regards education, residential segregation or integration, family life, work, sterilization and the provision of a range of services? Understanding how social policies are the product of the perception of the nature of a problem is an important contribution of this chapter.

In Chapter 5, Mental Retardation and Family Life, I look at how retardation affects the family in two situations--where a child is retarded and where a retarded adult enters marriage and perhaps becomes a parent. More attention is given to the first situation because it is much more common. The key questions I address where a retarded child is born into a family is what effects such a child has on the family, the kinds of responses family members make to this occurrence, the variables that influence these responses, and the outcomes on the life styles of all family members. I ask questions about how families make decisions and what decisions they make in caring for a retarded person. I look at how families feel about having a retarded member in their family including prenatal decisions when evidence suggests the child will be born with physical deformities and/or mental retardation.

While about 95% of all children with retardation stay with their natural families, we look at the stresses such families experience in locating community assistance and sufficient time to deal with the often extraordinary demands such a child can make on them. We also look at the 5% of the retarded who are placed in outside-of-home residential placements. Special attention is given to the stigma associated with being different, stresses on siblings, the care of older retarded persons in the homes of aging parents, and the return of institutionalized clients to their own homes. How are such releases initiated and how do they work out for both the family and the retarded person?

Since family home care seems to be the most natural setting and most cost efficient location for residential care, I investigate to what extent public policy supports family home care by natural parents. And lastly, I look at the rights of the retarded to not be sterilized, to marry, to bear and to raise children. A key question here is how much the states vary in protecting such rights.

In Chapter 6, Services, Advocacy Services, and Self Advocacy in Normalization, I look at the historical development of a range of services for the retarded not only in the United States but also in Europe. As in much social science writing, the question of norms and values arises in this as well as in other chapters. And so the question of what services should be provided to the mentally retarded is addressed in this chapter. But the question is more complicated than simply what services should be provided. Questions also arise as to how and when and where services should be provided as well as other policy issue questions such as who should bear the costs of special and generic services to not only the mentally retarded but persons with other or additional handicapping conditions.

The values and goals for assisting developmentally handicapped persons have been captured in the last 30 years in a number of value-laden theme terms--normalization, integration and deinstitutionalization. What do these terms mean in terms of concrete educational, residential, advocacy and prevention programs? These questions are explored. In this chapter I look at how and why the "rights" of the retarded have been expanded and clarified in recent decades. I also investigate how self-advocacy began among the handicapped and the directions it is taking.

In Chapter 7, Deinstitutionalization and the Residential Lives of the Retarded, I look at the roots of the deinstitutionalization movement--the movement to keep retardates out of large state asylums housing hundreds or thousands of clients or to move clients out of such large institutions back into smaller residences including that of their own families. I investigate the roots of this social movement which has affected not only the mentally retarded but also the mentally ill and other stigmatized handicapping conditions. I also raise questions about the meanings and goals of deinstitutionalization.

There are many possible classifications of residential settings. I describe these classifications to more fully understand the continuum of residential locations for retarded people that are usually related, at least in theory, to the severity and configuration of their impairments.

In this chapter I ask what are the long term trends in the residential locations of retardates. Next, I raise questions and give some answers on different methodological approaches to evaluating if particular residential locations are the most appropriate, effective and efficient methods of providing residential care for the retarded. Because the evaluation of outcomes of residential care services is quite

4

complex, I look at three particular research studies which attempt to evaluate the benefits and problems of residential services. And lastly, I look at how state and particularly federal policies which fund residential programs constrain it toward larger institutional models that are probably the most expensive. We ask why this is the case.

In Chapter 8, Education of the Mentally Retarded, I give particular attention to the major changes which have come about recently as a result of the 1975 passage of the Education for All Handicapped Children Act and other educational legislation and test court cases. I ask questions not only about what such legislation requires of schools but also the politics of its passage. I investigate the evolution of public education for the retarded by noting its progression from nothing being done, to special residential schools, to special classes, to special classes for the more severely retarded and finally the integration of retarded and other handicapped children into regular schools and classrooms in various degrees.

I provide evidence on the growth of federal financial support for the education of the handicapped and the key requirements of the federal legislation directed toward normalizing the developmental skills and environments of those with physical and mental impairments.

In attempting to answer the question of whether an integrated educational placement is beneficial, I explore the range of educational placements that have been worked out to deal with the general principle of the most appropriate educational environment for a given handicapped person. I look at different infant, preschool and school age programs that have been developed to deal with handicapping conditions as well as their results. What does educational research show as regards the outcomes of different educational strategies for children with varying degrees of retardation?

In the last chapter, Chapter 9, Vocational Services and Employment for the Retarded, I raise questions about the kinds of work people with varying mental deficiencies can do and what are the most appropriate training and work settings for them. I end up using a continuum of training and work sites that range from adult day programs to sheltered workshops to individual competitive employment to illustrate the range of alternatives that could be and are used to involve the retarded in work that is socially useful and personally meaningful.

In this chapter I explore questions about where the retarded work, their unemployment rates, their patterns of income, work adjustment and daily life. I also explore the impediments the mentally retarded face in getting training and getting and keeping jobs. In this discussion I explore seven myths that often hold back handicapped workers from participating in work that is most appropriate for them.

Since sheltered workshops are the work placements for many persons below the mild level of retardation, special attention is given to the problems such workshops face and the policy issues which stifle change.

The field of mental retardation has witnessed many dynamic changes in the past two decades. It provides an academic field to explore the many elements of what it is to be both human and different. It provides an employment field with many challenges as we explore ways to make us more competent as human beings.

Chapter 2

The Nature, Prevalence and Variations of Mental Retardation

OVERVIEW OF ISSUES

This book is about people who have varying degrees of difficulty in successfully coping with the adjustment tasks of life because of impaired intelligence. Variations in the degree to which they have difficulty coping with the tasks of living is primarily related to the extent of their intellectual impairment. But it can also be substantially influenced by their physical handicaps, their appearances, the attitudes of society toward developmentally disabled persons, the needs of the society in which they live and the quantity and quality of services provided to them to assist in coping with life's demands in our society. A critical point to be made is that there is a huge variation among the persons with mental retardation. Those labeled as mentally retarded vary greatly in measured intelligence, adaptive skills, personality, motivation and the presence or absence of one or more handicapping conditions. At one extreme of those classified as mentally retarded are the mildly retarded whose intellectual deficit primarily influences academic success during the school years and restricts opportunities in some adult jobs. At the other end of the extreme are those with such severe intellectual deficits that every aspect of their life is touched by it so that they become very highly dependent on others.

This book covers the three fundamental questions which can be raised about mental retardation--what is it?, what causes it?, and how have and are the mentally

7

retarded treated? While all of these are important, greater space is given to the treatment and management questions because of the complexity and rapid changes going on in the areas of prevention, detection and especially habilitation services for the mentally retarded from infancy to adulthood. The goal of habilitation services are the same for all people, whether handicapped or not, and that is to enable people to live full lives at the highest level of competence of which they are capable.

In this chapter we investigate:

(1)the nature of intelligence and its measurement;
(2)definitions of mental retardation;
(3)perspectives on the significance of mental retardation;
(4)the prevalence of mental retardation under different definitions of it;
(5)historical changes in the terminology relating to mental retardation; and
(6)the relationship of mental retardation to other handicaps.

THE MEANING AND MEASUREMENT OF INTELLIGENCE

The Meaning of Intelligence

The meaning and measurement of intelligence have been two of the central concerns that psychologists have investigated. Both the meaning and measurement of intelligence remain embroiled in controversy. Hundreds of definitions of intelligence have been offered and dozens of tests have been developed and modified over time in ongoing attempts to measure intelligence. Therefore, the reader should be aware that this is a complex area with thousands of books and articles on the subject.

While there is much disagreement on what intelligence is and how it can best be measured, there is some agreement on the key behaviors that are reflective of intelligence. Sternberg(1981) argues that the ability to learn and profit from experience, to acquire knowledge from experience, to reason and to adapt to changing conditions are the main cognitive components of intelligence. This

8

definition is not radically different from the *American Heritage Dictionary of the English Language*(1976, 682) which defines intelligence as (1)the capacity to acquire and supply knowledge, (2)the faculty of thought and reason, and (3)superior powers of mind. Binet, the originator of intelligence tests, defined intelligence as "the tendency to take and maintain a definite direction; the capacity to make adaptations for the purpose of attaining a desired end; and the power of autocriticism"(Terman, 1916, 45). Wechsler(1958, 7), a psychologist who developed a series of widely used intelligence tests, defined intelligence as the "aggregate or global capacity of the individual to act purposefully, to think rationally, and to deal effectively with his environment."

The word intelligence is a construct rather than a directly observable characteristic of individuals or directly observable processes that go on within the central nervous system. Therefore, it may be difficult to come to an agreement on how to define intelligence since its measurement involves assessing a variety of capabilities. How these capabilities are conceptualized and measured influences the interpretation of the nature of intelligence.

Differing Conceptual Approaches to the Nature of Intelligence

Since outward behaviors may be regarded as manifestations of intelligence, two major approaches have been used to conceptualize what intelligence is. One approach conceptualizes intelligence as a series of basic mental capacities while the other approach focuses on processes that are used in problem solving. The first approach attempts to identify and measure behaviors which underlie capacities or structures within an individual. The second approach, carried out by information-processing theorists, focuses on various components or steps of information processing that are involved in reasoning, generalization and other steps involved in information processing(Baroff, 1986).

Intelligence as a series of basic mental capacities. This conceptual model of intelligence as basic capacities has evolved over time with the development of IQ tests and the advancement of factor analysis as a statistical tool to identify "factors" that are correlated. In its early stages of

9

development, for example, Spearman saw intelligence as a relatively unitary concept that relied on a single general factor (g) and an indefinite factor and a series of two or more other abilities. For example, Hebb(1949) tried to resolve some of the issues over whether intelligence was inherited (as earlier assumed) or also influenced by the environment by distinguishing between what he labeled as Intelligence A and Intelligence B. He argued Intelligence A is genetically determined, located in the central nervous system and is the basic potentiality of the organism to learn and adapt to the environment. In contrast, Intelligence B, the product of genetic potential in interaction with the environment, is the only thing we can measure(Graham & Lilly, 1984).

In a similar vein, Cattell(1971) has identified two core abilities: (1)crystallized intelligence and (2)fluid intelligence. Crystallized intelligence involves capacity in dealing with verbal meanings and relies more heavily on cultural learning. In contrast, fluid intelligence involves capacities related to adapting to new situations, response time, learning in new areas, nonverbal tasks and is more genetically determined.

The Thurstones(1941) rejected an underlying general factor(g) and instead identified seven primary mental abilities: (1)verbal comprehension, (2)verbal fluency, (3)verbal reasoning, (4)memory, (5)spatial understanding, (6)perceptual speed, and (7)number fluency.

Guilford(1967) has developed one of the most complex multifactorial conceptualizations of intelligence. He argues that there are 120 abilities that can be measured by tests of intelligence. In his model there are five operations or primary abilities that deal with four forms of content that can yield six different types of products of information. Operations are basic cognitive capacities that include (1)cognition (knowing or understanding pieces of information), (2)memory (recalling information), (3)divergent production (generating alternative ideas), (4)convergent production (identifying a best solution among alternative possibilities), and (5)evaluation (reaching a judgment based on some standard). The content of mental operations can take four forms: (1)figural (pictorial), (2)symbolic (numbers, letters, codes), (3)semantic (words), and (4)behavioral (understanding the meaning of behavior). The six products of information that reflect the outcomes of

10

operations on content are (1)units, (2)classes, (3)relations, (4)systems, (5)transformations, and (6)implications.

Intelligence as Information Processing. Sternberg(1985, 59) distinguishes among three types of information-processing components after he defines a component as "an elementary information process that operates on internal representations of objects and symbols." Each of these three kinds of components can be applied in task performance for reaching some solution or goal. The three components in the Sternberg model are (1)metacomponents which are higher order control processes used in planning, monitoring, and evaluating some task performance, (2)lower-order performance components used in various strategies of carrying out a task, and (3)knowledge-acquisition components which involve learning new information and storing it in memory. The mentally retarded are often found to have deficits in all three areas of information processing but particularly in acquiring knowledge and knowing how to plan, monitor and evaluate their own task performance. Sternberg's theory is rather complex but reflects the difficulty of conceptualizing cognitive processes. For example, ten separate metacomponents are believed to be involved in intelligent functioning. These include (1)recognition of a problem, (2)determining the nature of the problem, (3)selecting a set of lower-order performance tasks to be executed like encoding the nature of a stimulus, inferring relations between two similar stimulus terms and applying a previously inferred relation to a new situation and/or acquiring new information and comparing it to earlier information, (4)selecting a strategy for task performance that combines relevant lower-order components, (5)selecting relevant information components, (6)deciding on how to allocate attentional resources, (7)monitoring task performance in terms of tasks completed and those needing completion, (8)understanding both internal and external feedback about the quality of task performance, (9)knowing how to act on the feedback information that is received, and (10)implementing action as a result of the feedback.

The two approaches described above to understand intelligence are not mutually exclusive but can be viewed as complementary. The capacities approach attempts to identify one or more factors or mental capabilities that help to identify what intelligent behavior is. It is like a "still" picture. The process approach is more like a movie that attempts to show the factors in operation. Piaget's developmental theory of intelligence combines these two approaches by showing that intelligence develops in stages over time as children mature biologically and psychologically from infancy to adulthood. Piaget(1966) identifies four stages in the development of intelligence among normal children:

Sensorimotor intelligence. This stage covers the first two years of life and is marked by a growing awareness of the self, the external world and of the distinction of these two. The infant begins to crawl, stand, walk, speak and planful "intelligent" behavior emerges.

Preoperational intelligence. This stage covers the years from 2-7 and sees the fuller development of language and the ability to deal with color, size, numbers and ideas of beauty. But the development of rationality has not begun yet inasmuch as the child cannot understand logic, consistency or the effect of more than one variable at a time on some outcome.

Concrete operations. This stage, from 7 to 11 years, shows greater logicalness and consistency in thought. The child can consider events from the perspective of others and not simply his own egocentric view dominant in the preoperational phase. The child can now begin to group things into categories and hierarchies, can understand multiple factors influencing outcomes, and make finer distinctions about the similarities and differences among things.

Formal operations. In this last stage of mental development, beginning at age 11, the child can begin dealing with abstract logical relationships, inspect theoretical and not only real world alternatives, deal with multicausal theories, deal with strategies to learn, and use formal reasoning in analyzing relationships.

The Measurement of Intelligence

The measurement of intelligence has gone through an evolution more complex than the attempt to define the term. Since Binet first developed an intelligence test in 1905 to help the French government distinguish between normal students and those intellectually limited so they could be removed from regular classrooms for special educational instruction, hundreds of tests of intelligence have been developed and modified(Kaplan & Saccuzzo, 1982). However, a few tests of intelligence have emerged as superior as marked by their widespread use and not necessarily because they are beyond criticism. We will give particular attention to several of these as follow:

> The Stanford-Binet Intelligence Scale(1960 revision).

> Wechsler Primary and Preschool Scale of Intelligence(WPPSI) for ages 4 to 16.

> Wechsler Intelligence Scale-Revised(WISC-R) for ages 6 to 16.

> Wechsler Adult Intelligence Scale-Revised(WAIS-R) for ages 16 to 74.

The Stanford-Binet Intelligence Scale. Alfred Binet eventually defined intelligence in terms of an individual's capacity to (1)find and maintain a definite direction or purpose, (2)adjust strategy if necessary to achieve that purpose, and (3)evaluate or criticize that strategy so that necessary adjustment could be made(Kaplan & Saccuzzo, 1982). Binet's first intelligence test was developed in conjunction with Simon. It was composed of thirty items of increasing difficulty and was individually rather than group-administered. It involved tasks to measure judgment, attention, and reasoning. Since then it has gone through numerous revisions with the last one in 1960 although it is currently being revised. Unlike the Wechsler intelligence scales, it has no subtest or subtest scores indicating performance in different areas such as verbal fluency, digit manipulation or arithmetic. Thus, it utilizes a single score to estimate general intelligence. Revisions of the test and its scoring have added to the concepts of chronological age, mental age, the intelligence quotient and the deviation IQ. Each of these terms is important. Chronological age is simply the number of months and years a person has lived. Mental age is determined by the total score on the test and whether that score is comparable to the average score of a large random sample of persons of the same chronological age. Thus a mental age of 7 sug-

13

gests that a seven year old person is functioning like a typical 7 year old as regard to mental functioning. At the outset Binet and Simon had suggested that a child be considered retarded if his mental age was two or more years below his chronological age. But a two-year lag in mental age would be a more serious deficit in a 4-year old than a 16-year old. Subsequently, in the 1916 American revision of the test, the mental age was divided by the chronological age of the person to produce a ratio. This is then multiplied by 100 to produce the <u>intelligence</u> <u>quotient</u>(Baroff, 1986). The formula for determining the intelligence quotient is:

$$\frac{\text{Mental Age (MA)}}{\text{Chronological Age (CA)}} \times 100 = IQ;$$

Some examples are: $\dfrac{MA}{CA} \quad \dfrac{6}{6} = 1(100) = 100$

$\dfrac{MA}{CA} \quad \dfrac{8}{6} = 1.33(100) = 133; \qquad \dfrac{MA}{CA} \quad \dfrac{8}{12} = .67(100) = 67$

Mental age is an important score for it can indicate the level of functioning of a person irrespective of their chronological age. At the same time it becomes a less useful tool in late adolescence and adulthood as mental growth as measured by IQ tests slows and then essentially ceases in adulthood. Later we will review some of the characteristics of persons at different mental ages. The IQ score is also useful--but in a comparative sense. It allows us to compare how the intellectual power of one person compares with that of another.

The <u>deviation</u> <u>IQ</u> was developed to deal with the fact that with the Stanford-Binet IQ test there is some variability in standard deviations at various age groupings with some revisions of this test. For some age groups one standard deviation was a little more or a little less than 16 scale points. But in 1960 the <u>deviation</u> <u>IQ</u> of 16 scale points was adopted so that IQ scores could be directly compared across age groups and interpreted in terms of standard deviations and percentiles for all age groups. Although the Stanford-Binet test is not as widely used as the Wechsler scales, it has shown to have predictive value for scholastic

14

achievement as it tends to be weighted toward verbal scores(Kaplan & Saccuzzo, 1982; Baroff, 1986).

Wechsler Intelligence Scales. David Wechsler, a clinical psychologist, first developed intelligence scales to assess the mental functioning of adults. His tests have been modified many times and variations of the tests have been developed to measure the performance of children at different age levels. One of the significant differences between the Stanford-Binet and Wechsler tests is that the latter includes multiple subtests which are first added into two subscale scores on (1)verbal scales and (2)performance scales, and these are then added together to produce (3)a full scale score. This reflects a somewhat different view of intelligence than Binet held. Wechsler believed intelligence was comprised of a number of specific abilities that could be separately defined and measured in subtests. However, these specific abilities were interrelated and therefore general intelligence was a global aggregate of these abilities which could be totaled into a full scale score (Wechsler, 1958).

The three Wechsler scales of intelligence are administered individually and each of the subtests are scored individually and then added up to produce separate verbal and performance scores as well as a full scale score. Table 2.1 lists the two major scales and the subtests of the 1970 revision of the Wechsler Adult Intelligence Scale. Scoring procedures are done differently for the Wechsler test than the Stanford-Binet test. Since there are different numbers of items in each of the Wechsler subtests, scores are converted into "standard" scores for the verbal, performance and full scale scores. A full scale IQ score has a deviation IQ with a mean of 100 and a standard deviation of 15(Kaplan & Saccuzzo, 1982). The advantage of the subtests is that analysis of scores on them allows the determination of specific areas of strength and weakness for the testee and this may allow for specification of educational intervention programming. For example, mentally retarded children often do better on nonverbal tasks or performance tasks in the Wechsler tests than they do on verbal tasks relative to normal children(Baroff, 1986).

Both the meaning and measurement of intelligence is exceedingly complex inasmuch as intelligence is a multi-faceted phenomena. While intelligence may be thought of as a set of distinct cognitive functions, it is influenced by a

15

Table 2.1

Subtests of Wechsler Adult Intelligence Scale--Revised

VERBAL SCORES	MAJOR FUNCTION MEASURED
Information	Range of Knowledge
Comprehension	Judgment
Arithmetic	Concentration
Similarities	Abstract Thinking
Digit Span	Immediate Memory, Anxiety
Vocabulary	Vocabulary Level

PERFORMANCE SCALES	MAJOR FUNCTION MEASURED
Digit Symbol	Visual Motor Functioning
Picture Completion	Alertness to Details
Picture Arrangement	Planning Ability
Block Design	Nonverbal Reasoning
Object Assembly	Analysis of part-whole relationships

Source: Kaplan & Saccuzzo (1982, 250)

multiplicity of variables including native ability (the structure of the nervous system), motives, experiential opportunities, attitudes and work habits all set in a social environment that is never alike for two people(Haywood & Wachs, 1981). Ideally all these things ought to be considered in interpreting any test score.

DEFINITIONS AND MEASUREMENT OF MENTAL RETARDATION

Just as there are varying definitions of intelligence there are also varying definitions of mental retardation as well as different ways of measuring it as individuals progress from infancy to adulthood. There are a number of reasons why there are multiple definitions of mental retardation. One reason is due to the fact that different investi-

reasons why there are multiple definitions of mental retardation. One reason is due to the fact that different investigators put relatively different emphases on the importance of the four interacting domains involved in the process of human development: intellectual, physical, emotional and social. Thus definitions concentrate on one of these domains, particularly the intellectual, to the relative slighting of motor, emotional or social skills. But since human development is a complex process, a definition is needed that will give due importance to each of these factors.

A second reason for multiple definitions of mental retardation is that some definitions assume or point to one or more causes of the retardation such as chromosomal defects, nutritional deficiencies or a deprived environment. But the cause of a condition does not have to be included in a description of it. The next chapter will examine the causal origins of mental retardation.

A third reason for the abundance of definitions is the function or functional origin of the definition. Thus, there will be scientific definitions that originate from scholars in the field concerned with understanding it while legal/administrative definitions originate from legislative bodies or administrators more concerned with demarcating cut-off points for the delivery of services. Scholars will be more interested in definitions which define, describe and classify or investigative reasons while those of legislators and service providers are more interested in definitions which relate to intervention issues such as incompetency, guardianship and the provision of medical, educational and residential services.

The AAMD Definition of Mental Retardation

While many definitions of mental retardation exist, one has emerged that today is widely accepted--the definition of the American Association of Mental Deficiency(AAMD), the premier organization dealing with mental deficiency. The AAMD has offered eight revisions of its definitions since 1921, four of them since 1959. The current, 1983, definition reads:

> Mental retardation refers to significantly subaverage general intellectual functioning

17

existing concurrently with deficits in adaptive behavior and manifested during the development period(Grossman, 1983, 1).

The AAMD manual on mental classification goes on to define four key terms used in this definition(Grossman, 1983, 1):

> GENERAL INTELLECTUAL FUNCTIONING is defined as the results obtained by assessment with one or more of the individually administered general intelligence tests developed for the purpose of assessing intellectual functioning.

> SIGNIFICANTLY SUBAVERAGE INTELLECTUAL FUNCTIONING is defined as approximately IQ 70 or below.

> ADAPTIVE BEHAVIOR is defined as the effectiveness or degree with which individuals meet the standards of personal independence and social responsibility expected for age and cultural group.

> DEVELOPMENTAL PERIOD is defined as the period of time between birth and the 18th birthday.

That there is some emerging congruence in defining mental retardation is seen in the fact that the American Psychiatric Association's latest definition is very similar to the AAMD definition:

> The essential features are: (1)significantly subaverage general intellectual functioning, (2)resulting in, or associated with, deficits or impairments in adaptive behavior, (3)with onset before age 18(American Psychiatric Association, 1980, 36).

The only difference between these two definitions is that the APA definition points out that deficits in adaptive behavior may be causally contingent upon subaverage

18

intellectual functioning and it says adaptive behavior may be either impaired or show deficits. Since these definitions are so similar, the AAMD definition will be used in this book although it is not beyond criticism as we shall note later in this chapter.

Deficits in <u>adaptive behavior</u> are to be distinguished from subaverage intellectual functioning. Determining deficits in adaptive behavior relies extensively on observation and clinical judgment whereas intellectual functioning is assessed almost entirely by individually administered paper and pencil or verbal IQ tests. Deficits in adaptive behavior may be assessed by <u>informal appraisal</u> methods such as observation and talking to people who have extensive contact with the subject such as parents, siblings, and teachers and/or by the use of <u>standardized adaptive scales</u> such as the following(Grossman, 1983):

> AAMD Adaptive Behavior Scales
> Adaptive Functioning Index
> BMT Instrument
> Camelot Behavior Systems Checklist
> Client Centered Evaluation Model
> Minnesota Developmental Programming System
> Progress Assessment Chart
> Vineland Social Maturity Scale

Expectations in adaptive behavior vary for different age groups in the following areas according to the AAMD(Grossman, 1983, 25):

> During INFANCY AND EARLY CHILDHOOD in:
> 1.   Sensorimotor Skill Development
> 2.   Communication Skills (including speech and language)
> 3.   Self-Help Skills
> 4.   Socialization (development of ability to interact with others)

> During CHILDHOOD AND EARLY ADOLES-CENCE in Areas 1 through 4 and/or:
> 5.   Application of Basic Academic Skills in Daily Life Activities

6.   Application of Appropriate Reasoning and Judgment in Mastery of the Environment
7.   Social Skills (participation in group activities and interpersonal relationships)

During LATE ADOLESCENCE AND ADULT LIFE in Areas 1 through 7 and/or:
8.   Vocational and Social Responsibilities and Performances

Whereas intelligence tests seek to measure the highest potential for performance, most scales of adaptive behavior are designed to assess a person's common or typical performance. And while intelligence tests emphasize language, reasoning, and abstract intellectual processes, adaptive behavior scales attempt to measure everyday proficiencies in self care in such areas as eating, dressing, toileting, communicating needs, developing appropriate emotions, motor skill development and meeting ordinary responsibilities for a person of a given age. Adaptive behavior scales can be scored to indicate at which of four levels a person is mentally retarded: mild, moderate, severe, or profound(Grossman, 1983).
Table 2.2 illustrates how a given level of performance at different chronological ages can yield four different clinical assignments as regards to the degree of retardation. Table 2.2 also points to an important concept with regard to the development of intelligence and that is the mental age growth period. The concept of retarded may suggest delay rather than arrest of mental growth. Thus, parents of retarded children may falsely believe that given enough time, their retarded child will eventually catch up with other children at the same age. Or they may believe that retardation can be overcome eventually with more years or more intensive study. But mental growth, like physical growth, essentially occurs during the first 18 years of life at which time it ends. This has significant implications for mental age differences between two persons with the same chronological ages. If we compare two persons at age 6 with IQs of 100 and 67, the person with the IQ of 67 shows a mental age of 4 with a mental deficit of 2 years. By chronological age 12 the person with a 67 IQ will show

a mental age of 8 in comparison to a mental age of 12 for the person with an IQ of 100. Now there is a mental age deficit of 4 years. And for two 18 year olds with IQs of

Table 2.2
Illustrations of Highest Level of Adaptive Behavior Functioning By Chronological Age and Level

3 years: MILD
6 years: MODERATE
9 years: SEVERE
12 years and above: PROFOUND

Independent functioning: Feeds self with spoon (cereals, soft foods) but may still spill or be messy; drinks unassisted; can pull off clothing and put on some (socks, underclothes, boxer pants, dress); tries to help with bath or hand washing but still needs a lot of help; indicates toilet accident and may indicate need and uses toilet when taken there.

Physical: Climbs up and down stairs but not alternating feet; runs and jumps; balances briefly on one foot; can pass ball to others; transfers objects; does 4- to 6-piece form board puzzle without aid.

Communication: Speaks in 2- or 3-word sentences (Daddy go work); names simple common objects (boy, car, ice cream, hat); understands simple directions (put the shoe on your foot, sit here, get your coat); knows people by name. (If nonverbal, may use as many as 10 to 15 gestures to convey needs or other information.)

Social: Interacts with others in simple play activities, usually with only one or two others unless guided into group activity; has preference for some persons over others.

---

6 years: MILD
9 years: MODERATE
12 years and above: SEVERE
15 years and above: PROFOUND

Independent functioning: Feeds self with spoon and/or fork, may spill occasionally; puts on clothing but

21

needs help with small buttons and jacket zipper; tries to bathe self but needs help; can wash and dry hands but not very efficiently; toilet trained but may have accidents, wet bed, or may need reminders and help with cleaning and clothes.

Physical: Hops or skips; climbs steps with alternating feet; rides tricycle (or bicycle over 8 years); climbs trees or jungle gym; plays dance games; throws ball and may hit target.

Communication: Has speaking vocabulary of over 300 to 400 words and uses grammatically correct sentences. If nonverbal, may use many gestures for communication. Understands simple verbal communications, including directions and questions ("Put it on the shelf." "Where do you live?"). May have some articulation problems. May recognize advertising words and signs (Ice cream, STOP, EXIT, MEN, LADIES). Relates experiences in simple language.

Social: Participates in group activities and simple group games; interacts with others in simple play ("Store," "House") and expressive activities (art, dance).

Source: Grossman, 1984, 204-5.

100 and 67, the 67 IQ person shows a mental age of 12 and a mental age deficit of 6 years. Thus, over time during the developmental period the mental age difference between two persons with stable but different IQs increases. The mental age growth curve is higher for those with normal intelligence but decreasingly depressed as we move from mild to profound retardation(Baroff, 1986).

Several key features of the AAMD definition of mental retardation need to be emphasized.

(1) The use of an IQ score alone is not an acceptable basis for there to be a diagnosis of mental retardation. Both individually measured subaverage intellectual functioning and deficits in adaptive behavior must coexist. A lack of congruence on the two criteria may result in a person being designated retarded by one criteria but not the other. This particularly occurs where persons are labeled mentally retarded by IQ test scores alone and creates prob-

lems for determining the true prevalence of mental retardation.

(2) Mental retardation is to be distinguished from other types of mental disability such as mental illness, autism and the learning disabled. While these other disabilities sometimes occur simultaneously with mental retardation and are often hard to diagnose and distinguish from it, they are not, by definition, the same as mental retardation which requires both subaverage intellectual functioning and deficits in adaptive behavior. In other words, persons who have deficits in adaptive behavior but not IQ are not retarded by the AAMD definition. Figure 2.1 shows the combinations that can result from using the dual criteria for retardation of the AAMD. The criteria should be employed sensitively by a skilled clinician to determine if a person is to be classified as mentally retarded.

Figure 2.1

Possible Combinations of Measured Intellectual
Functioning and Adaptive Behavior

Measured Intellectual Functioning

Adaptive Behavior	Retarded	Not Retarded
Retarded	Mentally Retarded	Not Mentally Retarded (Deficits in adaptive behavior only)
Not Retarded	Not Mentally Retarded	Not Mentally Retarded (Subaverage Intellectual Functioning Only)

Source: Adapted from Grossman, 1983, 12.

23

play the same symptoms as the mentally retarded but are not designated as being such. Rather, they are usually lab-

Table 2.3

Level of Retardation Indicated by IQ Range
Obtained on Measure of General Intellectual
Functioning

| Level of Mental Retardation | Intelligence Test Scores | | Educational Classification |
	Stanford-Binet	Wechsler	
(Borderline)*	69-84	70-84	Dull Normal
Mild	52-68	55-69	Educable
Moderate	36-51	40-54	Trainable
Severe	20-35	25-39	Dependent
Profound	>20	>25	Dependent
Standard Error of Measurement	3	4	
Standard Deviation	16	15	

*Beginning in 1973 the American Association of Mental
        Deficiency adopted a new definition of mental
        retardation which excluded the borderline range from
        inclusion in it.

Sources: American Psychiatric Association(1980);
        President's Committee on Mental Retardation(1975);
        Baroff(1986).

eled as brain injured. Baumeister and Muma(1975) critically suggest that the relevant criteria should be behavior rather than chronological age.

24

(4) The AAMD classification manual(Grossman, 1983) specifies four levels of mental retardation as indicated by Table 2.3 in the left hand margin. Columns 2 and 3 show the ranges of scores associated with each level of retardation depending on whether the Stanford-Binet or Wechsler tests are used. And the standard error of measurement for the Stanford-Binet is 3 while that of the Wechsler test is 4. This means, according to Grossman(1983), that the obtained or measured IQ score of any given individual may exist in a "zone of uncertainty." For example, if a person scored 68 on a Wechsler IQ test, his "true" score should be within ± 4 of that score 67% of the time (64-72 score range) and within ± 8 points of that score 95% of the time (60-76 score range). This "zone of uncertainty" allows for certain errors in measurement that exist with IQ testing and suggest the need for flexibility in clinically interpreting test results.

Problems remain in the classification of mental retardation even though there has been substantial closure in its meaning and measurement by the statements by the AAMD and the American Psychiatric Association. Three problems are:

1. Insofar as the classification of mental retardation depends on IQ testing, it is subject to the multiple criticisms that have been aimed at IQ testing in general. These criticisms include but are not limited to: (1)such testing devices may not adequately measure all the abilities that are related to intelligent behavior; (2)they measure both learning to date and native ability or potential and consequently reflect both environmental opportunities as well as genetic capabilities as are probably reflected in the lower average IQ scores of various disadvantaged and minority groups; (3)there will be variations in test scores over time that may reflect differences in the examining situation as well as differential growth curves in turn influenced by some mixture of potential, opportunity and a variety of factors that influence motivation; and (4)classification is subject to changing social definitions of mental retardation as seen in the deletion of that 13.5% of the population defined as of "borderline" intelligence in the AAMD redefinition of mental retardation in 1973(Evans & Waites, 1981; Turnbull & Wheatly, 1983; Vitello & Soskin, 1985; Oakland & Parmelee, 1985).

2. Insofar as the measure of adaptive behavior is a measure of mental retardation, it too involves making complex assessments about lags in development as regards motor skills, self-help skills, and socialization. For the profoundly and severely retarded, these clinical assessments are clearer than with the mildly and moderately retarded where lags may occur in some skill areas but not others or as children spurt or lag in some areas of growth with role changes or changes in the demands made by their environments. Thus, global clinical assessments of adaptive functioning as regards the degree of retardation are not always clear cut as they are made up of many changing elements(Grossman, 1983).

3. The assessment of mental retardation, especially borderline cases, by the two criteria of the AAMD is further compounded by difficulties where the subject may have other physical or mental problems. As we shall see more fully later in the chapter, many retarded individuals have developmental disabilities other than mental retardation such as autism, epilepsy, dyslexia, cerebral palsy and/or a variety of motor and physical health problems. Furthermore, some of them will have a "dual diagnosis" of both mental retardation and mental illness where either one can be the primary diagnosis or the secondary diagnosis.

All of this is not to say that the designation and classification of degrees of mental retardation is impossible. Various testing instruments as well as observation do show substantial predictive validity in assessing both academic performance and non-academic performance. What it does suggest is that there are "zones of uncertainty" in classifying persons as mentally retarded, especially in borderline cases and the assessments need to be made periodically and cautiously as people mature and change over time. Referring to the fourfold levels of retardation, developed by the AAMD, Vitello and Soskin(1985, 8-9) argue:

> Although the above classification system, based on degree of mental retardation, is useful in facilitating communication and research activities . . . , one should be particularly careful in using these rather gross demarcations in making decisions about the programmatic needs of mentally retarded individuals. Mentally retarded per-

sons represent an extremely heterogeneous group of individuals. Two individuals classified at the same level of mental retardation may be quite different in many attributes. Similarly, retarded persons at two different levels of retardation may exhibit overlapping characteristics.

THREE PERSPECTIVES ON MENTAL RETARDATION

Jane Mercer has developed a tripartite assessment model of mental retardation. Each of the three different models tends to be used by different occupations of people, have different purposes, make different assumptions, interpret scores of various tests differently, and use a distinct ethical code governing the assessment process(Cronbach, 1984). We will look at each of these models briefly but give greatest attention to the "social system perspective" and how it differs from the "clinical perspective."

The medical perspective is the one used predominantly by physicians. It concentrates on screening for biological anomalies which are found most frequently among severely and profoundly retarded persons. This model may also be called the pathological or defect or disease perspective since it focuses on biological or physical departures from normality and it is these pathological signs and not behavior alone which signal a defect. The assumptions of this model are that symptoms of mental retardation have a biological origin and the sociocultural factors are irrelevant to diagnosis or treatment since human organisms are transculturally the same. The ethical code operating here makes it a more serious error to overlook pathology and not treat than to treat in the case of an incorrect diagnosis that finds a pathology when none is present since an untreated pathology may worsen(Mercer & Lewis, 1978; Cronbach, 1984).

The clinical perspective is based primarily on the model of general intelligence developed by psychometricians or psychologists. Its purpose is to estimate learning potential in comparison to persons of the same age. Abnormality is scoring high or low on tests geared for age mates of the same sociocultural milieu. The assumptions

27

of this model are that tests can measure learning potential in a specific culture and inferences regarding normality are made by comparing children reared in similar sociocultural environments. Scores on such tests are believed to be valid indicators of intellectual competence in comparison to others in the same sociocultural environment. The ethical code governing intellectual assessment is that it is more serious to underestimate learning ability and thereby underestimate the child than to overestimate learning potential which could enhance experiential learning opportunities.

The <u>social systems perspective</u> is based on a model of deviance and/or social adaptation developed by sociologists. Its purpose is to identify deviant behavior which is defined as that which violates social norms. But this model assumes there are multiple definitions of deviant behavior since the behavior of people varies by both the roles they play and the specific social subsystem in which they are acting. This model further assumes there is no ultimate "right" behavior but that what is considered normal is shaped by political, familial and other sociocultural influences operating within a specific environmental setting. Consequently, scores on tests reflect a person's achievement in a particular role in a given social system in relation to the norms of that system. The ethical code governing behavioral assessment is that it is more serious error to falsely label behavior as deviant which may locate a person is a disabling social and psychological trajectory than to misdiagnose with an incorrect but positive label.

The social systems perspective on mental retardation comes from the labeling and deviance theories in the field of sociology. It takes the view that any form of deviance must be understood within its social context and not as an independent phenomena. Thus, deviance-- whether it be mental retardation, crime or alcoholism--is not solely a property inherent in a particular kind of behavior or person, but is a property or label applied by persons in contact with the person labeled(Erikson, 1966). While Mercer sees the appropriateness of the medical and clinical perspectives for severer forms of mental retardation, her formulation of the social systems model is most applicable to mild retardation where symptomology is often less clear and the application of labels may influence the life course of those labeled mentally retarded. For

Mercer(1973) mental retardation is an achieved social status associated with a role in relation to other roles. Thus, mental retardation is not an individual pathology but a label given to a person in a particular social system.

In contrast to the clinical perspective, the social systems perspective believes that the number of people who are viewed as retarded is a product of the social structure, culture and/or subculture of an area rather than a result of clinical diagnosis. This means, in a social sense, that retardation cannot remain undetected. It also means that the amount of retardation in a given population does not reside in individuals but comes about as people are labeled retarded by their perceived inability to meet the intellectual and behavioral demands of needs of one or more role positions. Jane Mercer(1976, 28) describes the centrality of the role of mental retardate in the social systems perspective:

> Sociologically, a person is a mental retardate when he acquires the status of mental retardate and plays the role of mental retardate. He is not a mental retardate by virtue of having certain personal attributes although these may play a part in his acquiring the status. Admittedly, persons who are assigned to the status of mental retardate do have many characteristics in common because they are sorted out and categorized by teachers, psychologists, medical doctors and other persons who have been trained in the clinical tradition and who share a common set of norms by which they evaluate behavior and assign persons to statuses. This type of regularity occurs in the characteristics of occupants of any social status. Indeed, we cannot even conceive of the notion of a social status at all except as an abstraction defined by the regularities and communalities which characterize persons who hold the status.

This perspective allows some people to be ascribed the retardate label in some settings but not other settings since mental deviance is partly a function of the needs of the system. In a school setting a child may be regarded by his teachers as retarded because of poor work in English and math. But his playmates and his parents may not label him so. His minister, Sunday school teacher, or girl or boy

Table 2.4
Two Perspectives on Mental Retardation

Clinical Perspective	Social Systems Perspective
Intelligence is a quality that resides in the individual independent of his sociological setting.	Intelligence is relative to the requirements of a cultural/historical era and a particular social system or subsystem.
If one is retarded by the statistical/testing standards of IQ tests, adaptive behavior scales or clinical medical judgments, he is retarded.	Individual persons can be retarded for some systems (like schools) but normal for others (like work or family life).
Determination of retardation is made by trained professionals. They can detect abnormalities not apparent to untrained laymen.	Retardation cannot remain undetected since it is the product of being labeled as such in particular social settings.
The number of retarded people in a given area or population can be scientifically determined by trained professionals without regard to the social system's structure or requirements.	The number of people labeled as retarded in a given social is determined by its expectations and levels of tolerance and may vary from one subsystem (like education) to another (like work or family life).

Source: Adapted and modified from Mercer, 1973.

scout leader may not label him or her as "dumb" or "slow" as may be occurring in the school system. Children so labeled in the school system may eventually have these labels carried over to other roles and social systems or remain "six-hour retards"--that is only viewed as retarded in the school setting but not in other places. But such ascribed roles may have powerful social effects on the life course of such individuals who once labeled may have their opportunities changed(Mercer, 1973).

Table 2.4 summarizes the clinical and social systems perspectives on mental retardation. These perspectives are not to be interpreted as true or false but as descriptions of social processes which occur and which will be illustrated shortly by the review of an empirical study carried out by Mercer in a California school.

While the clinical perspective is the dominant and normative procedure used in determining mental retardation in American society, the social systems perspective is also apparent in everyday life. As is shown in Table 2.5, the identification of the retarded by these two processes of clinical labeling and social labeling may or may not coincide. Clinical labeling is called "detection" while social system labeling is called "ascription."

Table 2.5

A Typology of Outcomes from the Labeling of Mental
Retardation by Clinicians and Laymen

		Clinical Retardation Detected	
		Yes	No
Retardation	Yes	(1) Retardation Detected and Ascribed	(2) Retardation not Detected but Ascribed
Ascribed			
by a Social	No	Retardation Detected but not Ascribed	Retardation Neither Detected or Ascribed
System		(3)	(4)

31

We would expect in the cell 1 case for the labels to be mutually reinforcing. The interesting question here is whether the labeling processes occurred independently of one another or whether one precipitated the other. In cell 2 we have the ascription of retardation in one or more social systems without the detection of it by clinicians. The interesting question here is whether this ascription may lead to testing to detect retardation and what effect this kind of labeling has when it is not reinforced by clinical substantiation. Cell 3 reverses the case of cell 2. In this cell there is professional detection but no popular ascription. Will such professional designation of mental retardation carry over into settings other than the clinician's office?

Jane Mercer did a fascinating study of 1,298 public school pupils, aged 8 to 14, in several sampled school systems in California. She was particularly interested in the question posed by a discrepancy between the numbers of persons who were clinically retarded but the lesser number of students who were ascribed retardation by placement in a special education class. At the time this study was done, mental retardation was defined by state law as pupils scoring below 80 on the Wechsler Intelligence Scale for Children. Of the 1,298 school children in regular classes, 122 or 9.3% of them fell below an IQ of 80. However, only 1.2% of the Anglos scored below 80 in comparison to 12.5% of the black pupils and 15.7% of the Mexican-American pupils. This pattern was interesting and could reflect bias in the test, lower verbal aptitudes among blacks and Chicano children or less stringent screening of Anglo children out of regular classes into special education classes than was true of the two minorities(Mercer, 1973). However, the central focus of this study was the question of why out of the 156 minority group students who had scored below 80 on the test, only 40(25%) of them were placed in special education classes. Thus, out of 156 students eligible for special education on the basis of intelligence test scores, only 40 were assigned this special retarded status and enrolled in special education classes. The 116 "eligibles" averaged only 2.1 points higher on the IQ tests than did the 40 "retardates." The psychological profiles and the home environments of the two groups were nearly comparable. The reason why some eligible students were assigned to this status and others remained in the regular classrooms were found to lie in (1)teacher's perceptions of what constituted mental retardation and (2)their referral of such students for further testing for mental retardation which subsequently led to their placement in special education classes. Of all the "eligibles," those that got assigned the retarded label were more likely to be perceived by teachers as displaying low academic competence, having lower English competence, having a poorer social adjustment, and coming from a worse home environment. The perceptions that teachers have of some students being retarded are frequently shared with other teachers and goes into a confidential file on each student. These cumulative files often provide the basis for a particular teacher suggesting that a student be further tested for placement in the special education class. Mercer(1976, 45) summarizes the selective process involved in how a child acquires the status of a retardate: "Low academic competence + poor adjustment + low competence in English + few friends = perceived low mental ability = retardation." Among the eligibles however the process is different: "Low academic competence + poor adjustment + relative competence in English + being easy to manage + being liked by peers + perceived low mental ability does not equal mental retardation." This study strongly shows the difference between the clinical perspective on mental retardation and the social systems perspective. It indicates that in some instances a child must demonstrate more than a low IQ to be assigned a retardate status; he must also be seen as having both low academic and English competence, plus providing problems to the teacher. Thus, behavioral deviation may be the critical point in moving a pupil who is technically a clinical retardate by administrative school standards into the ascribed role of a retardate.

The social systems perspective gives particular attention to labeling processes and outcomes. Deviancy theorists argue that labeling a person mentally retarded often has negative consequences both psychologically and socially. Psychologically, it lowers their self-esteem and initiates processes of lowered self-expectations and efforts. Socially, it is stigmatizing to be stereotyped as retarded where a person's worth is devalued, their skills discredited and they are treated as belonging to some dependent category who are treated all alike rather than as distinct persons. This too can initiate a self-fulfilling prophecy of lowered expectations, decreased opportunities and differential treatment. Various studies have pointed out that the label of EMR (Educationally Mentally Retarded) has disproportionately been applied to disadvantaged groups, especially Hispanics and blacks(Mercer, 1973; Kennedy, 1973). Mercer contends that disadvantaged and minority group children are not genetically inferior but that their statistical overrepresentation in the EMR category is due to the Anglocentric schools which use intelligence testing devices that are formulated around central core values of our society. Thus, in IQ testing in early grades, more minority children receive lower scores reflecting cultural differences in their home life. As a consequence they may receive a poorer education even though they may function adequately in noneducational settings such as the family or neighborhood.

As an attempted correction to these alleged discriminatory educational practices, in the mid 1970's, Mercer and Lewis(1978) developed a System of Multicultural Pluralistic Assessment that attempts to systematize the adjustment of a variety of IQ and adaptive behavior scale scores by scoring them in light of other information on a child's health, maturity and adjustment, and the child's family in terms of size and educational, social, economic and cultural resources. This pluralistic model of assessment yields an Estimated Learning Potential score that often elevates the learning potential of black and Hispanic students above the WISC-R norms which would otherwise find them mentally retarded(Cronbach, 1984). Grossman(1983) makes much the same point about the clinical assessment of scores on IQ and adaptive behavior scales. The AAMD manual recommends that assessments be made by fully qualified professionals, adjusted to account for specific deficits in vision, hearing, motor and cultural-language differences, use multiple assessment techniques, and periodically be repeated to reassess earlier performance and/or growth.

CHANGING TERMINOLOGY IN THE FIELD OF MENTAL RETARDATION

Both historically and currently the terminology referring to mental retardation has been in flux in English speaking countries. This reflects not only changes in the

34

scholarly and medical study of retardation but also changes in public attitudes and legislation. Some of the terms used in the past referred generically to all mentally retarded persons and some were used to designate degrees of retardation. This brief review of terminology will be helpful to persons interested in the historical treatment of the mentally retarded and will help to pinpoint the origins of slang usage still current. Table 2.6 compares the generic terms and terms indicating degree of retardation in both current terminology and the older terminology. However, it should be noted that many people still use terms like idiot, imbecile, moron, and mental retard as pejorative terms and not with any of the precise meaning they may have had with more informed persons.

Table 2.6

Current and Older Terminology in the Field of
Mental Retardation

Current Terminology	Older Terminology
GENERIC TERMS	
Mental retardation	Mentally deficient, mentally defective,
Mental subnormality**	mentally handicapped,
MR/DD***	feeble-minded
TERMS INDICATING DEGREE OF RETARDATION	
Mild retardation	Moron*, feeble-minded**
	High grade mental defectives
Moderate retardation	Imbeciles
Severe retardation	Low grade mental defectives
Profound retardation	Idiots

* Primarily a United States term.

** Primarily a British term.

*** Mental Retardation/Developmental Disability

Sources: Developed from Tyor and Bell, 1984; Tizard, 1965.

Tizard(1965) points out that "mentally deficient" and "mentally defective" were used in Great Britain as generic terms to identify all mentally subnormal people irrespective of their degree of retardation. But in Great Britain the term "mentally deficient" is no longer used in law having been replaced by the terms "mental subnormality" and "severe subnormality."

Tyor and Bell(1984, 6-7) say that in the U.S. before 1800 the terms idiot and imbecile were used almost interchangeably and generically. "After 1800, however, the generic denotation was gradually acquired by the term 'feeble-minded,' and idiot was increasingly restricted to the profoundly or severely retarded, the lowest and most helpless grades." On the other hand, "imbecile also had a generic connotation but it was more frequently used to indicate retardates with a higher level of capability than idiots, who nevertheless still required guidance and control." But during the 1800's "in the absence of any accepted standards, these terms as well as a plethora of others--such as dunce, fool, and simpleton--were used indiscriminately by physicians and laymen without reference to etiology, symptoms or prognosis." In the 1850's in the U.S. a more formal classification system was developed with the "feeble-minded" essentially equated with what we call mild retardation today, imbeciles were seen as an intermediate grade, and idiots the lowest grade of mental defectives.

In 1910 the Committee of the Classification of the Feeble-Minded of the American Association for the Feeble-Minded accepted Goddard's definition that said a person was retarded if a child was two or more years mentally below his chronological age or if as an adult he failed to score a mental age above twelve. This definition also specified three levels of retardation(Tyor & Bell, 1984): Idiots--mental age less than two years; Imbeciles--mental age of two to seven years; Morons--mental age eight to twelve years. In 1910 the British Royal Commission on the Care and Confinement of the Feeble-Minded defined mentally defectives in a functional way: Idiots--a person so deeply defective from birth or early age that he is unable to guard himself against common physical dangers. Imbeciles--were incapable of earning their own living but could guard against common physical dangers. Feeble-minded--were capable of earning a living under favorable

36

circumstances but incapable of competing on equal terms with their normal fellows or managing their affairs with ordinary prudence.

A recent piece of legislation has added to the growing complexity of terminology in this field and reflects the sociopolitical movement to assist people with disabilities. The term that was added is <u>developmental disabilities</u>. In a space of eight years this term went through three different congressional definitions. The first definition came in the Developmental Disabilities Services and Facilities Construction Act of 1970(P.L. 91-517):

> The term "developmental disability" means a disability attributable to mental retardation, cerebral palsy, epilepsy, or other neurological conditions of an individual found by the Secretary to be closely related to mental retardation or to require treatment similar to that required for mentally retarded individuals, which disability originates before such an individual attains age eighteen, which has continued or can be expected to continue indefinitely, and which constitutes a substantial handicap to such individuals(Breen & Richman, 1979, 3).

This definition cites three specific conditions plus a functional "other neurological conditions" which require a certain level of treatment originating before age 18 for people to be eligible for services under the legislation. The 1975 amendments to this act added "autism" to the specific disorders while maintaining the open-ended functional definition of other neurological disorders requiring a certain level of service because the handicap would be a continuing one. The 1978 Rehabilitation, Comprehensive Services and Developmental Disabilities Amendment (P.L. 95-602) redefined developmental disabilities in a totally functional way. This act also limited services to moderately, severely or profoundly retarded individuals thus excluding the mildly retarded, who make up roughly 89% of all the mentally retarded, unless they had additional handicapping conditions. This legislation defines a developmental disability as one that: (1)is attributable to a mental and/or physical impairment, (2)has an onset before age 22, (3)is chronic or likely to continue indefinitely, (4)is one that is likely to require treatment or other services for an indefinite time, and (5)results in substantial functional limitations in three or more of the following areas: (a) self care, (b)receptive or expressive language, (c)learning, (d)mobility, (e)self-direction, (f)capacity for independent living, and (g)economic self-sufficiency(Breen & Richman, 1979; Vitello & Soskin, 1985).

What appears to be happening currently is that sometimes the term "developmental disabilities" is replacing the term "mental retardation" since developmental disabilities(DD) is a more generic term that includes as a subset those who are mentally retarded. The term DD also has less stigma attached to it. Sometimes the two terms are used together in an abbreviated form: MR/DD, which indicates that the speaker is either referring to the mentally retarded as a subclass of the developmentally disabled or that he is referring to both.

The use of the developmentally disabled term will add complications to prevalence studies inasmuch as there will be overlapping subclassification categories within this somewhat vague term. For example, of the estimated 750,000 individuals with cerebral palsy, two thirds are also mentally retarded. Around 20 to 30% of the individuals with epilepsy are mentally retarded. It is estimated that 30% of all retarded children suffer physical handicaps while perhaps as many as 40% of them are "dual-diagnosed"--suffering from both mental illness and mental retardation(Breen & Richman, 1979).

However, how one defines and then redefines a condition can substantially influence the prevalence rate. For example, in 1978 the Developmental Disability Planning Council estimated there were 5,265,894 developmentally disabled persons in the United States using the 1975 definition. But later in 1978 Congress redefined developmental disability excluding the mildly retarded unless they had other defined handicaps. Thus, by 1981, using the new definition, the developmentally disabled population had shrunk 26% to an estimated 3,906,913. This estimated reduction of 26% is due to the fact that the mildly retarded make up about 89% of all the retarded who in turn constitute around 55% of the developmentally disabled(Keenan & Parker, 1983).

THE INCIDENCE AND PREVALENCE OF RETAR-
DATION

Epidemiology is the science that studies the distribution, determinants and correlates of disease and other
health problems that occur in populations. In formulating
policies to provide educational, medical, residential and
social services to the mentally retarded it is most helpful
for planners to have accurate epidemiological data on the
incidence and particularly the prevalence of mental retardation. Two interrelated measures, incidence and prevalence, are used to determine the need for services.

Incidence of mental retardation refers to the occurrence of new cases in a population that occur in a certain
time period. The time period is usually a year. However,
incidence rates may vary by the age period when they are
diagnosed. For example, it is estimated that about 125,000
children are born retarded each year. This is the incidence
of mental retardation. If we divide that number by the
number of all children born in a year(about 2.3 million), we
get an incidence rate of 5 retarded children per 1,000 population or .5%. However, many children born retarded are
not diagnosed as such until later, primarily when they enter
school. Consequently incidence rates have limited utility
for planning purposes and they may change over time if
prevention measures are effective.

Prevalence refers to the actual number of persons in
a given society who have some particular condition at a
given point in time. Estimates of the prevalence of mental
retardation vary greatly in the United States--from about 2
million to 6 million persons. These sizable and significant
differences can be explained by (1)different methods of
defining and measuring mental retardation, (2)different
assumptions epidemiologists make in estimating the
prevalence of mental retardation, and (3)the fact that we
have no agency that systematically collects data on the
prevalence of retardation.

Prevalence rates appear to vary most by how one
defines or measures mental retardation. If one uses only IQ
scores, as was extensively the case in the past and may still
be used as the prime indicator in educational settings, then
the prevalence rate will be higher--usually at the 2.5% to
3% range. Table 2.7 shows the expected frequency of IQ

scores below 70 if we assumed that IQ scores followed a normal distribution with 2.17% of all IQs below 70. How-

Table 2.7

Percentage and Numerical Distribution of Persons with Low IQ
Based on a Normal Distribution

MR Classification	Percentage Expected in Total Population	Percentage Expected in Retarded Population	Expected Number
Mild(-2 to -3 SD)	2.14000	94.066	5,107,067
Moderate(-3 to -4 SD)	.03182	5.794	75,938
Severe(-4 to -5 SD)	.00314	.138	7,494
Profound(over -5 SD)	.00003	.001	72
Total	2.17498	99.999	5,190,571

Source: Adapted from Ramey and Finkelstein(1981) with the
expected number calculated by the author based on an
estimated 1985 U.S. population of 238,648,000.

ever, mental retardation does not follow a normal distribution, most noticeably in the severe and profound range where they are much more frequent than would be expected if intelligence followed a normal curve. For example, in the 1960 Dingman and Tarjan study, updated by Vitello and Soskin(1985), as shown in Table 2.8, we find the estimated actual prevalence to be 6% higher than estimated by the normal curve. Their estimated actual prevalence was 6,857,041 retarded persons in a population of 210,000,000 for a prevalence rate of 3.265%. However, in the roughly mild range of retarded there was only a 1% excess over what was expected. But in the roughly moderate to severe range there was 125% more than expected and in the roughly profound range there was 185,400% excess over normal curve expectations.

40

Table 2.8

Estimates of Numbers and Percentages of Mentally Retarded
Persons Based on the Normal Curve and Estimated Actual
Prevalence

IQ Range	Number and Percent Calculated from Normal Curve		Estimated Actual Prevalence		"Excess"	Percent "Excess"
	N	%	N	%		
0-20	57	0.001	104,935	1.530	104,878	185,400
20-50	186,635	2.891	420,000	6.125	233,365	125
50-70	6,269,106	97.108	6,332,106	92.345	63,000	1
Totals	6,455,798	100.000	6,857,041	100.000	401,243	6

Source: Adapted from Vitello and Soskin(1985, 19) based
           on a population of 210,000,000 after Dingman and
           Tarjan(1960).

From the foregoing information on the prevalence
of mental retardation there are clearly widely differing
estimates. There are a number of reasons why there is a
lack of precision on the proportion of the population that is
estimated to be retarded:

1. As already shown, if IQ scores alone are used as
the criterion, estimates will be higher than if the AAMD's
double criteria for retardation is used. Furthermore, from
the social systems perspective, the labeling of mental retardation is often social system specific. Consequently, persons may be treated as retarded in one context but not in
another. And all of these factors change over time.

2. In the majority of cases of mental retardation the
cause(s) of it cannot be clearly specified. Therefore, incidence cannot be specified at the point of onset for most
mildly or moderately retarded individuals but usually can
be for most severely and profoundly retarded persons if it is
accompanied by physical abnormalities as is usually the
case.

3. Prevalence of mental retardation varies by age
for several reasons and this makes accurate prevalence

rates quite difficult to determine. Since most of it is not detected until school age and many of the mildly retarded lead fairly normal lives with less labeling and need for special services once schooling is completed, the prevalence of mental retardation reaches its peak during the school years. It follows an inverted U-shaped curve--low in the preschool years, higher in the school years, and then dropping lower during the adult years once schooling is completed. Prevalence by age is also influenced by age specific death rates among the retarded. More of the severely and profoundly retarded die during childhood or at earlier ages than normal people. And some will be aborted, induced or natural, because of obvious somatic problems that are present and/or detected(Cartwright & Cartwright, 1978).

Since we have no national registration or uniform case finding procedures for mental retardation and many cases of it exist in a "zone of uncertainty," its actual prevalence will remain in dispute as does its precise measurement. Cartwright and Cartwright(1978, 65) helpfully explain:

> Although 3 percent of the population may be diagnosed as mentally retarded at some point during their lives, only 1 percent of the population is so classified at any given point in time. . . Mercer's explanation of the discrepancy is that the 3 percent figure is based upon the sole criterion of psychometric score: i.e. 3 percent fall below IQ 70. If a multidimensional definition such as the AAMD definition is used, the figure will drop to 1 percent.

THE RELATIONSHIP OF MENTAL RETARDATION TO OTHER HANDICAPS

While mental retardation is itself a handicapping condition, it tends to be accompanied by other physical, neurological and/or emotional problems to be considered handicaps independent of the mental retardation itself. A handicap has been defined by the Department of Health, Education and Welfare as "any mental or physical impairment that limits at least one 'major life activity' such as walking, seeing, hearing, speaking, breathing, working and performing manual tasks"(Stroman, 1982, 42).

As one moves down the scale from mild to profound retardation the probability increases that there will be handicaps, that there will be multiple handicaps, and that the severity of the handicaps will be greater. While no precise data are available on the nature of handicapping conditions by level of retardation, a majority of the persons with moderate retardation and below will have one or more of the following: physical impairments, mental disturbance disorders, organic medical conditions needing treatment, and disfiguring biological abnormalities such as misshappened faces, heads or bodies, cleft palates or central nervous system disorders.

One piece of evidence on the extent of the overlap between mental retardation and a series of nine specific but not exhaustive handicapping conditions is found in Table 2.9. This information comes from a 1971 study of 14,068 persons designated as mentally retarded who lived in either community settings or residential facilities for the mentally retarded. In this broad based sample, only 12% of the men-

Table 2.9

Percentage Prevalence of Other Handicaps Among the Mentally Retarded

Function	No Handicap	Partial Handicap	Severe Handicap	Description of Severe Handicap
Ambulation	57.8	32.4	9.0	Able to take few steps with help or totally unable to walk.
Upper limbs, gross motor control	57.5	34.2	8.2	Unable to hold large objects or complete lack of muscle control.
Upper limbs, fine motor control	56.1	34.9	9.0	Minimal use of hands, cannot use eating tools.
Speech	45.1	33.4	21.5	Can possibly

43

				communicate needs or wants but uses few or no words.
Hearing	85.0	11.5	3.4	Functionally or totally deaf; hearing aid of limited or no help.
Vision	73.3	20.9	5.9	Minimally sighted or legally blind.
Seizures (epilepsy, convulsions)	82.3	15.1	2.7	Severe seizures partially controlled or uncontrolled.
Behavior, emotional disorders	58.1	35.7	6.3	Adjustment not possible in home environment, abnormal behavior, may be dangerous.
Toilet training	77.5	10.2	12.3	Dependent on others, slightly trained or not trained.

Source: President's Committee on Mental Retardation, 1975, 14.

tally retarded were free of one or more handicapping conditions. Thus, 88% of the retarded in this sample had one or more handicaps and 35% of these were rated as severe. Since the nine conditions listed in Table 2.8 are not mutually exclusive, some of the retarded are more than dual handicapped--they have three or more handicaps(Conroy & Derr, 1971).

Mentally retarded persons are also more likely to have organically based illnesses it was found in the same 1971 survey of 14,086 mentally retarded persons. While 68.9% of the mentally retarded had no organic illnesses, the remaining 31.5% had chronic respiratory problems; 5.4% had dental or orthodontic conditions; 4.9% had extreme obesity or severe chronic anemia; 3.45% had heart disease;

3.4% had metabolic and endocrine disorders; 2.9% had skin disorders; 2.1% were facially disfigured; 1.7% had a cleft palate or other oral deformity and 0.8% were diabetic(Conroy & Derr, 1971).

The effects of multiple handicaps and/or handicaps in conjunction with organic illnesses or defects should be noted. First, is that multiple disabilities often act in a cumulative or synergistic manner; the inability to engage in one activity may limit participation in some other activity. For example, a lack of toilet training for a mentally retarded child or highly disturbing hyperactive behavior often excludes a person from regular classes or other learning activities. This exclusion or other forms of differential treatment may exacerbate behavioral disorders. Or a person with ambulation problems may be excluded from many forms of physical exercise and games which may contribute to obesity, respiratory problems and heart problems(President's Committee on Mental Retardation, 1975).

We noted earlier that mental retardation is one form of developmental disability. Some other forms of developmental disability which often overlap with mental retardation are cerebral palsy, epilepsy, and autism. All of these appear to reflect defective development of the central nervous system(Caviness & Williams, 1983) and need further description.

Cerebral palsy is a nonprogressive disorder dating from birth or early infancy. It is characterized by aberrations in motor functioning such as paralysis, weakness, involuntary movements, imbalance and lack of coordination. It is often accompanied by sensory disorders, seizures, and behavioral disorders(Grossman, 1983). About one half of an estimated 750,000 persons with cerebral palsy are also retarded while the incidence rate is around 1 to 2 per 1,000 births. Cerebral palsy may come in one of three "pure" forms or a mixture of these three. In spastic cerebral palsy, which covers about two-thirds of all cases, the clinical picture is stiffness in one to four limbs-- sometimes on one side of the body only or more severe in either the top or lower limbs. Limb movement is stiff, slow, jerky, and limited in range. Dyskinetic cerebral palsy is characterized by jerky, uncontrolled, purposeless movements where the muscle tone varies from tense to flaccid. This form usually involves all four limbs, is exaggerated during volitional activity and disappears during sleep.

45

Only about 10% of the cerebral palsied have <u>ataxic</u> <u>cerebral</u> <u>palsy</u> characterized by poor balance when standing and walking, a wide-based gait, difficulty in turning rapidly or engaging in repetitive finger movements. About three quarters of all persons with cerebral palsy have speech problems as regards articulation of certain sounds, a monotone speech quality and irregular speech rhythms(Baroff, 1986).

<u>Epilepsy</u> is a clinical disorder characterized by single or recurring episodes of loss of consciousness, convulsive movements during these episodes or disturbances of feeling and behavior. The age of onset is usually in childhood and is associated with some organic brain dysfunction. Epilepsy, especially the kind associated with more severe seizures, is more prevalent among those with moderate to profound retardation than among the mildly retarded. About one out of five epileptics is also mentally retarded. The overall prevalence rate of epilepsy is around 1 or 2 per 100 people(Grossman, 1983; Baroff, 1986; Breen & Richman, 1979).

<u>Autism</u> is a pervasive lack of responsiveness to people with gross deficits in language and communication, cognitive deficits, and bizarre responses to the environment such as ritualistic and compulsive behavior. Infantile autism, with onset before 30 months of age, is accompanied by seizures about one fourth of the time. About 40% of the children with this disorder have IQs below 50 and 70% with IQs below 70(American Psychiatric Association, 1980).

<u>Mental</u> <u>illness</u> is a frequent problem among the mentally retarded with a prevalence rate at least twice that of the normal population. Because the system of services for the mentally ill and mentally retarded have become increasingly separate over time, the difficulty of getting services for those with a "dual diagnosis" of mental illness and mental retardation became recognized in the early 1980's. The frequent treatment bias in the past was to treat mental retardation but to disregard the person's accompanying mental illness or perceive it as part of retardation. Certain types of mental illness are more prevalent among the mentally retarded than are others. The most frequently located types of mental illness among the retarded are those with personality disorders(such as antisocial or passive aggressive disorders), schizophrenia, adjustment disorders

46

and neuroses. While it is unknown if the mentally retarded commit more crimes, their crimes are often directed against others rather than property. The defective delinquent or retarded offender often falls into gaps in the service system as well(Menolascino, 1983).

As the severity of retardation increases so does the probability of the development of emotional or behavioral disorders. Maladaptive behaviors and psychiatric syndromes reach as high as 50% among the severely and profoundly retarded. And while about 5% of all school age boys develop "attentional deficit disorders," usually with hyperactivity but sometimes without it, the rate is higher for the mentally retarded. While most of those who develop this problem are not retarded, it is a more frequent problem for mentally retarded boys. The key features of this syndrome are inappropriate inattention and impulsivity, and, with the more common hyperactive variant of it, excessive movement and fidgeting. In the past many names have been given to this disorder: hyperkinetic syndrome, minimal brain damage, minimal brain dysfunction and minimal cerebral dysfunction. It particularly presents problems in school settings because of the inability of boys to pay attention to academic material for significant periods of time(American Psychiatric Association, 1980; Grossman, 1983).

Mental retardation should also be distinguished from learning disabilities with which it is sometimes confused. While a mentally retarded child may have a learning disability, many do not. Most learning disabled children are of average or above intelligence. John Meir(1976) defines a "learning disability" as

> A disorder in one or more of the basic psychosocial processes involved in understanding and using language, spoken or written, which disorder may manifest itself in imperfect ability to listen, think, speak, read, write, spell, or do mathematical calculations. Such disorders include such conditions as perceptual handicaps, brain injury, minimal brain dysfunction, dyslexia, and developmental aphasia, but such a term does not include children who have learning problems which are primarily the result of

visual, hearing, or motor handicaps, or mental retardation, or emotional disturbances or of environmental disadvantage.

The central difficulty of a learning disabled child is some deficit in the psychological processing of information. At the same time, a number of other behavioral symptoms often accompany it but which should be distinguished from it are: hyperactivity, poor motor coordination, difficulty in switching from one topic to another, social immaturity, a short attention span, difficulty in following multi-level directions, and memory deficits. While learning disabilities are often thought to be due to a lack of development of the central nervous system or damage to it, other causes are not ruled out because it is a complex of behaviors which are not fully understood. The range of learning disabilities goes from slight to severe and estimates of its prevalence range from one to two percent to twenty percent(Weiner, 1973; Edgar, 1978). Extensive diagnostic testing needs to be undertaken to distinguish learning disabilities from mental retardation. Since neither one is often detected until the school age years and both may result in subaverage scholastic performance, the distinction is important because their treatments are substantially different(Peterson, 1973).

Meir(1976) puts mental retardation, learning disabilities and developmental disabilities together under the generic title of DLD(Developmental and Learning Disabilities) conditions. His "conservative" estimate for the prevalence of these conditions during the schooling years when they reach their peak is 25%. This 25% rate is the cumulation of about 10% attributable to learning disabilities, 5% to mental retardation, 4% to cerebral palsy, 3% to epilepsy, and 2% to autism. These are estimates in areas where definitional ambiguities and diagnostic uncertainties abound.

SUMMARY

The meaning and measurement of intelligence has involved the work of many psychologists and others for over 100 years. Despite the massive literature on the nature of intelligence, extensive disagreement still abounds on whether it is best conceptualized as a series of basic mental capacities or as mental processes used in problem solving. These two approaches may be complementary in that the mental capacities approach identifies the key elements of what we term intelligence at one point in time while the process approach looks at mental processing dynamics over time. Piaget's theory of intelligence attempts to combine these approaches by studying how intelligence develops as the human organism matures.

The measurement of intelligence has gone through a complex evolution. Today, many types of tests are available to measure both intelligence and adaptive behavior among adults and children of various ages and abilities. Several widely used tests such as the Stanford-Binet Intelligence Scale and various Wechsler intelligence scales are reviewed along with key terms used in the measurement of intelligence.

The definition and measurement of mental retardation has also evolved over time but today the definitions of the American Association of Mental Deficiency and the American Psychiatric Associations are nearly identical. These groups define mental retardation as subaverage intellectual functioning existing concurrently with deficits in adaptive behavior occurring before age 18. Particular attention is given to the meaning and measurement of Adaptive Behavior and how it is related to four levels of retardation. Extended attention is also given to three "perspectives" on retardation--the medical, clinical and social systems perspectives. These different perspectives point out how different occupational groups classify mental retardation and the implications that has for treatment and determining the prevalence of mental retardation.

Over the last century the terminology applied to mental retardation and the degrees of it have changed and become more exact. Generic terms such as mentally defective and feeble-minded have been dropped to a large extent. And older terms indicating the degree of retardation such as moron, imbecile and idiot have been replaced by mild, severe and profound designations with more precise meanings. The redefinition of the term "developmental disability" in 1978 federal legislation was done in such a way that it excludes mild retardation but includes retardation below that level as well as other disabilities with onset before age 22 that are chronic, likely to require treatment, and result in substantial functional limitations in at least three of seven skill areas.

Incidence and prevalence studies on the extent of mental retardation are often imprecise because of the use of different definitions of retardation. If IQ scores alone are used the prevalence rate appears to be around 3%. However, if both adaptive behavior and IQ scores are used together, then the prevalence rate appears to be about 1%.

The relationship between mental retardation and other handicapping conditions is examined. The evidence available shows that as the severity of retardation increases from mild to profound the probability also increases that there will be additional and multiple handicaps with greater severity. Particular attention is given to disorders which sometimes overlap mental retardation: cerebral palsy, epilepsy, autism, mental illness, and attentional deficit disorders.

Chapter 3

The Causes and Prevention of Mental Retardation

Exploring the causes of mental retardation is a complex undertaking for several reasons. First of all, there are hundreds of known biological abnormalities that can contribute to or be the cause of mental retardation. While great gains have been made in the last few decades in our understanding of the chromosomal and genetic origins of retardation, this science may only be in its infancy with large pieces of the puzzle on genetic and hormonal aberrations still undiscovered. Secondly, the role that the social and/or psychological environment plays in developing intelligence and adaptive behavior is an equally complex process that is not fully understood yet. And thirdly, the interactions that go on between heredity and environment are exceedingly complex and difficult to conceptualize and trace. Therefore, the causes and prevention of retardation are complex and their study requires a truly interdisciplinary approach because of the many scientific disciplines that have contributed to our knowledge in this area.

OVERVIEW OF CAUSES OF MENTAL RETARDATION

Historically and currently both "nature" and "nurture" have been seen as playing significant roles in the development of intelligent behavior or in deviations from it. At various points in history nature or genetic endowment has been emphasized while at other times the environment has been conceptualized as playing a more signifi-

51

Table 3.1

Major Characteristics of the Two Major Causes of Mental Retardation

General Classification of the Causes of Mental Retardation	Biological Abnormalities	Psychosocial Deprivation
Specific Causes of Mental Retardation	Present at Conception: 1. Chromosomal errors 2. Genetic errors Occur after Conception: 1. Prenatal hazards 2. Perinatal hazards 3. Postnatal hazards	Environmental deprivation that exists with variations
Approximate Percentage of all Retardates	25%	75%
Etiological factors are known in specific cases	Yes, as a general rule	No, as a general rule

Table 3.1

Major Characteristics of the Two Major Causes of Mental Retardation
(continued)

General Classification of the Causes of Mental Retardation	Biological Abnormalities	Psychosocial Deprivation
Prevalence Rate by Socioeconomic Class Structure	Prevalence rates are fairly even throughout the class structure	Disproportionately found in lowest socioeconomic class
Usual Detection Time	At birth or first several years of life	Around beginning of school
Severity of Retardation	More likely to be moderate to profound	Most likely to be mild

53

cant role in the occurrence and level of retardation. Both views exist today but a newer view is that in many ways genetic endowment and environment are in complex interaction from conception to adulthood so that it is often artificial to think of mental retardation as due to either nature or nurture alone. Rather, it is nature in ongoing interaction with environment with multiple variables at work under both of these heading and with complex feedback loops that best conceptualize the origins of mental retardation.

Table 3.1 gives an overview of the two major origins of mental retardation--biological abnormalities and psychosocial deprivation. (What is now called "psychosocial deprivation" was earlier labeled "cultural familial retardation" but this older model made it conceptually difficult to separate out family social inheritance from genetic inheritance. However, this problem still remains to some degree with the nature-environment interaction model.) In this chapter we will first look at the known biological abnormalities which cause mental retardation. These include: (1)chromosomal abnormalities, (2)genetic abnormalities, and (3)nongenetic abnormalities that occur after conception during the prenatal, perinatal, and postnatal periods of development. Biological abnormalities are increasingly prevalent as we move from the mildly to the profoundly retarded, are usually detected at birth or in the early years because they are often accompanied by clearly visible physical or behavioral differences, are proportionally distributed throughout the class structure and account for 25% of all retardation. In most instances the etiological factors causing the retardation can be delimited to a certain number of factors if not specifically pinpointed.

In contrast, environmental deprivation, which we will describe more fully later in the chapter, comes in many variations without known specific agents in most particular cases. This type of mental retardation is most likely to be mild, often not detected until around the start of schooling or later, more behaviorally academic in nature, disproportionately found in the lowest socioeconomic classes which includes larger proportions of minorities, and may account for roughly 75% of all retardation.

BIOLOGICAL CAUSES OF MENTAL RETARDA-
TION

Chromosomal Abnormalities

Some forms of mental retardation are initiated at the point of conception. These can be broken down into chromosomal defects and gene defects. Cells, the basic unit of composition of all living things, are either sex cells(egg and sperm) or somatic cells(all other cells in the body like tissue, hair, bone, blood and muscle). Cells grow and divide over time and during the process of division a material called chromatin in the nucleus of the cell arranges itself into pairs of threadlike structures called chromosomes. All human cells except the sperm and egg cells contain 23 distinct pairs of chromosomes or a total of 46 chromosomes. Hereditary units, called genes, are located on these chromosomes. In each somatic chromosome pair there is one maternal one and one paternal one inherited from our parents. In somatic cell division, called mitosis, each chromosome replicates itself so that the new cell has the same number of chromosomes that were in the parent cell before division takes place. But with the sex cells, the division goes through two steps after replication called meiosis whereby only 23 rather than 46 chromosomes are present. So far we have discussed normal cell division. However, in the process of cell division different errors can occur in the replication of chromosomes. Thousands of chromosomal errors can occur and fall into two categories: (1)either too few or too many chromosomes are reproduced--an error in number, or (2)material is missing or added to a chromosome--an error in structure. Many of these errors are associated with mental retardation(Hutt & Gibby, 1976; Berlin, 1978; Baroff, 1986).

The most frequent chromosomal error that is related to mental retardation is Down syndrome. About one in 700 children is born with this condition and about 7% of the institutionally located retardates have this chromosomal error. There are three variations of chromosomal error diagnosed as Down syndrome: trisomy contains an extra chromosome 21; translocation involves the extra chromosome attached to another, usually 14, and in mosaicism some cells have 46 chromosomes but others have 47. Trisomy makes up around 90% of all cases of Down syndrome(Coon, 1985; Hutt & Gibby, 1976).

Characteristics of Down Syndrome. While the clinical features of Down syndrome show some variability, the relatively common features are: small body stature and head size, flattening of the back of the head and nasal bridge, slanting, almond-shaped eyes, round face, high arched palate, small and irregularly aligned teeth, large and protruding tongue, and short hands. Many children with Down syndrome have a hyperflexibility of the joints and a shortened life expectancy mainly among the one-third who have congenital heart disease. Seizure disorders occur in about 8%. Most Down syndrome children are moderately to severely retarded, but significantly, mental development shows a slow decline in measured IQ over time--usually from mild retardation to severe retardation. This decline in retardation appears sharper if the children are placed in institutions rather than kept at home. Most Down syndrome children show a development lag of several years in gross motor skills such as walking and running and a one to two year lag in toileting. Speech often lags more than two years and is characterized by poor articulation, simplicity, short sentences and extensive supplementation by gestures. Fine motor skills usually show a greater lag than gross motor skills. By young adulthood many Down syndrome persons have developed some self-help skills but this will vary by level of retardation. Some will be capable of work in sheltered workshops and occasionally in nondemanding competitive work. They usually appear most impaired on tasks requiring initiative, planning, verbal and academic skills--tasks related to the concept of general intelligence. Behaviorally, many, but not all, appear cheerful, friendly, affectionate, have good imitative abilities, short attention spans, low frustration tolerances, low sexual interests and hyperactivity(Grossman, 1983; Baroff, 1986; Coon, 1985).

A significant factor in the incidence of Down syndrome is the mother's age at conception. While the overall incidence is about 1 per 700 births, for mothers in their twenties it is about 1 in 2,000 births. However, with increasing maternal age the probability of a Down syndrome birth appears to rise geometrically. For women in the 30-34 age range the risk is 1 in 750, but rises to 1 in 300 for women 40-44 and around 1 in 25 for women 45 and over(Smith & Wilson, 1973; Berlin, 1978). Knowledge about the relationship of maternal age to Down syndrome can be used in preventive ways to counsel women about the risks of such pregnancies or to proceed with amniocentesis or a chorion biopsy if they are already pregnant. While Down syndrome is genetic it is not hereditary.

Prior to birth and usually during the eleventh to eighteenth weeks, amniocentesis can be used to detect Down syndrome as well as many other chromosomal and metabolic disorders. Amniocentesis involves withdrawing fluid from the amniotic sac surrounding the fetus by means of a thin needle inserted into the woman's abdomen. This fluid contains shed fetal cells which can be analyzed in numerous ways to detect many chromosomal disorders and over sixty metabolic disorders. A new experimental prenatal diagnostic test that could replace amniocentesis is the chorion biopsy. It involves inserting a plastic tube into the womb and removing a snip of tissue from the outermost fetal membrane called the chorion. This tissue is inspected for abnormalities. This procedure is advantageous in that it involves a shorter reporting time due to different laboratory procedures, and allows for earlier and thereby a less risky abortion should that be the parent's choice(Baroff, 1986; Kazdin, 1978).

Other Autosomal Chromosomal Abnormalities

Autosomal abnormalities are those associated with the nonsex chromosomes. A number of these, in addition to Down syndrome, are known. Trisomy 18(Edward's Syndrome) has an incidence of 1 in 5,000 live births and is characterized by severe retardation, gross skull malformation, abnormalities in the heart, kidneys and nervous system with a 90% mortality rate during the first year of life. Trisomy 13-15(D)(Patau Syndrome) has an incidence rate of 1 in 10,000 live births and is characterized by absence of eyes, cleft lip and palate, cerebral malfunctions, extra toes and fingers, severe retardation and around an 80% mortality rate in the first year of life. Partial deletions of chromosomes sometimes occur. If the deletion is large it usually is fatal, but small deletions on some chromosomes are related to survivable but severe retardation(Baroff, 1986). A number of other syndromes occur that include Trisomy 8, 9p-Syndrome, 5p-Syndrome, 18p-Syndrome and 18Q Syndrome(Pueschel & Thuline, 1983).

Sex Chromosome Abnormalities

The sex chromosome for a normal male is XY and for a normal female it is XX. Of the two sex chromosomes present in normal people, an X is derived from the mother and X or Y from the father. Chromosomal abnormalities can be found in the sex chromosomes where there are one to three extra Xs and these extra Xs are related to mental impairment. The Klinefelter Syndrome(XXY) involves an extra X chromosome and is found only among males with an incidence rate of 1 in 600. The Klinefelter Syndrome is characterized by hypergonadism, infertility, small testes, slim bodies, enlarged breasts starting in adolescence, frequent personality problems and average lower IQs with about one fourth below 70. If additional extra Xs are present, the retardation is usually much more severe. Males with an XYY pattern of sex chromosomes have been described as more aggressive, more antisocial, more impulsive, and with IQ scores averaging ten points below normal(Berg, 1965; Baroff, 1986).

The XXX syndrome occurs in about 1 in 850 females but does not produce any physical abnormalities and mental impairment is only slightly more likely. However, the addition of more X chromosomes like XXXX, and XXXXX, increased the likelihood of more severe retardation(Baroff, 1986).

The Turner Syndrome(XO) is a condition found in about one of 2,200 females where there is only an X chromosome. Such females usually have small stature, experience sexual infantalism due to incomplete ovarian development, are infertile, may have elbow deformity, webbing of the neck, and congenital heart defects. But most Turner Syndrome females are in the normal range of mental development(Abuelo, 1983).

Another abnormality of the sex chromosome, called the "fragile X syndrome", appears to be more common among males and may help to explain why more males than females are retarded. The "fragile X syndrome" appears to run in some families, be associated primarily with moderate retardation and enlarged testes and occurs in about 1 in 100 live births but 2% of the retarded population(Abuelo, 1983; Baroff, 1986).

Genetic Abnormalities

Genes are the basic units of heredity which carry biochemical information to the cells which pattern the kinds of proteins the cells will utilize. Genes are located on the chromosomes. Genes are encoded in chain molecules of nucleic acids of two types--DNA(deoxyribonucleic acid) and RNA(ribonucleic acid). Since genes are located on the chromosomes and inherited this means that each gene contributed by one parent has a counterpart gene derived from the other parent with the exception of X-linked genes in the male which do not have counterparts on the Y chromosome. A gene may "mutate" or become abnormal as a result of some alteration in its DNA structure. If the mutated gene has the capability of producing some organic abnormality in the presence of a normal gene it is called a dominant gene. Recessive genes usually produce organic abnormalities only when both genes are abnormal. We will first discuss dominant and recessive single gene disorders and then look at multifactorial gene disorders. Multifactorial gene disorders are usually conceptualized as involving multiple genes and frequently interacting with environmental factors and more closely associated with mild, familial and/or psychosocial retardation(Abuelo, 1983; Baroff, 1986).

Since there are thousands of genes and hundreds of known genetic disorders, this section of the chapter does not have the space to catalogue all of the known dominant and recessive genetic disorders. Rather, it will illustrate a few of the more common ones which are also related to mental retardation. It should be pointed out that many dominant and recessive disorders may produce organic and/or physical disorders that are either independent or minimally related to mental retardation.

Dominant Genetic Disorders. In dominant genetic disorders only one of the parents is typically the carrier. Such a condition exists when the parent carrier transmits a single defective gene to statistically one-half of the offspring. However, it is possible that in reality all, none or some of the offspring will have the defective gene although the probability is that only half will have it. In addition, the parent who transmits the defective gene may have either inherited it or it is not inherited but it has developed as a new mutation in his own cells. In the latter case the parent will not suffer from it. In the case where the parent inherited it, he must have a sufficiently mild degree of it to be fertile and capable of reproductive behavior to transmit it(Berg, 1965.) In addition, dominantly inherited disorders have two other characteristics: (1)variable age of onset, and (2)variable expressivity which means the condition may range from being so mild that it cannot be detected to very severe(Abuelo, 1983).

Tuberous Sclerosis for example is a rare condition that occurs in about 1 out of 30,000 persons or less. Its clinical symptoms are abnormalities of the skin and nervous system although all of the manifestations of these two conditions may not appear simultaneously. The abnormal skin appearance include a butterfly-type of rash on the face and oval-shaped depigmented or "white spots" on the body and extremities with variable age of onset. In about 60% of the cases there is mental retardation which is often but not always severe and which is also progressive and associated with cerebral calcification. In the more severe cases epilepsy is also present. Common secondary symptoms include visual, lung, heart, and kidney problems. Many patients with this disorder do not live beyond age 25(Abuelo, 1983; Baroff, 1986).

Craniosynostosis Syndromes usually involve dominant inheritance patterns that are frequently accompanied by mental retardation. With these symptoms there are premature closures of skull sutures which produce deformities in the head and this in turn often damages the brain and eyes. The premature closure of the fibrous tissues between cranial bone plates may occur in the womb or after birth or some degree of both. Sometimes surgical opening of these sutures to allow normal brain growth may prevent or reduce the severity of head malformation and retardation. The most common form of craniosynostosis syndromes is the Alpert Syndrome. In this syndrome the skull is enlarged at the top, the eyes protrude but with a downward slant, there is an underdeveloped nasal bridge but a beaklike nose and the digits of the hands and feet are fused. Most persons with Alpert Syndrome are moderately to severely retarded and apparently from a mutant gene. Another form of craniosynostosis is Crouzon's Syndrome where there are cranial deformities much like in the Alpert Syndrome but without hand and feet webbing or fusion.

60

Dominant inheritance is found in 67% of these disorders(Abuelo, 1983; Baroff, 1986).

Neurofibromatosis, also called Von Recklinghausens Disease, has an incidence of about 1 in 3,000 births and is the most common of the dominant genetic disorders. This disorder is characterized by oval-shaped light brown splotches of skin pigmentation in 94% of the cases, scoliosis in 40%, large heads in 24%, seizures in 12%, and retardation, usually mild, in 10% of the cases and often accompanied by brain tumors. About half of these cases appear to be mutants and the other half dominant inheritance(Aubelo, 1983).

Myotonic Dystrophy is one form of muscular dystrophy with onset anywhere from infancy to old age and with highly variable degrees of severity. The symptoms usually include some mix of the following: weakness but rigidity in extremity muscles, dropping eyelids and mouth, a wasting of the temporal area, cataracts, endocrine and cardiac abnormalities, and varying degrees of mental retardation. Women with myotonic dystrophy often give birth to children who develop a severe case of it in infancy. They should receive genetic counseling as a possible preventive measure(Abuelo, 1983).

Recessive Genetic Disorders

Recessive genetic disorders are those where both parents carry the abnormal genes but are usually unaffected by the disorder themselves. The probability is 25% that any offspring of such parents will receive both abnormal genes. While most people carry several recessive genes, the probability of their being passed on increases with consanguanity(blood-relatedness). For example, if we assume that the risk for mental retardation is 3% for the general population, the risk for retardation increases with consanguinous matings to 6% for first cousins and to about 30% for incestuous matings(parent-child, brother-sister). There are many more kinds of recessive genetic disorders than dominant genetic disorders. Abuelo(1983, 111) states that "most recessively inherited disorders associated with mental retardation are either metabolic in origin, isolated CNS malformations, or multiple congenital anomaly-mental retardation(MCA/MR) syndromes." We will first look at those metabolic disturbances associated with mental retardation. These inborn errors of metabolism show great complexity in the processes by which they work and in the variability of the symptomology.

Inborn Errors of Metabolism

Phenylketonuria(PKU) is a rare inborn error of metabolism. Metabolism is a "stepwise series of biochemical reactions" with each reaction "catalyzed by a particular enzyme." Some defect in the enzyme, which is inborn, "produces a metabolic block which may have pathologic consequence"(Abuelo, 1983, 111). The things which may be metabolically blocked include amino acids(the most common), or proteins, or carbohydrates.

Phenylketonuria, if untreated, is almost always accompanied by severe to profound retardation. It is caused by a deficient liver enzyme called phenylaline hydroxylase which in turn causes excessively high levels of an amino acid called phenylaline which is toxic to the developing brain. In addition to mental retardation the PKU child usually has seizures, eczema, reduced stature and head size, lighter coloring and a musty odor to the urine. PKU is a rare condition with an incidence of about 1 in 12,000 newborns. The PKU infant is normal at birth but the process of progressive intellectual impairment begins when the newborn eats protein which contains about 5% phenylaline. PKU children are often autisticlike, hyperactive with sterotypic rocking or posturing movements, and unpredictable. PKU is one form of genetic retardation that is amenable to prevention or amelioration. If a diet low in phenylaline is introduced in the first few weeks or perhaps months of life, the evidence suggests PKU can be prevented. However, with increasing delay of beginning a low phenylaline diet the degree of retardation may be only reduced, not prevented, especially if it is not introduced before nine months. Limited information suggest this difficult diet may need to be maintained at least through adolescence or there may be retrogression in intellectual performance(Abuelo, 1983; Baroff, 1986).

Two unfortunate consequences could result from the successful treatment of PKU however. One is that those affected by it and who are carriers of it are likely to be normal people who are reproductive and not like the severely retarded and untreated PKU who is not reproductive. This means that over time the number of persons who carry this recessive gene would increase and in turn increase the probability of bearing PKU children as the gene pool of PKU widens. To deal with this, more genetic screening, genetic counseling and/or special diets would be necessary. A second consequence is that female PKU's who, if untreated would not bear children, now may bear children but expose them in utero to toxic levels of pheny-laline. Such "induced" PKU means the children may be born microcephalic, small in stature and retarded rather than having it occur after birth when the infant begins nourishment. To avoid this problem, PKU women would need to be counseled about three options available: avoiding pregnancy, therapeutic abortion, or keeping on the distasteful low phenylaline diet during pregnancy(Abuelo, 1983; Baroff, 1986).

Galactosemia is another inborn metabolic deficiency that is preventable with very early intervention. Galactosemia involves the newborn's inability to metabolize galactose, a constituent in milk. If milk and milk products are not removed early from a newborn's diet it will not thrive and may not live. Early infant symptoms include vomiting, diarrhea, jaundice, an enlarged liver, and increased susceptibility to neonatal infections. If the infant survives, it will later develop cataracts, cirrhosis of the liver, and mental retardation. However, if all milk products are eliminated soon after birth from their diets, such children then appear to have nearly average IQs. The incidence of galactosemia is estimated at between 1 in 40,000 and 200,000 births. Screening and intervention, to be effective, must be done shortly after birth(Abuelo, 1983; Baroff, 1986.)

Tay-Sachs disease is a disorder stemming from an infant's inability to metabolize fats(lipids). As these lipids accumulate in many tissues there is an early onset, after a few months of age, or blindness, seizures, spasticity, extreme sensitivity to sound, mental deterioration, and then death before age four. This too is a rare lethal disease but with a much higher incidence rate among Jews from Eastern European countries. The disease is preventable by biochemically testing prospective parents and/or amniocentesis during pregnancy or a therapeutic abortion(Abuelo, 1983; Baroff, 1986).

The Hurler Syndrome, like Tay-Sachs disease, is a lyssomal storage disease where certain chemical waste products are not excreted adequately because of a lack of a particular enzyme. These waste products accumulate in various body tissue. In infancy the symptoms of dwarfism, large head with cranial deformities, deafness, and mental retardation develop which usually lead to death by adolescence(Abuelo, 1983).

Some regressive disorders are sex-linked which means that the abnormal gene is located in the X-linked chromosome and therefore found only in males. The Hurler Syndrome appears to be sex-linked. The Lesch-Nyhan Syndrome is an inherited type of cerebral palsy that is accompanied by mental retardation and self-mutilation like severe lip and finger biting. This syndrome occurs only in males with an onset in infancy followed by a progression of the cerebral palsy in childhood(Abuelo, 1983).

NONGENETIC BIOLOGICAL CAUSES OF MENTAL RETARDATION

In this section of the chapter we will look at three sequential time periods in which retardation-producing disorders may occur. The first time period, the prenatal period, is the gestational period that normally lasts nine months during which time the fetus can be exposed to many hazards in the intrauterine environment. The second time period is the perinatal period that includes the many risks associated with birthing including those of prematurity. The third and longest period is the postnatal period that starts after the birthing process is completed. Table 3.2 lists both the genetic biological factors and nongenetic biological factors that can contribute to mental retardation.

Prenatal Hazards

While the role of prenatal biologic agents that contribute to mental retardation are fairly well understood, their particular influence must be understood within context

Table 3.2

Etiological Classification of Mental Retardation

Type	Example
GENETIC	

Type	Example
Chromosomal abnormalities	Down syndrome, trisomy 18 & 13
Disorders of amino acids metabolism	Phenylektonuria, maple syrup urine disease
Disorders of mucopoly-saccharide metabolism	Hunters's or Hurler's syndrome
Disorders of Lipid metabolism	Tay-Sachs disease
Disorders of carbohydrate metabolism	Fucosidosis, galacto-semia
Disorders of purine metabolism	Lesch-Nyhan syndrome
Miscellaneous inborn errors of metabolism	I-cell disease
Consanguinity, incest, etc.	
Hereditary degenerative disorders	Schilder's disease, retinal degeneration, etc.
Hormonal deficiency	Congenital hypothy-roidism, psuedohypo-parathyroidism
Hereditary syndromes or malformations	Primary microcephaly, X-linked hydrocephalus
Neuroectodermatoeses	Tuberous sclerosis
Unknown	

Type	Example
ACQUIRED	

Type	Example
PRENATAL	
Infection	Rubella, toxoplasmosis
Irradiation	Microcephaly
Toxins	Ethyl alcohol, mercury
Unknown	Malformations
PERINATAL	
Prematurity	
Anoxia	Birth injuries, hypo-glycemia
Cerebral Damage	Hemorrhage, trauma, infection

POSTNATAL

Brain injuries	Accidents, hemorrhage, ruptured aneurysm
Infection	Meningitis, brain abscess
Anoxia	Cardiac arrest, respiratory distress, hypoglycemia
Poisons	Lead, mercury, carbon monoxide
Hormonal deficiency	Hypothyrodism
Metabolic	Hypernatremia, hypoglycemia
Postimmunization encephalopathy	Rabies, pertussis, smallpox
Sociocultural Deprivation	
Kernicterus	
Epilepsy	

Source: Milunsky, 1983, 16.

of: (1)a frequent time lapse between the injurious event and its actual discovery, (2) the possibility of multiple causal agents operating simultaneously, and (3)the timetable of embryological development. This last concept refers to the fact that the cerebral and anatomic growth of the fetus follows a fixed sequence in time. Thus the impact of some hazard may be quite variable depending on when it occurs in the timetable of embryological development. Retrospectively, the nature of the disorder may indicate when the insult occurred to have the effect that it did.

Prenatal infections that are the most common include rubella, toxoplasmosis, syphilis, and cytomegalovirus. However, their overall contribution to the numbers of mentally retarded is small. Congenital rubella is caused by a virus that infects the pregnant woman and is totally preventable through a vaccine on the market since 1969. This disease often has few effects on the mother but it can cause massive damage to the fetus if the infection occurs in the first trimester of pregnancy. In fact, such undetected fetuses are often aborted naturally or therapeutically or stillborn. The symptoms are highly variable and largely dependent on fetal age. Fetuses infected in the first two months either do not survive half the time or show serious disorders in the other half. Those fetuses infected in the second trimester show malformation only 20% of the time and there appears to be no damage to the fetus from maternal rubella occurring in the last trimester. The extensiveness and severity of the symptoms vary widely but may include the following: heart defects, hearing and visual impairments, dental anomalies, hemorrhaging, cerebral palsy, seizures, delay in motor development, hyperactivity, restlessness, stereotyped movements and mental retardation. About half the children are retarded with severity ranging from borderline to profound(Baroff, 1986; Milunsky, 1983).

Congenital toxoplasmosis is a protozoan infection that has decreasing horrendous effects with the growing age of the fetus but which is rarely damaging to the pregnant mother. Those children who survive usually have some degree of blindness, psychomotor disturbance, microcephaly or hydrocephaly, and mental retardation ranging from mild to severe. The protozoan parasite is found in cat feces and raw meat which, clearly, should be avoided by pregnant women(Baroff, 1986).

Congenital cytomegalovirus affects about one percent of all newborns but is asymptomatic in 95% of these children. They frequently die in the first year due to enlargement of the spleen and liver, skin hemorrhages, cerebral calcification, microcephaly and jaundice. Survivors may be blind, deaf, neurologically abnormal, and show varying degrees of retardation(Baroff, 1986).

RH and ABO maternal-fetal blood incompatibilities are treatable; but if they go untreated may then cause fetal anemia which may damage the developing brain and precipitate some degree of retardation, motor disabilities and hearing loss in the newborn child. Rh blood incompatibility is a more common problem and occurs only when an Rh-negative mother bears a child from an Rh-positive father and where there is some mixing of the maternal and fetal blood. If the baby's blood enters the mother's bloodstream(a rather rare event), the mother produces antibodies against the Rh-positive blood of the child which can result in fetal anemia.

A number of maternal diseases and infections have been shown to correlate substantially with mental retarda-

67

tion as well as with other organically related handicapping conditions. Pregnant women who have diabetes mellitus, chronic renal disease, tuberculosis, herpes, thyroid abnormalities, hepatitis, influenza, mumps, and chicken pox increase the probability that the fetus' developing brain may be assaulted and damaged in some way and this may contribute to a lower level of mental functioning(Berlin, 1978; Baroff, 1986).

Teratogenic effects refer to abnormal conditions, diseases and disabilities which come from environmental insults on the developing fetus. A number of "teratogens" have been identified: x-rays, alcohol, tobacco, narcotic addictions, possible marijuana, as well as nonprescription and prescription drugs which may damage the growing fetus. The use and especially overuse of some of these drugs may cause a variety of interconnected anomalies including narcotic addiction, tremors, low birth weight, greater numbers of premature babies, respiratory disorders, retarded physical development, cardiac defects, microcephaly, more fetal problems and various levels of mental retardation(Berlin, 1978; Salvia, 1978; Milunsky, 1983).

Adequate maternal nutrition has been shown to be related to normal babies and inadequate nutrition to mental retardation. In early pregnancy the brain grows by increasing the number of brain cells while in later pregnancy it grows by increasing the number and size of cells. After birth no new cells are formed, only their size increases. Therefore, the average pregnant woman gains 25 pounds during pregnancy and this provides the biochemical fuels necessary to assure maximal brain growth. But once born, no amount of nutrition can reverse any brain damage that occurred during pregnancy. Consequently, inadequate maternal nutrition in the form of an unbalanced diet or inadequate levels of calories and proteins may contribute to mental retardation(Berlin, 1978).

Perinatal Hazards

The perinatal period is a short but important time period when damage can occur to the infant, particularly the head which is larger than other parts of the fetus. Four perinatal factors associated with mental retardation are: (1)premature birth, (2)mechanical injury to the brain, (3)anoxia where insufficient oxygen reaches the brain dur-

68

ing the period of labor and delivery, and (4)perinatal toxins in the new environment outside the womb against which the newborn has inadequate defenses(Lott, 1983; Berg, 1965).

Premature births are those born three or more weeks before the usual gestational period or weighing less than 5 1/2 pounds. Premature infants have a three times greater risk of suffering neurological damage than do full-term babies. And the earlier the prematurity the greater the risk of having low birth weight, dietary deficiency, respiratory problems and mental retardation. The premature infant is less ready to adjust to the extrauterine conditions of breathing, sucking, adjusting to outside temperatures, and infectious agents. Prematurity is more frequent among nonwhites and those without prenatal medical care which are undoubtedly correlated. Prematurity is also more likely among pregnant smokers and those under age 18 or over 35(Baroff, 1986; Berlin, 1978).

There are two risks that the fetus is exposed to as it passes through the birth canal and that are related to birth weight, head size, the size of the birth canal and the abnormality of fetus presentation at the birth canal opening. The first of these is the mechanical pressure on the head from the birth canal or forceps that may cause compression, hemorrhaging, and irreversible brain damage. The second factor is that during labor and delivery the fetus' body and brain needs adequate oxygen supplied by the blood of the mother through the umbilical cord. Should the umbilical cord become knotted, twisted or compressed so that an adequate oxygen supply does not reach the brain for some period of time, irreversible brain damage may result. Asphyxia(oxygen deprivation) may also be due to the premature separation of the placenta, excessive anesthesia which depresses respiration, obstruction of respiratory passage and difficult deliveries. Overlarge newborns often make labor and delivery more difficult. Progress in birth delivery and specialized fetal monitoring and care have reduced mortality due to head trauma but at the same time may salvage persons with a number of abnormalities who would have otherwise died(Berlin, 1978; Lott, 1983; Guillemin & Holmstrom, 1986).

Postnatal Hazards

As indicated in Table 3.2 there are a wide variety of factors which can contribute to mental retardation during infancy and up to maturity. The hazard of these factors is relatively greater during infancy when the child's immune system and defenses are less developed and growth more pronounced and critical. The major biological hazards to mental retardation during this time are infectious diseases which may damage the brain, cerebrovascular accidents, brain tumors, environmental poisons and protein malnutrition.

A number of infections can elevate temperature to critical levels or attack the brain itself including meningitis, poliomyletis, measles, mumps, diphtheria, encephalitis, and whooping cough. Both primary encephalitis, which attacks the brain itself, and secondary encephalitis, which infects other organ systems, may inflame the brain and cause permanent neurological deficits such as visual problems, seizures, epilepsy and mental retardation. Meningitis, while often treatable by drugs, often has crippling effects on the body and mind if it occurs in the first year of life(Baroff, 1986; Berlin, 1978).

Cerebral Trauma, injuries to the head, may occasionally contribute to cognitive deficits, particularly if severe and involving intracranial bleeding and pressure on the brain. There may be many sources of such accidents: falls, vehicular accidents, child abuse, firearms, and near suffocations and drownings. And both brain tumors and cerebrovascular accidents or intracranial hemorrhaging may impair brain functioning.

Environmental Toxins include chemicals that have been shown to impair neurological functioning and impairment. They include drug overdoses and their side effects, mercury, lead, thalium and arsenic poisoning. Perhaps the most critical of these is the ingestion and inhalation of lead from lead-based paints used in many old houses, lead found in many old waterpipes, and perhaps the breathing of lead exhaust emissions(Berlin, 1978).

The role of child malnutrition, except in severe malnutrition infancy, is not fully known yet as regards its role in cognitive functioning. However, it remains a strong suspect in contributing to mental deficiencies. Brain growth is more closely connected to protein intake than just

70

calorie intake. Severe protein deficits in infancy at least slow mental development in childhood, but whether this is permanent is not yet known. Research in this area is difficult because malnutrition usually occurs in homes where there are other confounding causes such as more disease, less medical care and a less stimulating environment(Baroff, 1986).

MULTIPLE BIOLOGICAL DISORDERS

A number of disorders that are frequently associated with mental retardation have multiple origins. This means they may be either/or or both/and: (1)biologically genetic-chromosomal abnormalities or dominant or recessive gene disorders, and (2)biologically non-genetic such as an infection in the womb that comes from the environment. For example, microcephaly, defined as head circumference two standard deviations below the mean for a child's age and sex, may come from multiple sources. It may be genetic in origin--chromosomal disorders or dominant, recessive, or X-linked disorders. And/or it may be non-genetic in origin from such sources as excessive alcohol intake during pregnancy, intrauterine infection during pregnancy or damage to the skull during delivery. The condition of macroecphaly, a generic term for abnormally large head size, can also be either genetic or non-genetic in origin(Abuelo, 1983).

Neural-tube Defects

Neural-tube defects are multifactorial congenital gene defects where the neural tube(the structure that develops into the brain and spinal cord) do not close properly. About 1 in 1,000 children are born with one of three variations of this defect: (1)amencephaly which is characterized by incomplete development of the brain and head, (2)enecphalocele characterized by the protrusion of the brain from the head, and (3)spina bifida where cystic lesions on the spinal cord protrude through the skin. The first two types of neural tube defects result in natural abortions, still births or early death. Some spina bifida infants who get surgical intervention to close the spinal protrusions may survive. About 90% of all neural tube defects can be detected in the prenatal period which allows prevention by means of therapeutic abortion. Tertiary prevention of hydrocephalis requires surgery in utero or shortly after birth that involves placing an intracranial shunt to draw off excessive fluids to other parts of the body when natural drainage channels are blocked(Vitello & Soskin, 1985).

ENVIRONMENTAL CAUSES OF MENTAL RE-TARDATION

A very substantial literature exists which suggests that the quality of the environment in which persons are born, reared and live has a substantial influence on the development of intelligence and adaptive behavior. Deficiencies in the environment have been viewed as capable of contributing in significant ways to mental retardation. But the concept of environment is a global concept that is made up of many smaller variables that elude precise conceptualization and measurement. Furthermore, some aspects of the environment overlap with biological factors which can contribute to mental and physical development such as intake of environmental toxins, nutrition in both the prenatal and postnatal periods, and access to variable qualities of prenatal, perinatal and postnatal health services. Despite the conceptual problems where psychosocial factors are less explicitly defined but more complexly interrelated, we need to try to understand what factors in the environment contribute to poor development as normatively defined by the AAMD definition of mental retardation.

Enriched, Normal and Deprived Environments

For purposes of analysis we will conceptualize the environment as a multidimensional continuum that ranges widely from enriched to deprived. These multidimensional factors will include physical well-being and psychosocial well-being with this latter factor much more complex and susceptible to highly variable formulations. Table 3.3 is an attempt to delineate some of these factors at two extreme type levels. But it should be recognized that each of the factors that we identify fall along highly variable continua of small gradations. The psychosocial environment relates to the biological, emotional, social and intellectual needs of

Table 3.3

Characteristics of Two Extreme Types of
Psychosocial Environments

PHYSICAL

1. Excellent protection
   from extremes of heat,
   cold, wetness, and
   noxious agents.

2. Rich variety of environmental stimuli that are
   explorable.

3. Excellent nutrition in
   quality and quantity.

4. Full access to high quality
   health care.

1. Extensive exposure
   to extremes of
   heat, cold, wetness
   and noxious agents.

2. Extreme deprivation
   of exposure to en-
   vironmental
   stimuli.

3. Extreme deprivation
   from an inadequate
   diet.

4. No access to health
   care.

PSYCHOSOCIAL

5. Loving, caring caretakers.

6. Responsive caretakers who
   guide the child's development in terms of developing
   competence skills, autonomy
   and self-esteem.

7. Child is exposed to a wide
   variety of stimulating
   sociocultural experiences.

8. Extensive verbal interaction
   with others.

9. Reward system that involves
   understanding contingencies.

5. Abusive, neglectful
   caretakers.

6. Unresponsive care-
   takers who do not
   guide the child's
   development of
   competence skills,
   autonomy and self-
   esteem and teach
   maladaptive
   behaviors.

7. Child is deprived
   of stimulating
   sociocultural
   experiences.

8. Gross absence of
   verbal interaction
   with others.

9. Authoritative-
   punitive reward
   systems.

individuals as they mature from infancy to adulthood. And the relative size of a particular influence may depend on when it happens in the child's developmental trajectory. Thus, early, loving contact between a child and its caretakers(usually parents) may be more important than the presence or absence of this contact later on. A lot of stimulation that is unrelated to the biological needs and/or mental age of the child may have little benefit. Enriched or deprived environments do not stand alone but are relative to the developmental needs of the child.

The nine factors listed in Table 3.3 do not stand alone as isolated variables but are interrelated to the others in the home and outside-of-home environment of the growing person. A deprived environment is often associated with economic poverty--inadequate income to provide good nutrition, housing, and a stimulating social environment. Poor families are often associated with large numbers of children whose parents do not give them adequate individual attention, lack the education to provide rich verbal stimulation and lack the time and abilities to give them the emotional and cognitive supports necessary to give the children success in developing their own personality, skills and achievement goals(Neisworth & Smith, 1978; Ainsworth & Wittig, 1969; Ramey & Finkelstein, 1981). Most children probably grow up in relatively "normal" environments--somewhere between enriched environments and brutalizing environments that deprive individuals from exposure to rich and caring sociocultural stimulation.

There is probably substantial agreement on what constitutes an enriched or deprived physical environment. An enriched physical environment is one where there is good protection from the elements, good nutrition and health care, and rich in visual, auditory and tactile stimuli to explore that are related to the child's developmental needs. In contrast the deprived environment is grossly deficient in all of these areas.

There is probably less agreement on what constitutes an enriched or deprived psychosocial environment because it is constituted by literally thousands of microevents and microprocesses between the growing child and parents, siblings, friends, teachers, and others. These microevents and microprocesses can be clustered into larger schemas. One of the characteristics of an enriched environment is loving, caring caretakers who show a

74

devoted interest in the child's total welfare in contrast to abusive and/or neglecting parents who physically, psychologically and perhaps sexually abuse the child or are totally neglectful of the child's total and changing needs. An enriched environment is one in which caretakers respond to the child's needs for intimacy, guidance, challenge, self-esteem, successes in developing adaptive skills, and in growing autonomy. Such caretakers will provide experiences in all these areas in such a way that the growing child is recognized as an independent person. In contrast, unresponsive caretakers do not guide the child in developing competency skills in these areas and may teach them maladaptive ways in dealing with problems such as crime, alcoholism, bitter and unproductive feuding, indifference and rigid authoritarianism. Such families do not provide their children a variety of positive growth-enhancing experiences with their environments. In the enriched environment, the child will be exposed to a variety of verbal mediators so that he can understand himself within that environment and develop skills in dealing with emotions, people and things. Particularly important here is the development of cognitive skills in analysis and problem solving that depend on abstract conceptualization of how events are interrelated. This stands in stark contrast to where there is a gross absence of verbal stimulation, social interaction or the interaction is of such a nature as not to encourage inquiry, independent analysis, verbal manipulation of ideas or verbal complexity. And lastly, the enriched environment uses reward systems that involve understanding contingencies on the part of the child. Contingent stimulation is one where the person's reactions produce some meaningful effect on the environment. This type of stimulation appears to develop reasoning ability in responding to the world. Authoritative reward systems, in contrast, develop conformity of thought and behavior rather than independent reasoning ability. They appear to diminish independence, motivation for accomplishment and cognitive skills in the manipulation of ideas(Bronfenbrenner, 1972; Miller, 1970; Baroff, 1986; Neisworth & Smith, 1978).

The psychosocial explanation for retardation is primarily used to explain about 75% of all retardation--that which is usually mild and where no clear biological etiology is presently detectable to explain it. Psychosocial retardation is found to be statistically concentrated in homes described as psychologically, socially, and economically impoverished. Housing and hygiene are poor, nutrition and medical care inadequate, infectious diseases are more common. While these conditions characterize many poor families in general and may help to explain why about three times(or about 9%) as many of the poor are retarded, they do not explain why 90% of the poor are not retarded. To explain why only about 9% of the poor and around only 0.5% of the upper classes are mildly retarded we need to look more intensively at the area of family life-- particularly child rearing practices and mother-child relationships. "Disadvantaged children" may suffer a range of deprivation from unresponsive parents who are concerned more about themselves or survival than the nature and quality of the stimulation their children receive. These homes have been described as disorganized homes involving inept parenting with adults living from crisis to crisis like separation, desertion, divorce, illness, job loss, and child abandonment. Parents lack the communication skills to stimulate childhood acquisition of good verbal and thinking skills. Children are without toys and possessions of their own and often unattended to except in demanding do's and don't's. Crowding is frequent with large families, exploratory opportunities limited, reading to the children rare or absent, and chaos rather than organization characteristic of mealtime, bedtimes and other activities. But such descriptive findings of homes most characteristic of the origin of mildly retarded children do not easily lend themselves to research using more precise instrumentation and quantification(Begab, 1981).

The relationship of IQ and environment is a complex area to investigate because of the hundreds of variables that can be conceptualized in various ways and levels. Bouchard and Segal(1985) reviewed hundreds of studies on the relationship of IQ and malnutrition, family occupation, language development, achievement motivation, provisions for general learning, press for language development, family size, birth order, and inequalities in the quality of preschool and school programs. With such "small" variables, the size of such correlations was usually small. Bouchard and Segal(1985, 452) conclude:

> The principal finding in this review of environmental effects on IQ is that no single

environment factor appears to have a large influence on IQ. Variables widely believed to be important are usually weak. Some social scientists have been discouraged by this finding, and they have argued that we simply do not know very much about how environment works. We would like to argue differently: Even though many studies fail to find strong environmental effects, and some misinterpret genetic for environmental variance, most of the factors studied do influence IQ in the direction predicted by the investigator. What does not exist is a small subset of variables, which, when manipulated simultaneously, leads to substantial improvement in IQ. The message here is straightforward and does not originate with us. It is simply that environmental effects are multifactorial and largely unrelated to each other.

There may be substantial influence of this global thing we call environment on mental ability. The problem is in defining it and measuring it. As Jensen(1981, 33) observes, "My hunch is that the nongenetic variance in IQ is the result of such a myriad of microenvironmental events as to make it extremely difficult, if not impossible, to bring more than a small fraction of these influences under experimental control." And without experimental control, hypotheses about the relationship of "environment" and IQ or retardation may remain largely as hypotheses. Thus a major research agenda awaits those who want to more definitively show the relationship of the polysocial environment to IQ.

Because of the difficulty of separating environment from familial genetic inheritance, we now turn to the analysis of multifactor causes of mental retardation.

Multifactorial Causes of Mental Retardation

Multifactorial studies involve the study of both genetic and environmental factors, possibly present simultaneously, and perhaps, as we shall discuss shortly, in an interactive or transactive way. The American Psychiatric

Association(1980, 38) describes multifactorial retardation as follows:

> In the remaining 75% of the cases, no known specific biological factor accounts for the disorder; the level of impairment is usually mild, with IQs between 50 and 70; and the diagnosis is commonly not made until school entrance. The lower socioeconomic classes are overrepresented in these cases of Mental Retardation; the significance of this is not clear. There is often a familial pattern of similar degrees of severity of Mental Retardation in parents and siblings.
>
> Mental Retardation without known biological etiology may be associated with psychosocial deprivation of various types, such as deprivation of social, linguistic, and intellectual stimulation. However, the specific etiology of these forms of Mental Retardation is unknown. Three sets of etiologic factors are probably involved either singly or in combination: genetic factors, environmental biological factors such as malnutrition, and early childhood rearing experiences.

The multifactorial model of mental retardation can also be called the "polysociogenic model"(Begab, 1981) made up of both polygenetic and polysocial origins of mental retardation. The polygenetic origins of intelligence are the characteristics that persons inherit from their parents. However, instead of dominant or recessive genes that often have a "present of absent" character to them such as height or five or six digits on each limb which are determined by single genes, the thing we label as intelligence has many genes which influence it and which therefore results in many gradations of it as indicated on the scale scores of IQ tests. And as we described earlier, the environment contains many variables of many gradations between enriched and deprived environments which may be also labeled a polysocial.

In looking at the relative role of genetics versus environment in the development of intelligence we may note four possible positions or models in this regard(Ramey and Finkelstein, 1981).

1. *Genetic Model*. Intelligence is here defined as a function of genetic inheritance alone. In its simplest form it argues smart people pass on their genes and so do retarded people and consequently intelligence or retardation runs in families. This model sees intelligence as innate, fixed at birth and constant in individuals over time.

2. *Environmental Model*. This model sees human beings as raw tablets upon whom are written the experiences they have in their environment. This model, in its simplest version, sees human intellect or social competence as a product of learning opportunities presented by the environment. Both this and the genetic model have modified versions where a limited role is given to the other factor--either inheritance with the environmental model or the environment with the genetic model(Neisworth & Smith, 1978).

3. *Genetic-Environmental Interaction Model*. This model attempts to sidestep the obvious one-sided shortcomings of the prior two models particularly with mild familial retardation by saying that both genetic inheritance and environmental deprivation could contribute to mental retardation in either known proportions or in unknown proportions in an interactive way. However, some proponents of this model argue that the greater of the two causes is genetic(the genetic-social model) while other proponents support the environment as the greater contributor(the social-genetic model). Extensive research has been carried out to determine the percentage of retardation which is attributable to each. Some of this research will be reviewed shortly. However, this model and its two variants are criticized because users of it try to measure the separate effects of the two types of causes as if they were both stable over time and noninteractive with each other.

4. *Transactional Model*. This model argues that both biological(including genetic) and environmental factors are in ongoing transaction for all levels of retardation and that these transactions involve the person who is labeled as retarded by the demands he makes on persons in the environment and the responses they give which in turn influences the biological-social interplay of factors. Ramey

and Finkelstein(1981, 83) give the following example to illustrate this more complex model.

> Full term but fetally malnourished infants(low ponderal indices) who have been randomly assigned to a supportive environment or to a presumably nonsupportive environment differed in Bayley and Stanford-Binet performance up to at least 2 years of age. Mothers initially treated these two groups of infants alike. However, coincident with the decline of intellectual performance by the fetally malnourished infants in the nonsupportive home environment, the mothers were rated as less involved with their infants than mothers of similar infants in the supportive day care environment in which no such intellectual decline was observed. Thus, it appeared that children with potentially dysfunctional conditions who were placed in nonsupportive environments declined in intelligence and presented demand characteristics which were then reacted to less than optimally by their primary caregivers. No such trend was observed for similar infants who were provided supplemental care via preschool education. That is, the infants neither declined intellectually nor did their mothers withdraw from them.

This model notes that the quality of the environment will interact with biological factors over time to yield outcomes not predictable from either factor alone. Thus, we have to look at the demand characteristics of the infant and the response of the environment in a dynamic way. While a child born with PKU might die or be severely retarded, with a proper dietary intervention at the right time by caregivers his biography may be rather indistinguishable from normal peers.

To further illustrate the transactive model we need to look at genetic and environmental factors in interplay. To do this we need to introduce the concepts of genotype and

Table 3.4

Theoretical Illustrative Phenotype IQ Ranges as a Function of Genotype Endowment and Environmental Favorableness

Genotype Endowment for Intelligence	Favorableness of Environment			
	Deprived	Average	Enriched	Total Range
Low (40)	20-30	30-50	50-60	20-60
Medium (100)	65-85	85-115	115-125	65-125
High (120)	95-110	110-130	130-145	95-145

Note: These IQ ranges are theoretical and for illustrative purposes only.

Source: Adapted from Neisworth & Smith, 1978, 142.

phenotype. The genotype of a newborn infant is its array of genes as inherited from its parents. These genes determine physical characteristics and provide a mental constitution that can be developed along many continua of variability depending on the relative richness or poverty of environmental stimuli. The phenotype of an individual are those measured attributes and features of a person such as intelligence, height, adaptive behavior, musical and other talents whether measured at age 4, 14, or 24. The phenotype of an individual is thus a function of (1)a person's genotype in interaction with (2)a person's environment. Measured intelligence reflects what is called a reaction range--the same person might have a range of different IQ scores if he were reared in different environments. In a deprived environment he would show a lower IQ score than in either a normal or enriched environment. The size of the reaction range may also vary by genotype--with smaller ranges associated with lower genotype "potential." Table 3.4 illustrates how genotype and environmental favorableness interact to produce a range of measured phenotypic IQ scores. There is no way to measure accurately the genotype endowment for intelligence, artistic ability, emotionality or any other behavioral trait unaffected by environment. It is a hypothetic construct and the figures in this table are only illustrative ideas, not empirical data. In this table if we hold environment constant(by comparing numbers within one column at a time) phenotypic intelligence will vary among individuals as a result of individual variation in genotype. In contrast, if we hold genotype constant(by comparing numbers across one row at a time) phenotypic intelligence will vary as a result of environmental difference. The reaction range of phenotypic intelligence is shown in the right hand margin under "total range." It shows that environmental impact can variably affect phenotypic intelligence depending on the genotypic intelligence one starts with. Thus, if one starts with a low genotypic intelligence not much can be done to amplify it by environmental richness. But with higher genotypic intelligence the environment may have a greater impact on phenotypic intelligence.

The Question of the Hereditability of Intelligence

One of the central questions that psychologists have sought to answer is to what extent is intelligence hereditable. "Hereditability is the proportion of the population variance of a trait that is attributable to genetic difference"(Nichols, 1981, 128). What is not attributable to heredity is attributable to environment it is assumed in some studies although this assumption leaves open the questions about the interaction of these two variables. Many types of correlational studies have been carried out to test this hypothesis: (1)correlation of parental IQs and off-spring IQs in all types of families including those with one or two retarded parents; (2)correlation of sibling IQs reared together and apart; (3)correlation of own and foster children IQs; (4)correlation of IQs of unrelated persons reared together and apart; (5)IQ correlations of fraternal twins of the same sex and opposite sex; and (6)correlations of IQ scores of identical twins with identical genes reared together and apart. These are fascinating studies, fraught with methological problems, that are too extensive to review here. But we will summarize the range of conclusions that different investigators have reached about such research.

One conclusion that can generally be reached is that as blood relatedness increases so does the size of the correlation. Thus, unrelated persons have either negative or low positive correlations of their IQs. Correlations between parents and children, between siblings, between two-egg fraternal twins are higher than unrelated persons although the range of correlation magnitudes varies sizably in different studies. The highest correlations of IQ occur among identical twins who share the same genes. A second conclusion can be reached by comparing, in each of the above named groups, those reared together and apart. When we aggregate these various studies by type of study, we find that IQ correlations among persons of the same degree of relatedness are higher if they are reared together than apart. Thus unrelated persons who grow up in the same family environment have a higher correlation of their IQ scores than if they are reared in different family environments. This is also true of siblings and twins. These two conclusions stand from these studies: both environment and genetic inheritance influence intelligence, but we do not know how much without further analysis(Westling, 1986).

Jensen and Jencks have looked at about the same correlational data sets in an attempt to determine how influential each of these two factors was. But they come to substantially different conclusions. Jensen concluded that the hereditability of IQ is approximately 80% with 20% attributed to environment while Jencks concluded that hereditability of IQ was 45% with 35% of intelligence due to environment and the remaining 20% due to covariance or the interactions of genes and heredity(Nichols, 1981). They do agree in a general way, however, that the role of genes is more important than environment. Many other investigators fall in between "conservative" hereditarian and liberal "environmentalist" positions.

The research on the hereditability of intelligence thus shows that both environment and heredity play a role. We may never know how much each contributes if we take seriously transactive effects going on in an interactive way between environment and genotype both before and after birth since it may be statistically impossible to factor out the relative size of each of these effects. It is quite clear, however, that environment can either enhance or depress mental development. And if Scarr-Salapatek(1975) is right in her estimate of a reaction range of 25 IQ points for persons within about two standard deviations of a normal IQ, then a disadvantageous environment could depress a normal genotype into the range of retardation.

Other types of research involving early environment intervention also suggests that the quality of environmental stimulation can either enhance or depress the development of intellectual and adaptive functioning. Many of these programs are now underway because of the apparent success of some of the early programs in enhancing performance. We will look at several of these studies.

The first of these studies began in the depression and involved the removal of two girls, aged 13 and 16 months with Kulhman-Binet intelligence test scores of 46 and 35, from an orphanage and placing them in an institution for the mentally retarded. While in the orphanage, the two girls lived in a hospital wing where their physical needs were met but they had little personal attention, few toys, and ward attendants showed no interest in them. When in the orphanage they had delayed motor skill development, were emaciated and undersized for their age. But in the institution for the mentally retarded they were placed in wings housing mildly retarded adolescent girls who were told to take good care of them. The girls lavished mothering attention on them as they became ward pets. The young girls spurted in motor, speech and intellectual development. When tested six months later, the younger girl's IQ had changed from 46 to 87 and the older girl moved from an IQ of 35 to 77. When they were adopted a little over two years later, both girls had IQs in the 90 to 100 range. Skeels and Dye were impressed by the results of this change of environment and in the following years moved an additional 13 infants(average age: 19 months; mean IQ of 64 with a range of 35 to 89) from the orphanage to an institution for the retarded. Nineteen months later they were remeasured on intelligence tests which showed an average IQ of 92 with the range of gains from 7 to 58 IQ score points. None of the children had biological abnormalities. Twenty-five years after the initial placement, Skeels found that all of these children were leading normal lives outside an institution(Skeels, 1966; Nichols, 1981). While all of these children had IQ tests given to them at young ages when they are less reliable and there was an absence of matched controls and a careful measurement of the environment, this study is suggestive of the powerful role of environment in modifying behavior.

The Milwaukee Project study of Heber and his colleagues was more ambitious and somewhat better designed than the Skeels and Dye study. This longitudinal program was designed for a group of children considered at risk for mental retardation because their mothers had IQs below 80. And many of the mothers involved in this early stimulation program had other children under six of whom 80% had IQs below 80 which suggested a pattern of cultural-familial retardation. The mothers all lived in a section of Milwaukee with high population density, low family income and primarily black families. This intervention program was aimed at very early stimulation rather than a preschool program beginning at age 4 or 5.

As children were born to mothers in high risk families they were put into a control group or an experimental group. Nothing special was done for the 20 children in the control group but the mothers and especially the 20 children in the experimental group were given special attention. Some of the mothers in the experimental group, those with IQs above 75, received instruction in child care, home economics and job skills. From early infancy up to about six months of age a project staff member worked with both the mother and infant on stimulation. From about 6 months of age up to two years of age the children all attended a special infant education center where one staff member worked with each child in providing care and stimulation. Beginning at age two and for seven hours a day one teacher worked with three children in six structured learning periods, a motor development period, two meals and a snack, and watching Sesame Street. The six structured learning activities involved language training, arithmetic, reading awareness, problem solving, art, and music. Multiple measurements were taken on both the experimental and control groups. At the age of 18 months the experimental group children were 3 to 4 months ahead of the control group who were at the norm of the Gesell Scales used to measure intellectual development. By 22 months the experimental group was 4 to 6 months ahead of the control group on this scale. The experimental group spurted one year ahead of the control group in vocabulary development by age of two and a half. At 54 months, the experimental group had a mean psycholinguistic age of 63 months in comparison to a mean of 45 months for the control group. During the preschool years when the children were measured on the Stanford-Binet IQ test three different times, the experimental group children averaged around 25 to 30 points higher--around 91 IQ to 124 IQ. After schooling was started they were measured three times on either the WPPSI or WISC and these tests usually produce lower scores than the Stanford-Binet. But on this test at ages 7.2, 8, and 8.8 the experimental group had mean scores of 105, 106 and 109 while the mean control group scores were 81, 84 and 81 so that the earlier differential was maintained(Heber & Garber, 1975). While this study has been criticized for incompleteness of data, sampling and design problems, it too suggests that the quality of early environmental life can have a major impact on adaptive and intellectual adjustment.

THE CURE AND PREVENTION OF MENTAL RE-TARDATION

When we hear the word cure, we usually think of somebody who had some disease or condition, they are then treated for it or it goes away spontaneously after which we say they are "cured" which implies the disease or condition is no longer there. In this chapter, however, we will use a broader definition of cure as developed by Stark(1983, 2). He defines "'cure' as significantly increasing the current level of intellectual functioning and the concomitant level of social adaptation." Stark illustrates this idea by saying at time 1 we have somebody who is retarded by the AAMD definition of it. Subsequently a specific curative intervention is undertaken. And then later, at time 2, we have a level of intellectual and adaptive functioning that exceeds the upper level of the mental retardation range. If this occurs we have a "cure." If we as a nation could cure some mental retardation, then its prevalence should decline over time. This would be a tremendous individual and social benefit as mental retardation is a major health problem in our society and the cost of care for the mentally retarded is a high one.

Stark and Menolascino(1983) define three levels of prevention that can be used to reduce or ameliorate retardation. These three levels or kinds of prevention are:

> *Primary Prevention.* This kind of prevention removes the causal agent from operating to cause a disorder. It totally prevents the handicapping condition.

> *Secondary Prevention.* This kind of prevention substantially removes or reduces the symptom of mental retardation. It usually involves early diagnosis and intervention and returns a person to a normal state or a better state than he would have been without the intervention. This concept is most like the traditional conception of cure.

> *Tertiary Prevention.* This kind of prevention involves minimizing residual handicaps and

Figure 3.1
Curative and Research Emphases Related to Levels of
Retardation

	Primary Prevention	Secondary Prevention	Tertiary Prevention
CURATIVE EMPHASES	Total Prevention of Retardation	Reversal	Amelioration
Research Empahses	Biomedical Emphasis on Severe/Profound and Moderate Retardation	Behavioral Emphasis on Moderate and Mild Retardation	
I.Q. Level	Severe and Profound 0-34	Moderate 35-49	Mild 50-69
Percentage of MR	5%	10%	85%
Etiological Factors	**Biomedical Causes** (25% of MR) -Genetic Disorders -Prenatal Influences and Disorders -Trauma -Nutritional or Metabolic Disorders -Infectious Diseases & Toxic Dirorders -Brain Diseases-- Postnatal	**Sociocultural Causes** (75% of MR) -Environmental Factors -Familial Factors -Psychological Factors -Other Factors	

Source: Stark(1983, 5).

maximizing future development. It is usually most associated with educational efforts
to remediate existing impairments so as to
lessen the severity of their impact.

These three types of prevention are differentially
applicable to mental retardation since there are so many
origins of it.

88

Figure 3.1 depicts how the three levels of prevention are generally related to different kinds of research--biomedical and behavioral, the level of retardation and its relative prevalence and the kinds of etiological factors investigators are likely to look at.

How much retardation is preventable? In 1972, the President's Committee on Mental Retardation set a national goal of reducing retardation by 50% by the year 2000. While this may be an achievable goal it is probably over optimistic in light of several problems. Many scientists feel we are investing too little in the necessary research to reach this goal. Secondly, there must be a tremendous education effort of the public to make them aware of their role in various preventive strategies. Thirdly, most retardation is of the mild kind whose origins are still frequently described as "obscure" and "unknown" and whose prevention might involve massive intervention programs. But while such programs might be expensive, in the long run they might be less expensive than the estimated 11.7 billion dollars we annually spend to care for retarded persons(Vitello & Soskin, 1985).

There are over 350 known causes of retardation(Menolascino, 1983). In the last several decades there have been significant gains in our understanding and control of these causes by means of one of the three types of "cure" or prevention. In 1975 the President's Committee on Mental Retardation presented a general outline of the many steps that can be taken at various points in time to toally prevent or reduce the seriousness of mental retardation(President's Committee on Mental Retardation, 1975, 19):

(1) During Pre-Conception: (1)genetic assessment to determine potential chromosomal-genetic risks in pregnancy; (2)timing and spacing of pregnancies through family planning strategies; (3)adequate nutrition for women of child-bearing age; and (4)immunization.

(2) During Pregnancy: (1)protection of mother and fetus against diseases; (2)proper nutrition; (3)monitoring pregnancy through

medical supervision; (4)use of amniocentesis to determine the condition of the fetus in high risk mothers; (5)parental choice of pregnancy when amniocentesis confirms that the fetus is defective.

(3) At Delivery: Medical supervision of delivery in a hospital, including: (1)screening for conditions causing mental retardation to determine newborn children at risk, and taking remedial action; (2)protection of Rh-mothers with gamma globulin within 72 hours of delivery; and (3)intensive care of children who are born ill or premature.

(4) In Early Childhood: (1)proper nutrition for nursing mothers and for infants and very young children; (2)dietary management of metabolic conditions leading to mental retardation; (3)removal of environmental hazards such as lead-based paint; and (4)early social stimulation and education for infants and young children who are at risk of developing mental retardation(for prevention) and for children who exhibit early mental retardation(to lessen handicap).

The Cure and Prevention of Biological Causes of Mental Retardation

Earlier in this chapter we looked at the many biological causes of mental retardation. About 1 in 200 births show some chromosomal abnormality many of which are related to mental retardation. There are over 100 different inborn errors of metabolism many of which are related to the onset of retardation. About 3% of retardation is due to perinatal causes some of which are preventable or their severity reduced by immediate treatment. And it is estimated that one-half of the individuals with IQ under 50 have genetically based causes of retardation. In one study of severely and profoundly retarded institutionalized persons it was estimated that 31% to 44% had conditions that were preventable. Another estimate is that 30% of all severe and profound retardation is preventable(Abuelo, 1983; Menolascino, 1983).

The outline above on the ways to prevent mental retardation prepared by the President's Committee on Mental Retardation shows that prevention is a complex undertaking due to the variety of steps that usually need to be taken at critical time junctures. Carrier detection of autosomal recessive genes like Tay Sachs disease or metabolic enzyme deficiencies needs to be done before conception. Usually massive screening programs for quite rare disorders are not cost effective and also often entail painful parental decisions about weighing probabilistic evidence about the reproduction of defective children. Some immunizations before conception are vitally important and cost effective. Prenatal monitoring by means of amniocentesis, fetoscopy and senography are cost effective for women at risk but cost-questionable as massive screening programs. They, too, often involve ethical questions as regards therapeutic abortions. Newborn screening for metabolic deficiencies, such as PKU, is another technique that allows for effective secondary prevention(Westling, 1986).

Earlier in this chapter, as we discussed specific chromosomal and genetic disorders and nongenetic biological causes of mental retardation, we often indicated if there were particular preventive or interventive therapeutic steps that could be taken. Substantial gains have and are being made and will be made in the future in our understanding of the biological origins and medical interventions and treatment of retardation. Fetal surgery, enzyme replacement therapy, genetic engineering, and advances in screening programs all offer promise in reducing the incidence of retardation through prevention and/or detection and intervention(Vitello & Soskin, 1985; Clarke, 1982).

Since mild mental retardation composes about 75% of all mental retardation, the major area where gains would be most helpful in reducing the numbers of retardates would be in the prevention of mild retardation and primarily by means of early intervention techniques.

A related and interesting facet of mild retardation is that its prevalence tends to increase from infancy up to age 15 when it begins to decline. The apparent best explanation for this is what Berkson(1983) calls a "cumulative deficit." The cumulative defecit in adaptive behavior and IQ test scores occurs because retarded children are given fewer opportunities to learn or the nature of their learning opportunities are somehow restricted in comparison to their normal peers. Consequently, their deficits in behavior accumulate over their early histories partially as a result of a more depriving environment.

Bijou(1983) has identified three types of early intervention programs which can help avoid the cumulative deficit and prevent some youngsters from falling into the category of the mildly retarded. These three early intervention programs are: (1)Parent Training Programs, (2)Preschool Programs, and (3)Special Elementary School Programs.

Many Parent Training Programs have been developed in the last two decades to help stimulate children at home. Programs of this type fall into two main categories: how-to books and multimedia packages of face-to-face instructional programs where professionals train parents on what to do with their children. The latter have been found to be more effective. Teachers can better train parents on how to assess and observe their children on concrete behaviors, provide information on explicit teaching methods, and provide guidelines on modifying materials and instructional practices. A grant from the Bureau of Education for the Handicapped in the U.S. Office of Education helped develop a demonstration program that proved to be effective. The Portage Project, begun in 1969, involved providing services to parents of 205 children. Activities in this project included: (1)a weekly home education program implemented by teachers who visit the home and work with parents, (2)ongoing child assessment to determine curriculum goals, (3)the implementation of a behavioral teaching model with appropriate record keeping of techniques used and goals reached, (4)a weekly curriculum plan with prescribed goals, and (5)weekly meetings for problem solving and curriculum modification. The data from the Portage study that intensively involved parents show that before the program was begun the children in it had an average IQ score of 75 on the Cattell Infant Scale and Stanford-Binet Intelligence Scale. After eight months, there was an average gain of 18.3 IQ points which raised the group IQ average to 93. A comparison of these children with children attending local classroom programs for culturally and economically disadvantaged preschoolers showed the Portage study children to have higher IQs and better language, academic and socialization skills as measured by the Halpern-Boll Developmental Profile(Bijou, 1983).

Various models of preschool programs have been developed. They usually start at about age 3 and last until regular schooling begins. They are usually targeted at "disadvantaged children." One example of such a program was the Abecedarian program carried out in South Carolina. Much like the Milwaukee project, it was targeted on children of mothers with low IQs who averaged in the 80's as did the older siblings of these children. These children were involved in day nurseries and then preschool programs since the age of 3 months. They were compared to a control group who were not exposed to such a preschool program that focused on cognitive, linguistic and social development. During the first four years of the project, the experimental group scored in the mid-90 range on IQ tests compared to the mid-80s for the controls. By age 5 the mean IQ in the experimental group was 98 with a range of 71-119 compared to 91 for the controls with a range of 68 to 123. While the gains were about one-half those found in the Milwaukee project, they are still significant(Baroff, 1986; Begab, 1981).

The third type of program is a special elementary education program usually designed for the first four grades of school. The objective of such programs, designed for disadvantaged students, is to teach social, academic acquisition, and knowledge skills(language, reading, spelling and math) to such a level that they are intrinsically reinforcing and have carryover effects. To reach these objectives, teachers work in smaller groups than usual, have more face-to-face contact with students, and use carefully sequented daily lessons in all content areas. In one follow-up study of 5,000 children in 20 communities who participated in such a program, it was shown that the children (1)performed around or above the national average in reading, math, spelling and language according to the Metropolitan Achievement Test and the Wide Range Achievement Test; (2)gains in IQ were maintained throughout the 4 years, (3)there were significant gains in self-esteem and intellectual responsibility, and (4)that low IQ students(under 80) made significant gains(Bijou, 1983).

Bijou(1983) believes that an ideal program would incorporate all three of the above named components of an early intervention program. He suggests the integration of

93

parent training, preschool, and special elementary programs into one ongoing program that goes from early infancy to about age ten when children finish fourth grade.

Such a wide variety of intervention programs have been developed and evaluated that it is impossible to review all of them here. Nevertheless, we do need to discuss some of the controversy surrounding the operation and effects of such programs.

One controversy has to do with how successful such programs are. Some programs show sizable IQ gains, others moderate gains, and still others no or minimal gains. The question then arises as to whether IQ is as plastic and subject to environmental alteration as environmentalists believe, or whether the differences are due to methodological differences in the research techniques used, or whether high success is attributable to "better" programs while low success is attributable to "poor" programs. This question also relates to a second controversy which has to do with what are the most important elements in those programs which are found to be the most successful. Some research findings indicate it is primarily the earliness of the intervention that is important. Other research indicates that mother verbal stimulation, and perhaps of a particular contingent nature, with growing children, is the most critical factor while still others say it is best to have a highly structured stimulation program at the outset with prescribed goals and methods of reaching those goals that is most critical. Another controversy has to do with whether the gains are long lasting. One view here is that the explanation of the sizable IQ gain children make in experimental groups in comparison to control groups is due to a "hothouse" effect. That is, early intervention programs force measured IQ development to occur at an earlier age but that given enough time the children in the control group will catch up. In contrast, the "fertilizer" view is that children in the experimental group not only spurt ahead but stay ahead because early intervention gives them a cumulative advantage. Many of these controversies can be resolved, perhaps, by longitudinal studies which look at long range effects of early intervention programs under carefully controlled conditions which pinpoint inputs and outputs. A last controversy has to do with the cost of the early intervention programs. They are expensive inasmuch as they require case finding, assessment, labor intensive instruction by parents and/or teachers with small classes and involve dealing with disadvantaged parents who have other ongoing problems. Will such programs "pay off" in significantly reducing retardation and economic dependence? Or should there be other programs that eliminate poverty and lack of access to health care either as a substitute or supplement to early intervention programs? In the final analysis, the reduction of mental retardation and its associated costs involve not only personal decisions but national policies(Bijou, 1983; Baroff, 1986; Begab, 1981; Bijou, 1981; Neisworth & Smith, 1978; Bronfenbrenner, 1972; Vitello & Soskin, 1985).

SUMMARY

This chapter has reviewed the genetic and nongenetic biological causes of mental retardation as well as the suspected environmental origins of mental retardation. Genetic biological causes of mental retardation are those occurring at or near the point of conception when either chromosomal or genetic defects happen. Hundreds of different chromosomal defects have been identified some of which are related to mental retardation. Both dominant and recessive genetic disorders and inborn errors of metabolism are discussed as they contribute to mental retardation.

The nongenetic biological causes of mental retardation are discussed as hazards which are faced at three time periods: prenatally, during delivery and postnatally. Such hazards include infections and exposure to toxins while in the womb, premature birth and cerebral damage during the birth process and infection and brain injury during infancy.

The environmental origins of mental retardation are conceptualized as stemming from deprivations in either the physical or psychosocial environments. The role of enriched and deprived environments are discussed as they contribute to the development of intelligence. A transactive model of genetic factors and sociocultural factors in constant interplay is seen as the best way to conceptualize the relative role of nature and nurture in the development of intelligence. The question of the hereditability of intelligence is discussed with the point made that both genetic and environment contribute to it but in unknown amounts.

The prevention of mental retardation is discussed with the point being made that primary and secondary prevention techniques follow a biomedical model that are most applicable to biological causes of mental retardation while teritiary prevention is most applicable to psychosocial deprivation. Parent training, preschool, and individualized school training programs are discussed as methods to ameliorate or reduce retardation that stems from psychosocial deprivation. Research indicated that early intervention programs can reduce levels of retardation but such results are not universally accepted by all investigators.

Chapter 4

The Treatment of the Mentally Retarded in Historical Perspective

To better understand contemporary attitudes toward and policies affecting the mentally retarded it is helpful to see how they have been perceived and treated in the past. The past will be limited to American history. However, it should be recognized that there are Biblical, Grecian, Roman and western European roots which preceded and helped to shape our historical treatment of the retarded.

One important point should be remembered in reading this chapter. That is that it primarily covers the perception and treatment of about only 25% of the retarded--those with IQs below 50 or the moderately to profoundly retarded. For the most part, the mildly retarded have walked through their biographies much like other people. But with the rise of formal schooling and the shift away from back and hand labor with the rise of an industrial and now a post-industrial economy, the importance of social and intellectual competence has been elevated. Even now, once schooling is over, many of the mildly retarded with few physical stigmata lead normal lives that involve integration into the mainstream of everyday life in their families, work and recreational outlets.

In his "closing comments" in *A History of Mental Retardation*, Scheerenberger(1983, 254) makes three points that serve as a prelude to our understanding of the history of retardation. One is that "attitudes about mentally retarded persons, their place in the community, and society's responsibilities toward them have frequently and dramatically changed." A second point is that the "science" of any era may be seriously flawed and that scientific opinion at any point in time may only objectify what society wants to hear. Thus, the science of each era, including our own, needs to be approached cautiously. A third point he makes is that "in many instances, mentally retarded persons have been treated in a manner that seemed to meet the needs of the professional community rather than themselves." He quotes Trilling to the effect that once we take an enlightened interest in people, we "'go on to make them objects of our pity, then our wisdom, ultimately of our coercion.'" Thus, he warns that once professionals develop a philosophy or position, "mentally retarded persons were often shaped to conform to those levels of professional expectancy."

Tyor and Bell(1984, 153) also note some dramatic changes in the treatment of the retarded over time, but observe "the sheltered facility has remained the constant in the history of American mental retardation care." While the shape, the size, the objectives and the underlying philosophy for the sheltered facility have changed, it remains a rather constant and paternalistic program for the retarded.

MODELS OF PERCEPTIONS OF THE MENTALLY RETARDED

In the past and yet today there are a wide range of attitudes toward the retarded. Each of us as individuals may have a variety of perceptions of the mentally retarded which we draw upon to fit our mood or situation. Society also has swings of perception. These generally held perceptions and attitudes are important for they help shape policy formulation, legislation, program development and implementation, architectural designs for institutions for the mentally retarded and the daily interactions between normal and retarded people. Wolfensberger(1976) has described seven such perceptual models that have been used in the course of American history as follows:

1. *As sick persons*. Mental retardation has been viewed as an illness, disease or organically-based illness. This view has been most dominant among physicians and related medical personnel. This conception of illness has had the following implications: (1)Doctors and other medically trained people were seen as central in diagnosis and therapy, and in making decisions about non-medical

matters. (2)Therapy tends to center on "patients" in the form of prevention where possible or custodial caretaking where prevention and cure is not possible. (3)Therapy is offered in clinics or hospitals, particularly large state hospitals, where living units become nursing units and wards and hospital routines and nomenclature become standardized. (4)Treatments usually center on medical techniques such as drug therapy, restraints, dentistry and orthopedics rather than education, training or behavior shaping modalities.

2. *As subhuman organisms*. In this view the mentally retarded are consciously perceived or labeled as subhuman, animal-like or vegetables who consequently do not deserve treatment as human beings with rights. This attitude dehumanizes them of the needs or attributes of other humans. They are seen as animals who lack reason, sensitivity to heat and cold, and basic human needs and who therefore need to be tamed or broken as are wild animals. This animal-like conception of the mentally retarded sees them as a threat to normal social life and consequently it leads to caretaker institutions and policies where subhumans are housed in unattractive buildings, their movements restricted in segregated environments that limit choice, their rights to privacy and to communication restricted and only their bare "animal" needs are met.

3. *As a menace*. This model substantially overlaps with the view of them as subhumans but even more heavily justifies their separation from society in prison-like institutions. In this view they are seen as a menace to social values and other humans in one or more ways. They are seen as a menace because of: (1)alleged propensities toward crimes against persons or property, (2)deviance from norms of civilized social interaction increases social disorganization, and (3)because they contribute to genetic decline if allowed to propagate. This model often ascribes an evil intent and evil consequences if "defectives" are not removed from society. Therefore it leads to policies of segregation from society and a segregation of the sexes to reduce genetic decline in order to protect other persons and the genetic health of society.

4. *As objects of pity*. People who hold this view see the mentally retarded as (1)eternal children who will never grow up, (2)people suffering from a condition that needs to be alleviated as far as possible, (3)blameless for

their behavior and therefore not to be held accountable or punished for it. This model tends to lead to residential placements and programs that are paternalistic in sheltering the retardates from injury, that make few demands for personal development or responsibility, and that tries to bestow happiness by involving the retarded in games, fun, picnics, music, crafts, religious nurture and activity as ends in themselves. This model is dehumanizing however because it treats the retarded as children who can never be taken seriously. It infantalizes their condition.

5. *As a burden of charity*. This view is part of a larger welfare ethic that sees those dependent on public taxes for the basic necessities of food and shelter should expect no luxuries or frills and should be grateful for what they do receive. This sour humanitarianism also expects that those who are dependent on public support should do as much work or maintenance as possible in order to reduce the size of the burden of charity on taxpayers. Consequently, these burdens of charity may be educated or trained, not for development purposes, but in order to defray the expenses of charity. They need not be residentially segregated from society for this might reduce their sense of privation and the development of work programs that will reduce the burden of charity.

6. *As a holy innocent*. Occasionally the mentally retarded are seen as special children of God, holy innocents incapable of voluntarily committing evil, and as persons sent by God to serve some special purpose. Viewed as harmless children, this view often led to the mentally retarded being seen as needing extra love, care and attention and therefore being maintained in their own homes and communities or in boarding homes. While humanitarian in many ways, it could dehumanize by not seeing and emphasizing the growth and development of the mentally retarded.

7. *As capable of development*. This developmental model takes an optimistic view of the modifiability of human behavior. This view undermines negative attitudes toward the mentally retarded by emphasizing their variable capability of growth, learning and development. It emphasizes individual assessment and the development of appropriate training, educational, and residential services so that the lives of the mentally retarded can be as normal and socially integrated as is possible. Rather than emphasizing

100

deviance, differentness and apartment, it emphasizes alikeness, progressive integration and progressive normalization of the mentally retarded into the mainstream of public life. This view is a humanitarian one that is currently under development.

Some of these perceptual models have been more dominant during some periods of our history than others. While elements of all these models are sometimes currently articulated by citizens and policymakers, the last one is more predominant today.

EARLY AMERICAN TREATMENT OF THE MENTALLY RETARDED

In the period up to 1850 not a lot is known about the treatment of the mentally retarded. For the most part they were not clearly distinguished from other citizens unless they also fit into the category of deviant such as criminals, the insane or the worthless poor. In colonial times several were among those accused of being witches. During labor shortages, which were frequent in colonial America, they were sometimes brought over from Europe or England as indentured servants. Some were also known to be trained in simple apprentice programs. If they were not cared for at home, as most were, they came under treatment of the Elizabethan "poor laws" in effect in the colonies. This meant if they were not self-supporting they were put into jail, or a few institutions slowly developing then called almshouses, workhouses, lunatic asylums or poorhouses or they were "placed out" with families willing to take care of them for a small fee from the local political jurisdiction responsible for local taxation and taking care of the poor. For the most part the retarded were kept at home and trained as their capacities permitted to do work on the farms where most other Americans then worked or in other simple jobs. If they ended up lodged in institutions, they were often not distinguished from the criminals and particularly the insane(Zastrow, 1982; Scheerenberger, 1983).

A few minor exceptions to the predominant pattern of treatment of the retarded in this time period do exist however. Prior to the 19th century there were no public or private facilities for the care of retarded children. However, several were placed in the asylum for the deaf and dumb in Hartford, Connecticut in 1818 where efforts were made to instruct them. A few "idiots" were taken in by the Commercial Hospital and Lunatic Asylum established in 1821 in Cincinnati, the Ohio Deaf and Dumb Asylum begun in 1827, and the Perkins Institution for Blind in Boston in 1839. And in 1848, Dr. Henry B. Wilbur, one of the early giants in the education of the mentally retarded, opened a private facility in Barre, Massachusetts by the title of Private Institution for the Education of Feeble-Minded Children(Kanner, 1964; Tyor & Bell, 1984).

Prior to mid-century, several developments in Europe emerged that were transferred to the United States. First was the emergence of different theories of human nature that began to distinguish mental retardation from insanity and both from various physical disabilities which often accompanied them such as blindness, deafness, and various motor disabilities. The second was the development of institutions for the mentally ill.

PERIOD OF OPTIMISTIC INSTITUTION BUILDING: 1850-80

During the pre-civil war period a rationale developed for the building of institutions to house the mentally ill and the mentally retarded and to separate them from the poor in almshouses and criminals in prison. After 1850 the mentally ill and mentally retarded were increasingly housed in separate institutions as separate institutions were developed for the retarded. However, many of the conditions in lunatic asylums were wretched in the 1840s. People of all ages, sexes, and conditions were crowded together in damp, cold, ill-ventilated rooms. Sometimes they were ill fed and put in tranquilizer chairs to inhibit all movement or tied to their beds. For the most part there were no daytime rehabilitative activities. It was to the reform of horrendous conditions in many lunatic asylums, jails and almshouses that Dorothy Dix gave her efforts from about 1840 to her death in 1877.

Because of Samuel Gridley Howe's success in improving the condition of three blind idiots at the Perkins School for the Blind in Massachusetts, the state legislature formed a three-person committee in 1846 to determine the extent of the problem in the state and what should be done

102

about it. This committee, with Howe on it, visited 574 individuals considered mentally retarded in some 60 communities in the state. In 1848 the committee submitted its report recommending the beginning of a school for such persons. The school would not only help retardates but be a model program for others to copy in how to train persons, remove filthy habits and free them from restraints, the report said. The legislature gave them $2,500 for a 3 year experimental school for 10 idiot children to be operated in a wing of the Perkins School for the Blind. By the end of the school year Howe reported the students were improved in health, strength and activity of the body, had decent habits, dressed themselves, were well mannered and obedient, were learning to speak and some to write and were gentle, affectionate and well-behaved. As a result of Howe's work, the state legislature established the Massachusetts School for Idiots and Feeble-Minded Youth in 1855(Scheerenberger, 1983).

The period of 1850 to 1880 was a period of developing new institutions for the mentally retarded: the State Asylum for Idiots in New York state in 1851, the Pennsylvania Training School for Feebleminded Children in 1853(later moved to Elwyn where it became the Elwyn Training School), the Institution for Feebleminded Youth in Ohio in 1857, the Connecticut School of Imbeciles in 1858. By 1898, twenty four public institutions were maintained by 19 states plus another one in New York City. There were also a number of private schools which catered to those families who could pay the expense of such private schooling(Kanner, 1964).

The philosophy behind the development of these new institutions was an optimistic one described by Wolfensberger(1976) as "making the deviant undeviant." The founders of these institutions usually believed they could either cure or more likely ameliorate feeble-mindedness and idiocy by training and education during the growing years. And it was believed this education and training could most efficiently and effectively take place in schools where the retarded would be congregated together so they could receive intensive attention from experts. They were perceived as capable of development under the right environment.

While there were some variations among the schools in the first twenty years of development, let us look at some of the predominant characteristics of institutions during this time period(Scheerenberger, 1983; Tyor & Bell, 1964; Wolfensberger, 1976).

1. They had selective admission policies. They denied admission to unsuitable cases, to those below school age and above 16. School administrators wanted to develop good success records to insure continued legislative funding.

2. School authorities were committed to ideals of education and rehabilitation. They did not want their institutions to become custodial warehouses but <u>schools</u> for slow learners who were to be discharged for work when they were ready but no later than the usual schooling period.

3. They were based on a developmental model of human growth--that is that many of the retarded could learn and develop even if at a slower rate than their age peers.

4. The schools were run as limited institutions in the sense that students went home for periods up to two months during the summer and sometimes for other vacations. This allowed the students to become reacquainted with their families and everyday life and kept the early institutions from having the quality of permanent residential institutions.

5. The legislative rationale for the operation of these institutions was reflective of this era's humanitarianism and reformist ideals in the perfectibility of man. Thus, the support of these schools was seen as a moral obligation of society. The expenses of such special schooling were as much a <u>right</u> for retarded individuals as public schooling was for the normal. Such schooling was not viewed as a privilege or a worthy charity of benefactors or only on expedient grounds of making retarded citizens economically productive but as a fundamental right of individuals and a correspondent responsibility of society.

6.   Most of the institutions were located in urban areas, were small and had a regular schedule of activities and classes where each person could receive individual attention. The homes were operated on family principles where teaching morality and correct social behavior was very important. Their goals were restorative--to return students to their homes and communities.

7.   The funding came from a variety of sources - the state treasury, county gifts, neighboring states who sent pupils to it, parents and benevolent donors which made centralized control impossible.

During this time period as the population of the country was growing, these schools repeatedly went through a cycle of first having a waiting list, then expanding the facility as state monies were made available, and then finding itself filled to capacity with another waiting list. Four factors during this time period began to dull the high optimism with which these small schools began. (1)Some of the clients were not helped much--especially the idiots or those with severe or profound levels of retardation. Thus the goal of releasing all clients to their homes after schooling was completed did not work out. For example in the 1870s and 1880s only 26% of the residents released in Connecticut were found to be self-supporting while 19% of the new admissions into Kentucky institutions were released for community employment while another 30 to 40% were released to their families and reported to be less burdensome because they were self-helped. (2)Some potential releasees had no place to return to and began accumulating in the institutions. Some parents didn't want the child back home, had died or had moved and couldn't be located. And since some of the clients could not become self-supporting, they had no place to which to return. (3)An expanding population, fueled by heavy immigration of the poor from abroad, created waiting lists of entrants some of whom had poor chances of restoration to self-support. (4)The accumulation of residents in institutions that were growing in size led to more custodial practices and undermined the misperceived objective that all such persons who attended such schools would be completely or substantially rehabilitated(Wolfensberger, 1976; Tyor & Bell, 1984).

GROWING PESSIMISM AND INSTITUTIONAL CHANGE: 1880-1990

During this time period a number of changes were taking place in American society: rapid industrialization, heavy immigration, urbanization, and the concentration of wealth and power. There was a growing concern about the rapid increase in the number of retardates. The U.S. Government made attempts to ascertain the number of retardates and by its estimates these numbers of retardates were found in the decennial censuses: 15,707 in 1850; 18,865 in 1860; 24,527 in 1870; 76,895 in 1880 and 95,571 in 1900. These sizable increases were variously interpreted to mean that heredity or immigration were responsible and that more prevention and more institutions were needed(Scheerenberger, 1983).

During the period of 1870-90 Wolfensberger(1976) believes that the ideology underlying the care and treatment of the retarded changed and it was largely concomitant with the growth of these institutions and other changes occurring in them. During this period he believes the optimism of developmental theories of the founding period were substantially replaced by the attitudes that the retarded were to be pitied, protected and that they increasingly became objects of charity.

A number of changes occurred during this time(Tyor & Bell, 1984; Wolfensberger, 1976):

1.   The number of size of institutions increased. New institutions were begun in states that had none before. And as residents accumulated in them and as the population base of the nation grew many institutions were expanded from 40 to 60 residents and then into hundreds of residents.
2.   Since many of the residents, if released, could not fully support themselves(maybe 20% could) or only partially support themselves(perhaps 30%), many were not released. Those who were kept in institu-

106

tions often performed some chores and services to help defray their expenses. Proposals were often made to state legislatures to establish separate institutions for those hopelessly dependent who needed custodial care, but legislatures usually responded by expanding existing institutions. This was responded to by superintendents by segregating classes by level of retardation and putting a greater emphasis on basic skill training and manual trades and less on traditional school subjects.

3. As new institutions were developed or older smaller ones relocated they were usually placed in rural areas. Such locations were seen as promoting idyllic comfort and happiness for its permanent childlike residents. It also permitted the development of farming, training in farm-related work and greater economic self-sufficiency since residents could grow some of their own food.

4. A fourth characteristic of institutional change during this time was economization. Increasingly the residents worked on the farms or produced objects in workshops located at these institutions. Over time the emphasis shifted from such labor being rehabilitative to productively occupying residents time for purposes of self-support. The more capable workers were interpreted as helping to support the less capable at such institutions and lowering the tax burden on state citizens.

5. A name change often symbolically covered these changes listed above. The term "school" was used less often and replaced by the term asylum or institution. This name change reflected the shift from a residential boarding school to a permanent custodial institution.

PROTECTING SOCIETY FROM DEVIANCY: 1900-1920

The "Progressive Era" was marked by many changes going on in society with the predominant focus on reforms in many areas: controlling big business, changing the working conditions of children, upgrading salaries and improving working conditions for all people but especially the poor, and eliminating slums. Reforms were sought in politics, business and human services.

In this era up to about World War I we find a crescendo of concern about mental retardation with the negativism of the prior period being turned into programs to prevent retardation and control the many forms of deviancy alleged to be associated with it. During these reform years the professionals debated the causes of retardation and generally agreed it was primarily inherited and therefore should be controlled. But toward the end of the period, professional and public attitudes began to change which laid the groundwork for changes in the next period.

Beginning in the 1880s and perhaps climaxing around 1910 was the belief that retardation was associated with many forms of deviance and this was a threat to social order if not controlled. One other theme emerged in the first decade of this period that was to grow stronger in the 1990s and become ideologically dominant in the first two decades after the turn of the century. This was the growing conviction that retardation was an inherited condition characteristic of a pauper class of criminal and immoral families. Richard Dugdale's research on the Jukes family over six generations convinced him that pauperism, harlotry, illegitimacy, syphilis, deformed youngsters, crime and idiocy tend to run in families. While he saw both hereditary and environmental forces at work in his poorly researched study, the next generation was to give this and later studies a more hereditary interpretation(Scheerenberger, 1983).

Walter Fernald, the resident superintendent of the Massachusetts School for the Feeble-Minded, was one of the most outspoken leaders regarding the social debilitation associated with retardation. Although he reversed his ideas greatly after 1915, in 1903 Fernald(1903, 34-35) observed:

The brighter class of the feeble-minded with their weak will power and deficient judgment are easily influenced for evil, and are prone to become vagrants, drunkards and thieves. The modern scientific study of the deficient and delinquent classes as a whole has demonstrated that a large proportion of our criminals, inebriates and prostitutes are congenital imbeciles, who have been allowed to grow up without any attempt being made to improve or discipline them. Society suffers the penalty of this neglect in an increase of pauperism and vice, and finally at a great increased cost, is compelled to take charge of adult imbeciles in almshouses and hospitals; and of imbecile criminals in jails and prisons, generally for the remainder of their natural lives. As a matter of mere economy, it is now believed that it is better and cheaper for the community to assume the permanent care of this class before they have carried out a long career of expensive crime.

A few years later Fernald(1912, 88) described imbeciles as:

a parasitic, predatory class, never capable of self-support or of managing their own affairs. The great majority ultimately become public charges in some form. They cause unutterable sorrow at home and are a menace and a danger to the community.

The scientific community of the time found substantial evidence, although retrospectively highly questionable, that feeble-mindedness was (1)hereditary--especially susceptible were feeble-minded women who were seen as prone to immorality and licentiousness, and (2)associated with all manner of vice, immorality and criminality. The moral imbecile of the previous era became the "defective delinquent". A spate of studies, such as Goddard's study of the Kallikak family, attempted to show all manner of degeneracies ran in families(Scheerenberger, 1983).

These scientific studies were influential in leading to three major attempts to control the social effects of feeble-mindedness: (1)prevention by means of segregating retarded people in institutions and segregating the sexes within them to prohibit procreation; (2)the prohibition against mental defectives marrying; and (3)the sterilization movement. The eugenics movement of the time saw all three of these steps as necessary to reduce the prevalence of mental defectives(Scheerenberger, 1983; Wolfensberger, 1976).

The method of prevention and control by segregation in institutions and segregation of the sexes was extensively undertaken during this time period. More asylums were built and others enlarged. By 1917 there were 37,200 patients in such places in 31 states. Of this number, 31,361 were in state sponsored ones, 3,043 in other public supported institutions such as jails and poorhouses, and 2,816 in private institutions. Even so, probably no more than ten percent of all the retarded were institutionalized so that the effectiveness of this method of prevention would have to be severely limited(Kanner, 1964).

The second method of prevention was to reduce the number of retardates who married or had sexual relations either among themselves or with nonretardates. Eventually 39 states had laws prohibiting marriage among or with retardates. In some states persons had to take an oath that they had never been insane or mentally defective or if they had been they were cured. Connecticut passed a law which imposed a minimum prison sentence of three years for those below age 45 who were either retarded or not retarded if such persons had sexual relations with each other(Tyor & Bell, 1984; Scheerenberger, 1983). While such laws assumed the hereditability of intelligence, they would have to prove ineffective because of the ease with which persons can lie about their mental condition, the difficulty of identifying mental defectives and the nearly impossible task of detecting private acts of cohabitation involving such persons.

The third solution to deal with the "menace" or feeble-mindedness and moral imbecility was sterilization. This solution was hotly debated. While some thought this measure would be effective in reducing retardation, others thought it would not be. This solution was part of the larger Eugenics movement to improve the human race.

110

Michigan was the first state to pass such a law in 1907. By 1912, eight states had passed such laws and by 1917 fifteen states had some variety of eugenical sterilization law. These states, in addition to including idiots, imbeciles and the feeble-minded, also variably included habitual drunkards, drug fiends, syphilitics, rapists, confirmed criminals, prostitutes and procurers. Between 1907 and 1958 a total of 31,038 retarded persons, 20,048 of them females, were sterilized in 30 states. But in retrospect, sterilization has had little impact on prevention even though it caused furious debate. It had little impact because most states did not adopt such laws, it was used selectively on only some persons residing in institutions but not on the roughly 90% of retardates living outside institutions, it was based on faulty assumptions about the relatively strict hereditability of retardation, and many found sterilization morally repugnant and were unwilling to support or use it(Tyor & Bell, 1984; Scheerenberger, 1983; Wolfensberger, 1976).

Other developments in this period were significant. First, the separate institutions to serve the mentally retarded grew in number and size and there was a shift to a more custodial approach during this time period. While education remained an important goal in these institutions a much greater emphasis was put on manual training and work so that residents could be more helpful in defraying the costs of operating institutions. The value of inmate labor running the institution and in making products or providing services in the local community was increasingly emphasized in many institutions(Tyor & Bell, 1984).

As the institutions grew the number of buildings increased and their functional use was differentiated. Some institutions had hundreds of residents and some over a thousand. On these "campuses" was usually a central administrative building, housing for staff quarters, classroom buildings, a hospital for the lowest grade of retardates, a series of dormitories or cottages as residences, and a number of outbuildings for shops, workrooms, and farm machinery storage. Services were more comprehensive in this era. There was hospital care for the most profoundly retarded, education classes for the feeble-minded and training programs and work areas for the lower grade defectives. There were custodial facilities for the morally defective--the "moral imbeciles" who would not be returned to society inasmuch as they were seen as without

111

conscience. Over time there was increasing sex segregation in dormitories, classes and workshops to prevent sexual contact(Tyor & Bell, 1984).

A new development during this time period was the emergence of "off-campus" "colonies" which were developed in several ways. Fernald introduced the idea in 1901 when 50 boys were transferred from the main institution to a "farm colony" 61 miles away. Both "brighter" and "low grade" retardates lived at and operated the farm under the direction of a matron, 2 female cooks, 2 female attendants and 3 male farm workers. Fernald developed a second farm colony where residents had greater freedom. This idea was copied by a few other institutions. Charles Bernstein developed "community colonies" as well as farm colonies in New York state on the conviction that institutional environments were abnormal and did not contribute to normal development. For example, he rented a house in Rome, New York, where retarded girls lived and were hired out in the local area for a variety of domestic jobs. After some experience in the program, many of the young women were released to live on their own in the community. By 1935 his community colonies had expanded to 52 in number. Contrary to some beliefs, there were discharges from some institutions where those who were either self-sufficient or had caretakers on the outside were released(Scheerenberger, 1983).

At the turn of the century some pessimistic people believed that all the retarded should be institutionalized. However, there were undercurrents of disagreement with this position which became more pronounced by the end of World War I when a new optimism began to emerge about the amelioration and benevolent care of the retarded. This new optimistic thrust toward better care and more community based treatment came, according to Scheerenberger(1983), due to (1)the recognition that there was not enough money to put all retardates in institutions, (2)the fact that many institutions got a bad press for their crowdedness, poor environment and lack of rehabilitation, (3)the unwillingness of most parents to send their children to such understaffed and underprogrammed asylums, and (4)the fact that more community services, particularly special education classes, were slowly becoming available, and (5)the fact that mostly mentally retarded persons could meet the demands of society.

Perhaps one of the most significant and positive developments during this era was the rapid rise and spread of special education classes which undermined much of the need for residential institutional care. The first documented special education class was begun in 1896 in Providence, Rhode Island, followed by Springfield, Massachusetts the next year, Chicago in 1898, Boston in 1899 and New York in 1900. The adoption of special education programs spread across the country rapidly so that by 1922 133 cities in 23 states had 23,252 pupils enrolled in a variety of special education classes. There was also rapid expansion within single cities. For example, New York had one class in special education in 1900, 14 by 1906, 103 by 1910 and 131 in 1914. By the mid 1920s special education had become a state responsibility. At least for the first decade of the new century, special classes were mainly a way to get problem students out of normal classes. Into them were grouped students with what we now call "developmental disabilities," all levels of retardation, physical defects, epileptics, and delinquents--most of whom were from poor backgrounds and various ages. Over time and with the introduction of intelligence tests, the level of students permitted into such classes were elevated from around an IQ of 40 to about 50 with lower functioning students excluded. While there were variations in how different schools taught the retarded, the predominant pattern that was to last for 60 years was to spend morning classes on the R's and the afternoon classes in manual and domestic arts, music, physical education and art. Many of those in special education classes were able to gain and hold low level skill jobs when they left school although some lived unemployed at home or ended up in institutions(Scheerenberger, 1983; Tyor & Bell, 1984).

One other significant development occurred in this era--the development and proliferation of use of intelligence tests along with a better classification system of levels of retardation. Binet, Simon, Goddard, Terman and Kuhlman were all early developers of intelligence tests with a special interest in retardation. Many of the debates we hear today were heated then too as regards the stability of IQ over time, the reliability of such IQ tests, whether they measure some innate potential or some potential as influenced by experience and environment, and to what extent intelligence is a product of heredity or environment.

Table 4.1

Two Sets of Definitions of Three Levels of Retardation

1907 Definitions of Binet and Simon	1910 Definitions of the American Association of Mental Deficiency

IDIOT

An idiot is any child who never learns to communicate with his kind by speech--that is to say, one who can neither express his thoughts verbally nor understand the verbally expressed thoughts of others, this inability being due solely to defective intelligence, and not to any affection of the organs of phonation.	Those so deeply defective that their mental development does not exceed that of a normal child of about 2.

IMBECILE

An imbecile is any child who fails to learn how to communicate with his kind by means of writing--that is to say, one who can neither express his thoughts in writing, nor read writing or print, or correctly understand what he reads, this failure being due to defective intelligence, and not to any defect of vision or any paralysis of the arms which would explain his inability.	Those whose mental development is higher than that of an idiot but does not exceed that of a normal child of about 7 years.

MORON

A moron is one who can communicate with his kind by speech or writing, but who shows a retardation not being due to insufficient or irregular attendance.	Those whose mental development is above that of an imbecile but does not exceed that of a child of about 12 years.
Source: Binet & Simon, 1907, 74-5.	Source: Committee on Classification of Feeble-minded(1910, 61).

One of the outcomes of this work as well as developments in medicine and the professional field of mental retardation was a clearer classification system of three levels of feeble-mindedness which was used as a generic term to describe all levels of mental defect(Scheerenberger, 1983). Table 4.1 compares two sets of definitions of three levels of retardation. The 1910 definitions are a sizable step in specificity over those of 1907.

In summarizing the period from 1900 to 1920 Scheerenberger(1983, 175) observes it was a remarkable one:

> Attitudes toward mentally retarded persons changed dramatically from the idea that such individuals were inherently amoral and incorrigible, requiring life-long institutionalization to the belief that education and community support would result in productive citizens. Direct services for mentally retarded persons and their families, however, were at best fragmentary and not universally preferred. Nevertheless, communities were more alert and sensitive to the value and unique problems of such youngsters and adults and began to develop a variety of appropriate services.

PERIOD OF GRADUAL CHANGES: 1920-1945

The era of the 1920s was not a period of major reforms or national concern with social issues other than immigration, prohibition and crime. The depression years, with the exception of new federal initiatives to deal with economic issues such as the Social Security Act of 1935, continued the general lull. And during the war years the retarded were neglected and institutional care declined during a period of labor shortage when winning the war became the national priority. Still some changes did occur that were significant for the perception and treatment of the mentally retarded in this period.

One of the significant philosophical changes in this time period was the reversal of views by Fernald and Goddard, two leaders in the mental retardation services system. They changed their views from pessimistic hereditarism views that emphasized segregation to environmental views that many retarded could be trained and educated and safely returned to the community without being a menace to society. These dramatic reversals of their former positions were prompted by the success of a number of programs which paroled residents from institutions for the retarded into successful community placement, the failure of intelligence testing to demonstrate that only heredity shaped intelligence, and the widely shared experience that most of the retarded were not pathological delinquents but persons who adjusted well when they lived at home with their parents in a normal environment(Scheerenberger, 1983).

A number of new services were devised and older services to the mentally retarded were expanded during this time. Special education classes were adopted in many more school districts. Enrollment in such programs increased from 46,625 enrollees in 1929, to 84,458 in 1934, to 98,416 in 1940. But only about 10% of all mildly retarded persons were enrolled in such classes by 1950. Many school districts excluded some retarded children from school. And the quality of the teachers and curriculum varied substantially in these areas(Scheerenberger, 1983).

While a few community services were begun in the opening two decades of the twentieth century, they were expanded somewhat during this period and often in conjunction with the mental hygiene movement begun in the 1920s. These community services included diagnostic services for the mentally retarded and their families, school mental clinics, home-based programs for families of retarded children, community placement and follow up programs for releasees from mental retardation institutions. While the philosophy developed for the desirability of such programs they were not widely available during this time period(Tyor & Bell, 1984; Scheerenberger, 1983).

The quality of residential services for the retarded generally declined during the depression and war years when budgets were slashed. Many of the institutions now contained thousands of residents in little more than warehouses or custodial facilities. There were long waiting lists to get into such institutions in many states. There was often high staff turnover of people untrained for the kind of work they were doing. Tyor and Bell(1984, 137) comment:

> During World War II, mental retardation care continually deteriorated and at many places grim, oppressive conditions developed. . . . The harsh picture of life at the Rainier State School, Buckley, Washington, reflected institutional realities throughout the country. Inadequate and insufficient equipment and rooms, a shortage of key personnel, including teachers and psychologists, and limited training and education programs created a snake-pit atmosphere.

There was a growing recognition that some of the persons in institutions should not be there and that many of the higher grades of the retarded could be trained and released. However, the lack of school-based special education programs in many areas, especially rural areas, and the lack of funds for training and community based parole programs meant that many were confined to institutions that did little for them beyond caring for their basic needs of food and shelter. Wolfensberger(1976) sees the period of 1920 to 1950 as largely a continuation of practices begun in the previous period but with an end to the indictment of the mentally retarded as a menace to society.

Several experimental programs showed promise during this time but would have to wait decades before they were widely adopted. Charles L. Vaux, Superintendent of the Newark State School, placed over 100 residents, with an average IQ of 50, in private homes with families sensitive to the needs of such persons. The boarders performed household chores, participated in social life at a community center and had their medical needs provided in the community. This program was found beneficial in several ways: more freedom and development for the children, an altruistic outlet for the caretakers, and it cost less money than institutional care(Tyor & Bell, 1984). Another experimental program for retarded offenders was undertaken at the State Institution for Defective Delinquents in Napanoch, New York. This program involved academic and industrial training, sequentially less restrictive housing going from dormitory cells to colony housing, and judi-

117

cious parole and parole supervision. While few were paroled, the ones that were were successful. Other experimental programs in task training and carefully sequenced learning models enabled more severely retarded persons to learn a variety of self-help skills formerly thought impossible. However this forerunner of behavior modification strategies would have to wait decades for development(Scheerenberger, 1983).

AN ERA OF CHANGE: 1945-1985

The four decades following World War II were a period of unprecedented change in both the larger society and in the treatment of the mentally retarded. These changes occurred in interdependent areas of society and can be categorized according to six types of change.
1.   *Research*. Major gains were made in understanding the complex biological and environmental origin of retardation as well as the effect of educational and social programs on them.
2.   *Legal*. Changes in the legal sphere included extensive state and federal legislation, which radically changed the provision of services for the retarded, and court cases which much more clearly established their rights as persons and their rights to a wide range of services and opportunities which had formerly been denied to them or unavailable to them.
3.   *Education*. The spread of special education continued and then in about the last half of this period the mainstreaming of developmentally disabled(which includes retarded) children into regular classrooms was developed and widely implemented.
4.   *Residential*. With the exposé of the poor living and habilitation services in large institutions, major steps were taken to reform residential institutions and primarily by means of deinstitutionalization that involves preventing unnecessary admission to such state hospitals, and, more importantly, moving residents to smaller residential facilities in normal communities.
5.   *Attitudinal*. A major attitudinal change occurred in both the profession and popular mind. The developmental model became dominant again which emphasized the retarded's variable capability of growth,

118

their sameness rather than differentness, and their need for normal experiences if they were to be integrated into normal community experiences.

6. *Services*. Many new and/or existing services were expanded to meet the special needs of retarded people and their parents. This idea will be explained largely in later chapters.

It is interesting to note that during both World War I and II substantial numbers of retarded men served in the military and many of them also worked in defense plants or other occupations during a time of manpower shortages(Scheerenberger, 1983).

Three major pieces of legislation were passed which promoted research into behavioral and organic problems of mental patients--both the mentally ill and retarded. The first of these was the 1946 National Mental Health Act that funded a tremendous increase in basic, clinical and administrative research on mental problems and which also paid for training mental health workers and in planning and implementing community service programs. The second of these was the creation of the National Institute of Mental Health in 1946 which funded many research programs in both its own laboratories and those of hospitals and universities. The third was the Mental Health Study Act of 1955 which established the Joint Commission on Mental Illness and Mental Health(Cockerham, 1981). This last piece of legislation was to bear fruit in expanded service programs beginning in the Kennedy administration. These legislative acts funded many types of research that would be useful in understanding the chromosomal, genetic, prenatal, natal and postnatal biological origins of retardation as well as environmental causes. For example, Watson and Crick developed a model of the molecular structure and replication of DNA which led to advances in genetics. The chromosomal structure of Down's Syndrome, Klinefelter's Syndrome, and Turner's Syndrome were identified. Gains were made in understanding and screening for biological abnormalities. The learning processes of retarded children were studied extensively and led to gains in instruction and behavior modification. The role of environmental causes was extensively researched and substantial gains made in understanding the emotional origins of infantile autism, the variations in learning disabilities, the role of labeling and social deprivation. Consequently, there were substantial gains made in distinguishing between biological and environmental factors(Scheerenberger, 1983).

Education of the mildly mentally retarded was stated more definitely by a variety of educators, legislators and lobbying groups in this period. Attitudes changed here to the developmental model that such students could be educated to become productive law-abiding, tax-paying citizens, marriage partners, and parents. The curricula of most schools variously emphasized social competence, personal adequacy and occupational adequacy. Increasingly in the 1950s and 1960s special education programs became more widespread, were increasingly divided into classes according to age and ability, were more likely to get teachers with specialized training, and increasingly involved vocational rehabilitation training. In 1953 109,000 students were enrolled in special education programs, but ten years later this had more than tripled to 361,000. By 1963, still only 20% of mildly retarded persons, mainly boys, were enrolled in such programs. Programs for the trainable mentally retarded were also expanded during the 1950s and 1960s when public schools accepted for the first time a clear responsibility for their education. The number of TMR students increased from around 5,000 students in 1953 to 30,000 in 1963 reflecting the growing commitment of public schools to their education. Such education usually centered on language development, motor development, progress in self-help skills, health, safety, sensory training and intellectual development(Scheerenberger, 1983; Tyor & Bell, 1984).

However, the most important piece of legislation to affect education of the retarded did not occur until the mid 1970s. In 1975 Congress passed Public Law 94-142, The Education for All Handicapped Children Act, which was the product of a long effort to provide free and appropriate educational services for the retarded and other handicapped students. This legislation engendered a lot of controversy because it was seen as expensive, required teacher skills many existing teachers were untrained for, and largely substituted "mainstreaming" handicapped students into regular classrooms under the concept of the "least restrictive environment" for the segregated special education classes that had existed for a long time(Stroman, 1982). We shall discuss this controversy, this legislation and its effects more fully in a later chapter.

Both public and lay attitudes toward the retarded became more optimistic during this era which emphasized individual rights ushered in by the civil rights movement that began in the 1960s. One element in this change of attitudes was the proliferation of parents and friend advocacy groups and their rise to substantial influence. The first such advocacy group was developed in Ohio in 1933--the Cuyahoga County Council for the Retarded Child which developed, financed, and ran the first parent-supported class for the gravely retarded. By 1950 there were 88 such local groups with 19,300 members advocating for retarded citizens in 19 states. In 1950 a national gathering of parents and friends formed the Parents and Friends of Mentally Retarded Children organization. In the following year it changed its name to The National Association for Retarded Children and in 1974 changed its name again to reflect its broader age concerns to the National Association for Retarded Citizens(NARC). In 1980 it became the Association for Retarded Citizens(ARC). By 1970 it had 250,000 members that engaged in a variety of programs in conjunction with state and local chapters: (1)local, state and federal lobbying activities; (2)support for educational programming for the retarded in schools and in vocational rehabilitation programs; (3)development of Youth (N)ARC which in 1974 had 40,000 teenage and young adult members who befriend retarded persons their age through a variety of social service activities; (4)support of a wide variety of service projects at the local level such as recreation, parent counseling, parent education classes, summer camps, sheltered workshops and special clinics, and (5)taking cases to court to appeal the rights of the retarded for education or other services(President's Committee on Mental Retardation, 1975; Scheerenberger, 1983).

One of the most significant court cases affecting the educational rights of retarded persons and supported by the National Association for Retarded Citizens was the 1971 case of the Pennsylvania Association for Retarded Citizens(PARC) et al v. David H. Kurtzman, et al. Prior to this time, many retarded children, especially the severely and profoundly retarded, had been denied a right taken for granted by most Americans: a free public education. The PARC attorneys argued that all children should be given equal protection under the law to education and due process if this right were to be fully and equitably achieved. The court found for the plaintiffs and ordered that by the start of the next school year "every retarded person between the ages of six and twenty-one years . . . [have] access to a free public program of education and training appropriate to his learning capacities"(quoted in President's Committee on Mental Retardation, 1975, 80). Within the first year after the State of Pennsylvania signed a consent decree, the State's Right to Education Office estimated 10,000 additional retarded children were in public classrooms including 2,551 severely and profoundly retarded children. In 1972 in a similar court case, Mills et al v. Bd. of Education of the District of Columbia, the court ruled that not only mentally handicapped but also physically handicapped students had a right to a free public education(President's Committee on Mental Retardation, 1975). In 1972 and 1974 state associations of retarded citizens of New York and Maryland respectively went to court with similar claims about the denial of rights. Between 1971 and 1974, 111 lawsuits were filed on behalf of retarded citizens that they might gain rights that they believed had been denied them--rights: (1)to equal educational opportunity; (2)to be free from inappropriate educational classification, labeling and placement; (3)to community services and the right to treatment in the least restrictive environment; (4)to be free from peonage; (5)to be free from restrictive zoning ordinances; (6)to be free from unconstitutional commitment practices; (7)to procreate; (8)to equal access to adequate medical service; and (9)of free access to buildings. Of the 74 lawsuits settled in this time period, 70 were for the retarded plaintiffs(President's Committee on Mental Retardation, 1975). Thus the 1970s and continuing on into the 1980s was an explosive era of testing and procuring the rights of handicapped people. Prior to 1970 only a few court cases relative to the rights of the retarded were filed and decided(Kindred, 1984).

What prompted the civil rights explosion for the handicapped in the 1970s? One of the roots is the civil rights movement of the 1960s where minorities made legal and other gains under both court test cases and legislative enactments. These methods and goals of acquiring rights by minorities were widely adopted by the "developmental disabilities movement"(Stroman, 1982; Wiegerink & Petossi, 1979). Another and more specific root was the humanitarian interest of President John F. Kennedy, who had a retarded sister, in the quality of life of the mentally ill and retarded. He appointed a 26-member President's Panel on October 11, 1961 and prefaced his charge to them by stating(President's Panel on Mental Retardation, 1962, 196):

> Both wisdom and humanity dictate a deep interest in the physically handicapped, the mentally ill, and the mentally retarded. Yet, although we have made considerable progress in the treatment of physical handicaps, although we have attacked on a broad front the problems of mental illness, although we have made great strides in the battle against disease, we as a nation have too long postponed an intensive search for solutions to the problems of the mentally retarded. That failure should be corrected.

In 1962 this panel made 112 recommendations under the following eight headings(President's Panel on Mental Retardation, 1962, 14-15):

> **Research** in the causes of retardation and in methods of care, rehabilitation, and learning.
> **Preventive health measures** including (a)a greatly strengthened program of maternal and infant care directed first at the centers of population where prematurity and rate of "damaged" children are high; (b)protection against such known hazards to pregnancy as radiation and harmful drugs; and (c)extended diagnostic and screening services.
> **Strengthened education programs generally,** and extensive and enriched programs of special education in public and private schools closely coordinated with vocational guidance, vocational rehabilitation, and specific training preparation for employment; education for the adult mentally retarded, and workshops geared to their needs.
> **More comprehensive and improved clinical and social services.**

Improved methods and facilities for care, with emphasis on the home and the development of a wide range of local and community facilities.

A new legal, as well as social, concept of the retarded, including protection of their civil rights, life guardianship provisions when needed; and enlightened attitudes on the part of the law and the courts; and clarification of the theory of responsibility in criminal acts.

Helping overcome the serious problems of manpower as they affect the field of science and every type of service, through extended support, and increased opportunities for students to observe and learn the nature of mental retardation.

Programs of education and information to increase public awareness of the problem of mental retardation.

In response to the clear need for better intervention services for the mentally ill and retarded, Congress passed, in 1963, the most important piece of federal legislation to date in this field: the Mental Retardation Facilities and Community Mental Health Center Construction Act. This act blanketed the country with facilities and programs to serve these two groups(Stroman, 1982). Over the next 20 years Congress passed 116 acts or amendments to these acts to provide retarded individuals and their families programs for income maintenance, education, employment, housing, health and nutrition, vocational rehabilitation, social services, and rights. Scheerenberger(1983, 250) summarizes the gains made in this era:

By 1976, 11 major federal agencies administered 135 special funding programs. . . . By 1980, the federal government was spending an estimated $4 billion per year on mental retardation. During the 1980-81 fiscal year 852,000 mentally retarded children received special education services, 165,000 mentally retarded persons received vocational rehabilitation services, and 640,000

124

mentally retarded persons received some form of support or assistance through Social Security legislation, including approximately 130,000 persons in public institutions.

A third factor which contributed to the civil rights demands and legislation for the retarded was the 1971 adoption, by the United Nations General Assembly, of the Declaration of Rights of Mentally Retarded persons given below(President's Committee on Mental Retardation, 1975, 76):

1. The mentally retarded person has, to the maximum degree of feasibility, the same rights as other human beings.
2. The mentally retarded person has a right to proper medical care and physical therapy and to such education, training, rehabilitation, and guidance as will enable him to develop his ability and maximum potential.
3. The mentally retarded person has a right to economic security and to a decent standard of living. He has a right to perform productive work or to engage in any other meaningful occupation to the fullest extent of his capabilities.
4. Whenever possible, the mentally retarded person should live with his own family or with foster parents and participate in different forms of community life. The family with which he lives should receive assistance. If care in an institution becomes necessary, it should be provided in surroundings and other circumstances as close as possible to those of normal life.
5. The mentally retarded person has a right to a qualified guardian when this is required to protect his personal well-being and interests.
6. The mentally retarded person has a right to protection from exploitation, abuse and degrading treatment. If prosecuted for any offense, he shall have a right to due process

of law with full recognition being given to his degree of mental responsibility.

7. Whenever mentally retarded persons are unable, because of the severity of their handicap, to exercise all their rights in a meaningful way or it should become necessary to restrict or deny some or all of these rights, the procedure used for that restriction or denial of rights must contain proper legal safeguards against every form of abuse. This procedure must be based on an evaluation of the social capability of the mentally retarded person by qualified experts and must be subject to periodic review and to the right of appeal to higher authorities.

These rights have been extensively promulgated and have been adopted in the United States. They have been used as a platform for reform and program development.

A fourth factor, intertwined with the activities of advocacy groups, court cases, and progressive legislation, was the enunciation of developmental principles that have come under the generic heading of "normalization." Normalization has been specifically applied to institutional residential programs under the idea of "deinstitutionalization" and to public education and service programs under the idea of "mainstreaming".

The concept of normalization appears to have begun with Neils E. Bank-Mikkelsen(1980, 56), head of the Danish Mental Retardation Service, who phrased it as "letting the mentally retarded obtain an existence as close to the normal" as possible. This principle was written into a 1959 Danish law governing services for the mentally retarded. In 1969, the executive director of the Swedish Association for Retarded Children, Bengt Nirje, first gave it written expression. It was made popular in this country by Wolf Wolfensberger starting in 1972 with his textbook on *The Principle of Normalization in Human Services*. Since then it has become an international paradigm for human services and not only for the mentally retarded(Wolfensberger, 1980).

The apparent originator of the concept of normalization, Bank-Mikkelsen(1980, 56), explains the meaning of the term this way:

> There have been semantic problems about the very word "normalization." Some have misinterpreted it to mean converting mentally retarded people into so-called "normals." Normalization does not mean normality. A mentally retarded person is not normal--who is? What is normality, and does anyone want to be "normal" at a time when there is so much understanding for people who are trying not to be uniform. Normalization means making normal mentally retarded people's housing, education, working and leisure conditions. It means bringing them the legal and human rights of all other citizens.
>
> Normalization is basically an attack on the various dogmas, especially protectionism, which have for centuries worried mentally retarded people. Normalization is an antidogma. It means that mentally retarded people should not be treated in any special way.... This, of course, does not mean that mentally retarded people do not have a right to special education or special treatment. But this should be provided according to the need and not merely because they are mentally handicapped and the same should apply to other citizens who need special provision for a short period of time or for their whole lives.

Bengt Nirje(1980, 32-33) describes what the "normalization" principle means to him:

> Normalization means sharing a normal rhythm of the day, with privacy, with activities, and mutual responsibilities; a normal rhythm of the week, with a home to live in, a school or work to go to, and leisure time with a modicum of social interaction; a

normal rhythm of the year, with the changing modes and ways of life and of family and community customs as experienced in the different seasons of the year.

Normalization also means opportunity to undergo the normal developmental experiences of the life cycle: infanthood, with security and the respective steps of early childhood development; school age, with exploration and the increase of skills and experience; adolescence with development towards adult life and options.... Like everybody else, retarded people should experience the coming of adulthood and maturity through marked changes in the settings and circumstances of their lives.

Normalization also means that the normal respect and understanding should be given to the silent wishes or expressed self-determination of retarded persons; that relationships between sexes should follow the regular patterns and variations of society; that the same basic economic patterns of life followed by others should apply also to retarded persons.

Finally, normalization also means that if retarded persons cannot or should not any longer live in their family or own home, the homes provided should be of normal size and situated in normal residential areas, being neither isolated nor larger than is consistent with regular mutually respectful or disinterested social interaction and integration.

The normalization principle means making available to all mentally retarded people patterns of life and conditions of everyday living which are as close as possible to the regular circumstances and ways of life of society.

Nirje(1980) goes on to point out that the practical implementation of the normalization principle involves six types of <u>integration</u>: (1)<u>physical</u> <u>integration</u> involves retarded people living in homes in residential areas and going to school in regular school buildings and working in available industrial and business areas and engaging in leisure activities at the same places other people use; (2)functional integration involves having physical access to, even if physically handicapped, and using ordinary segments of the environment from restaurants and barbershops to rest rooms and transportation; (3)social integration involves mutually respectful social and interpersonal relationships in neighborhoods, schools, work and community institutions; (4)personal integration means having opportunities for meaningful activities and relationships as one moves through the life cycle and the cycle of the days, weeks, seasons and years as are available to other people; (5)societal integration means that insofar as the retarded need services these should either be the use of generic services or the use of specialized services that are patterned and operated like services available to other people as much as possible; and (6)organizational integration means using generic community services when available but if unavailable specialized services for the retarded should be patterned after generic services as much as possible.

One prong of normalization has to do with the residential location(and thereby treatment programs) for the retarded. The National Association of Superintendents of Public Residential Facilities for the mentally retarded(1974, 5) identify three types of "deinstitutionalization":

1. The prevention of admission to the institution by finding and developing community methods of care and training.
2. The return to the community of all residents who have been prepared through programs of habilitation and training to function in appropriate local settings.
3. The establishment and maintenance of a responsive residential environment which protects human and civil rights and which contributes to the expeditious return of the individual to resume community living, whenever possible.

The indicators for evidence of deinstitutionalization are: (1)admission rates and numbers over time, (2)release rates and release numbers and the total numbers of persons in large state hospitals over time, and (3)the quality of care of residents in such institutions. We will later present evidence on the rate of deinstitutionalization in the 1970's and 1980's. However, at this point, let us look at a brief overview of the deinstitutionalization record. In 1950 there were 128,145 persons resident in public institutions for the retarded. This number increased steadily up until 1967 when it reached a peak of 193,188. Since then it has been dropping, declining to 181,058 in 1971 and 128,637 in 1982. This decline is primarily due to the release of residents to community residential facilities since death rates in institutions have remained steady while admission rates have increased only slowly(Butterfield, 1976; Hauber, 1982). In a later chapter we will examine the pattern of residential location of retardates and issues related to institutional care and deinstitutionalization.

Several court cases prompted the translation of deinstitutionalization from an ideal into reality. The landmark case of Judicial Activism was *Wyatt v. Stickney*(1972) which established the right to habilitation. Judicial factfinding and extensive testimony indicated that Partlow State School and Hospital in Alabama was only a warehouse for retardates that was incapable of providing habilitation and which instead contributed to their deterioration and debilitation. The court declared(Kindred, 1984, 197): "Because the only constitutional justification for civilly committing a mental retardate is habilitation, it follows ineluctably that once committed such a person is possessed of an inviolable right to habilitation." The court ordered extensive changes in the staffing and operation of this institution. A number of similar cases followed. In the 1975 Willowbrook State School case(New York State Association for Retarded Citizens, Inc. v. Rockefeller), more than 50 witnesses reported harmful conditions at the school including beatings, assembly-line-bathing, cruel restraints, inadequate clothing and medical care. In *The Willowbrook Wars*, Rothman and Rothman(1984) report that the consent decree by the state promulgated standards to protect the residents from abuse and harm such as protection from peonage, human experimentation, use of unnecessary medication, and involuntary sterilization.

Later court cases orders called for phasing out of this institution primarily by placing most of the residents in community programs.

Later court cases have sought to affirm plaintiff rights to "the least restrictive alternative" in residential placement and the receipt of other services. In the much heralded case of Halderman v. Pennhurst State School and Hospital(1977), a federal district court found such terrible conditions at this Pennsylvania school that were inadequate for habilitation and normalization that it ordered it closed when the residents could be properly placed in community programs. The court also ruled it was the duty of Pennsylvania to place all residents of state schools in community residences. On appeal, however, the Third Circuit Court of Appeals ruled in 1979 that while there was a clear preference for habilitation in the least restrictive environment it was not an unconstitutional denial of due process or equal protection to place retarded residents in state institutions(Vitello & Soskin, 1985).

Other legislation was passed in this era that not only helped improve the services and quality of life for retarded persons but also for other developmentally disabled persons. One of these acts was Public Law 90-480, the 1968 Architectural Barriers Act, which required that new public buildings be made accessible to and internally useable by the disabled(Stroman, 1982).

Several other acts were Public Law 91-517, the Developmental Disabilities Services and Construction Act of 1970, and Public Law 94-103, the Developmentally Disabled Assistance and Bill of Rights Act of 1975 and 1978(Public Law 95-602) which have established a bill of rights for such persons, established state Developmental Disability Councils to plan and coordinate a variety of services for those with disabilities, and act as an ombudsperson agency for the disabled(Wiegerink & Petossi, 1979).

SUMMARY

The history of the perception and treatment of the mentally retarded has varied greatly in the course of American history. Seven different perceptual models of the retarded were reviewed to illustrate the range and types of attitudes that have existed. Initially the retarded were usu-

131

ally kept at home for there were no specialized programs for them up to about 1850 unless they got into trouble which landed them in lunatic asylums, jails or poorhouses. From 1850 to 1880 an optimistic environmental view prevailed that saw the retarded as capable of development. Schools were developed on a small residential model to educate and train them. But toward the end of this period and in the 1880 to 1890 decade a pessimistic view developed that they were to be protected from society and then society from them. They were to be segregated from society to protect it from their reproduction and amoral behavior. During this time asylums became larger and more custodial in nature and were to be shelters for these pitiable creatures. The depth of pessimism and efforts at social control reached a maximum in the 1900 to 1920 period characterized by large institutions, permanent custodial care, stereotypes of the retarded as a social menace who ought to be segregated and sterilized. From 1920 to 1950 more optimistic views began to emerge and a wider range of services advocated even though the depression and war years made such efforts small in comparison to need. The more affluent period from 1950 to 1985 saw the reemergence of the developmental model in theory and research and its gradual expansion as an operational model as new professional ideals, court challenges, and progressive legislation came together to lead to new changes in educational, residential and social services for the retarded.

132

Chapter 5

Mental Retardation and Family Life

In this chapter we want to look at two different family situations that involve retardation--families in which the parents conceive, bear and, perhaps, raise, a child who is retarded, and families in which one or both of the married partners are retarded and who may have children. Since the first type of family situation involving parents with retarded children is much more common and better researched it will occupy most of our attention.

Retardation occurs in an institution, the family, which has the traditional function of not only creating the child but being responsible for its care and development until the child reaches independence. The National Association for Retarded Children(1976) estimates that one in ten Americans has contact with a retarded person in their family. Thus, having a retarded member either in the immediate or extended family is not an exceptionally rare experience but one which can have profound effects on each of the members in the family and on family relationships. But in discussing the effects of retardation on family life we need to recall that there are large variations in retardation--large variations in the level of intellectual and adaptive behavior, in physical defects, and in personality and emotional functioning. Therefore, one of the critical variables in how families respond to retardation is the degree of its severity and how this influences a variety of interventions.

MODELS OF FAMILY CARE

Caring for a dependent family member is a universal situation for all parents who have children. However, when that dependency is greater or longer or abnormal in comparison to other families it may create greater stress. Perlman and Giele(1983) have developed a model of a Family Care System that can be applied to a variety of situations: a retarded child or adult living at home, a mentally disturbed family member, a physically handicapped family member, or someone who is either acutely or chronically ill or impaired such as an aged parent who can no longer live alone. Figure 5.1 delineates the three key variables in this model.

Figure 5.1

Model of the Family Care System

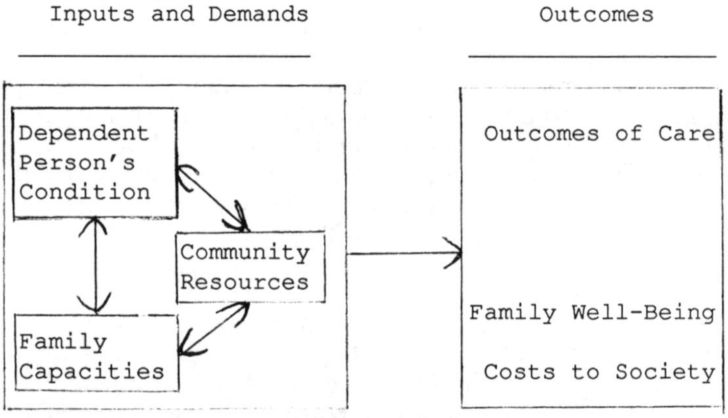

Inputs and Demands   Outcomes

Source: Perlman & Giele(1983, 15).

The three key variables are(Perlman & Giele, 1983, 12):

1.   **the physical and emotional needs and demands** that the dependent person places on the family;
2.   **the material and non-material capacities of the families** to meet the dependent

person's needs and simultaneously to fulfill other family functions; and

3. **the availability and use of community resources** such as social services.

These three key elements form an "unstable triad" because as any of the elements changes it may affect inputs or outputs. Further, each of these variables may have a wide range of variation. Among the mentally retarded, for example, the "need" range might go from a mildly retarded individual who needs some additional assistance with schoolwork and leisure activities to an incontinent, nonambulatory, profoundly retarded person who needs 24-hour a day care. And family capacities will vary in terms of financial assets and income, the number and ages of family members, how many are working outside the home, the amount of time they are willing to allocate to caregiving, the physical and emotional strength of each and all family members, and their values with regard to caretaking responsibilities. Community resources may also vary by the number, kind and cost of services available to assist in caretaking. This model also looks at three outcomes: (1)outcomes for the dependent individual, (2)outcomes for the well-being of the family as an ongoing systems of relationships and meeting of the needs and demands of each individual in it, and (3)outcomes to society in terms of cost of services, manpower utilization, and the quality of life of other people impacted by family home care. This model provides key variables to investigate as we look at the effects of retardation on family life.

Horejsi(1983) also develops a family care model that is useful in helping to identify stresses involved in home care for the retarded, or other dependent persons, and why some families decide out-of-home-care(placement in some type of residential facility other than their own home) is the best alternative. Horejsi uses a formula to show the relationships of the key variable in his "Motivation, Capacity and Opportunity Framework" shown in Figure 5.2. One of the points Horejsi makes about this model is that as you elevate or depress any one of the variables in the formula this may (1)affect in a synergistic way one or

Figure 5.2

Motivation, Capacity and Opportunity Framework

$$FC = \frac{M \times C \times 0}{P}$$

Key: FC = Ability to provide **F**amily **C**are
    M = **M**otivation to cope with the
         problem.
    C = **C**apacity(physical, emotional,
         intellectual) to deal with the
         problem.
    O = **O**pportunities in the environment to
         use formal and informal resources.
    P = **P**roblems, needs, demands of develop-
         mentally disabled family member.

Source: Adapted from Horejsi(1983, 59).

more of the variables in the numerator or denominator, and (2)indicate the feasibility and/or quality of family care. For example, if there are few "opportunities" for using environmental resources in the community for day care and physical therapy for a physically disabled, severely retarded child, this may exacerbate the child's condition, exhaust the parents in trying to provide such care themselves and lower the quality of the family care that is offered. With these models available as analytical tools, we now turn to an analysis of the decision points and processes involved in dealing with the stresses retardation can introduce into family life.

THE DIAGNOSIS OF MENTAL RETARDATION

The time at which parents find out about the likelihood or fact of retardation is not uniform. When they find out is usually related to its severity and whether it is accompanied by physical abnormalities. A few find out in the prenatal period from the results of amniocentesis or other diagnostic tests. Some find out at the point of birth or within the first few months of the newborn's life either by

136

the visible presence of physical defects and/or the delay of development or the health condition of the infant. This is particularly true for severely and profoundly retarded children. Most parents do not find out until about ages 3 to 8, or even later, when the child is slow in development or having problems at school. This is primarily the case with mildly retarded children.

Prenatal Diagnosis

Advances in medical diagnostic techniques now make it possible to know before birth that a child definitely will be or may be born with defects that are always or usually accompanied by retardation. Rather than confronting a defective baby at birth, the parents may have to make a decision whether or not to have a therapeutic abortion. This is often an agonizing decision because the parents are confronted with questions of why the baby is defective, how defective it may be, what the child's life might be like if it is carried to term, and what demands would be placed on them for years to come. The decision on abortion will involve their religious values, the effects such a child could have on other children, and the quality of their own life as parents. And the parents may experience greater stress if they are not unanimous in their decision on abortion.

The decision on abortion will also be influenced by the wider values in society. Because of the high economic and personal costs associated with raising a severely retarded child, the parents may feel obligated to have an abortion of a genetically defective fetus. A survey by Yankelovich, Skelly, and Wright(1981) found that 87% of the respondents in a poll agreed with the statement that a woman with a severely defective fetus should be allowed to obtain a legal abortion. At the same time, Pro-life advocates argue that since they believe life begins at conception and not at some later time, the rights of the unborn child to life outweigh the woman's right to control her body or that of an unborn fetus. These issues remain hotly debated and raise questions about individual versus social responsibility. For example, if the abortion of a defective fetus is not allowed even though that is the mother's wish, does this mean that society should then be responsible for the care of the child? Can society force a woman to give birth to a child whose quality of life would be very low and burden a family with the high cost of its care?

Early Postnatal Decisions and Problems

Early postnatal diagnoses that the child is retarded usually occur when the child is visibly different and is likely to be severely or profoundly retarded. When parents are told a few hours or days or months after birth that their child is retarded there is often a shock and denial experience. There is a disbelief that this had happened to them(Kugel, 1976). After reviewing the literature on the nature and sequence of events following the disclosure of a diagnosis of a handicapped child, Fortier and Wanless(1984) developed a five stage model of the crisis a family goes through after the pronouncement:

1. *Impact.* The family members experience shock, anxiety, numbness, bewilderment, disorganization, protest and agitation. It is an occasion of unexpected grave disappointment when the usual expectation is to have a healthy, normal baby.
2. *Denial.* The second stage often overlaps the first and third stages as parents go through a wide range of emotions. The second stage is characterized by disbelief that this could happen to them. They may deny this unexpected outcome by engaging in "shopping for cures"-- getting other medical diagnoses which they hope will reverse the first diagnosis that their child is "not normal." They may engage in imaginary explanations of why this has happened, regress to magical thinking that somehow the baby will be cured, or give evasive explanations about the baby's condition because they are still disbelieving it has really happened to them.
3. *Grief.* Anger, guilt, feelings of loss, isolation, self-pity, hopelessness, despair, and remorse mark the third stage. A pervasive sadness and depression may set in that is mixed with anger about this unexpected turn of events. Parents often feel helpless at this time. They feel they are "different" because this happened to them and express self-doubt about their ability to cope with it. They may feel humiliated because a defective child is a reflection on them.

138

4. *Focusing outward.* In this fourth stage the parents begin seeking information about the origins of the condition so they will "understand." They consider intervention options and formulate plans. This acceptance of reality is often accompanied by anxiety as to whether they can deal with the options they have considered.

5. *Closure.* This last stage is marked by growing family solidarity as they orient themselves to and plan together to meet the child's needs.

One of the early decisions that sometimes arises is whether to give treatment to a highly defective newborn. This treatment may involve surgery, the use of life sustaining support equipment, or food, without which things the child would die. It is usually the parents who make this decision in concurrence with their physician. If the decision is made to let the infant die by withholding treatment, the moral justifications for this decision include: (1)the infant may never have a meaningful life, (2)the defective person will suffer a great deal of physical and emotional pain, and (3)the social and economic costs to either the parents or society or both are intolerably high.

While passive euthanasia is sometimes practiced on defective infants without reaching the courts, in some cases the courts have been resorted to in an effort to resolve complex issues or questions. Vitello and Soskin(1985) say these issues include: (1)should parents decide what is in the best interests of the child when this may conflict with their own best interests? (2)are parents or physicians or courts best qualified to judge what constitutes a meaningful life? and (3)if a defective infant is ordered to receive treatment by judicial intervention, who is responsible for the cost of lifetime care? With regard to passive euthanasia as well as with more active treatment programs, like surgery which, if withheld, could lead to death, Vitello and Soskin(1985, 77) conclude,

> Both in law and morality, there is a lack of social consensus to guide parental decisions. This ambiguity adds to the confusion and sense of guilt as to what is the "right" thing to do. Parents must often feel that no matter what decision is made, they will be damned if they do and damned if they don't.

139

The research on family stress induced by having a retarded child has focused on both family dynamics and outcomes. Much of the early research emphasized the problems that such families experience while later research shows that although families go through a period of shock, disbelief and denial, many families eventually learn to cope quite well with the presence of a retarded member. One of the critical elements is how and when parents are told. Carr(1984) says that research reveals that parents want to be told early, honestly and sympathetically that they have a retarded child. And the trend seems to be more in this direction as medical personnel come to know more about retardation. Some earlier studies and reports indicated physicians often delayed telling parents, told them the clinical conditions but without much sympathy, and often gave pessimistic prognoses.

Kanner(1953) categorizes parental reactions of having a mentally retarded child into three patterns: denial, disguise and acceptance. These patterns are not mutually exclusive. Parents may fluctuate from one response to another at different points in time ranging from a few minutes apart to months or years apart. But many move from denial, then to disguise, and finally to an acceptance pattern of coping.

The Denial Response. The denial response is often a first and temporary response. But sometimes this severe emotional reaction to stress continues as parents deny to themselves and others the reality of the child's disability. Deniers often feel some misdiagnosis has been made or that the child is just a slow developer who will catch up with his age mates with a developmental spurt. This response is more likely to occur when the retardation is mild and is not accompanied by obvious physical blemishes. It may also be a function of the parent's own maturity level, their knowledge about retardation and their personality needs, and it can hamper the realistic adjustment of the parents to the child and the provision of beneficial services in the child's development.

The Disguise Response. This response may overlap the denial response particularly with regards to admitting the child's condition to other family members or to other people in the community. But in disguising the retardation to others the parents may be trying to hide the full meaning of retardation from themselves. The disguising response

140

may take several forms and any one family may engage in multiple forms of it. One form is "doctor shopping" where it is hoped a new diagnosis will be made that the child really isn't retarded or that some "cure" will be found. Parents may suspect the child has a vision or hearing problem or some other malady that will explain the slow development. But doctor shopping often results in disillusionment, that is, the problem is not a false diagnosis but real.

A second form that disguising takes is to blame the child for the apparent retardation. The child's retardation is interpreted primarily as a behavioral problem of uncooperative behavior, or the child not wanting to try. By blaming the child the parents disguise the real nature of the problem. But in the process the parents often become punitive toward the child for perceived laziness, indifference, and lack of interest and effort.

A third form of disguising is to blame psychologists, social workers, physicians or teachers either for being unable to make a clear diagnosis or unable to properly apply some therapy or instructional technique. Teachers in regular or special education classes may be blamed for their child's slow educational progress. They may be misperceived as being poor teachers or not motivating their children, or of not giving them enough individual attention. Other therapists may also be interpreted as lacking the skill to alter their child's behavior. Disguising, then, involves some misperception of the location of the problem(Hutt & Gibby, 1976).

Both denial and disguise responses may be due in part to the stigma of a handicap which reflects on both the parents and child. These responses are a way for parents to avoid the blame for their child's retardation by either denying the problem or placing the blame on the child or "helping" professionals.

The Acceptance Response. This response is more constructive and adaptive for it accepts the reality of the child's disability. Rather than trying to blame someone for the disability or not recognizing it, the accepting parent realizes the disability as a given that needs to be dealt with in a constructive problem solving approach. These types of parents will not feel threatened by having a retarded child. Rather, they will intellectually accept this fact and deal constructively with the emotions this situation engenders.

141

They will seek information and guidance from informed professionals and parental groups on how to deal with questions regarding home care, instruction, the most appropriate residential location and services for their child. The acceptance response is a dynamic one that often emerges over time as parents deal with anxieties about what to do with their retarded child. Rosen(1955) found that many parents went through about five stages of dealing with a mildly or moderately retarded child. The first stage, <u>awareness</u> that their child is different, occurred around age two and a half. At about five years of age, the second state emerged--this was the <u>recognition</u> stage where it becomes clearly known that the child is retarded. In the third stage, <u>causes</u> for the retardation are sought. Next, the <u>solution seeking</u> stage involves parents investigating alternative ways of dealing with the problem. And the final stage, <u>acceptance</u>, occurs when both the child and the problem are accepted by the parents. There is no inevitable progression through these stages. Thus, acceptance involves a growth process in the parents as they gradually become aware of their child's handicap, its origins, and how to deal with it. Some parents may misperceive the nature of the problem and get stuck permanently or temporarily in denial or disguise responses. Parents of more severely retarded children must work through these stages in a more highly compressed time period. They may experience panic reactions of not knowing where to turn for help. They often feel guilty--wondering what they did to deserve this or feeling guilty about not loving the defective child as much as they would a normal one. The typical vicarious satisfaction that parents hope to achieve through their children seems to be denied to the parents of a retarded child. Olshansky believes that most parents who have a mentally retarded child suffer from a pervasive psychological reaction that he calls "chronic sorrow." Such parents know or find out that the demands that a retarded child makes on them are time consuming, energy draining and often permanent in the sense the child may not become an independent, self-sufficient adult(Olshansky, 1970).

Lawrence Goodman(1970, 373) describes the experience this way:

>The birth of a congenitally defective infant
>transforms a joyously awaited experience

into one of catastrophe and profound threat. The apprehension of failure that is a normal part of the psychic anticipation of parenthood turns into reality--and the family finds itself in crisis.

Silvia Schild(1970, 358) describes the ambivalence parents of retarded children go through based on her counseling experience:

Enormous ambivalence of feeling is evoked in a parent when he learns that his child is retarded. Feelings of rejection, dejection, and disappointment collide with anxious hopefulness, doubt, anger, and self-pity. Strong emotions of guilt mix with protective parental reactions; resentment, confusion, and insecurity become pervasive. . . . These conflicting emotions are never completely resolved, as the long-term aspect of the problem and the repeated crises that stem directly from the fact of the child's handicap stir up the ambivalence from time to time.

LATER POSTNATAL ISSUES

We have already looked at some adjustment processes that parents have to work through whenever retardation is discovered--whether early or later in the postnatal period. Many of the stresses that families of retarded members are exposed to are continuing ones--particularly the responsibility of additional care that many retardates require. In this section of the chapter we will give attention to several other issues: (1)expectations about and problems in home care, (2)relationships to and stresses on siblings, (3)stigma, (4)care of the retarded by aging parents, and (5)factors involved in making a decision about out-of-home residential placement.

Home Care Problems. The great majority of retardates, about 95%, live with their parents. They are primarily mildly or moderately retarded persons. It is a normative assumption in our society that the natural family is the best place for a retarded person to live unless his condition is truly extraordinary. It is presumed that in his own home a person will receive loving attention. However, today's smaller family, which involves a majority of women working outside the home, is subject to a time stress in caring for a child or teenager who may require extra attention. While nonretarded children usually require less attention and supervision as they mature, this is often not true of a retarded person. Thus, one of the "chronic stresses" in families of retarded children is both the additional and continuing nature of the burden of supervision that falls heaviest on the mother. "Respite care," wherein parents get sitter services and relief from providing care full time seven days a week, has been shown to decrease negative maternal attitudes toward the mentally retarded child and to put less stress on the marital relationship(Wikler, 1983; Carr, 1984).

One of the particular problems in home care is the setting of realistic expectations for the retarded child. Two contrary expectations seem to be made by some families with retarded children: setting either unrealistically high goals for the retarded person or overprotection and overindulgence of the child. If unrealistically high goals are set, this provides a setting for disappointment, failure, and blame. It may precipitate family tensions over the goals for the retarded person or over how those goals are to be reached. Such expectations engender a chronic sorrow over a lack of achievement. On the other hand, some parents of retarded children expect too little of them. This sets the stage of overprotecting them from the outside world and low expectations of what they can accomplish. It may involve keeping the child sheltered at home and away from the normal experience of other children. In protecting them from normal socialization experiences, including the right to fail and make mistakes, the retarded person is not given the opportunity to learn from his mistakes. Overindulgence involves excessive catering to the child's wants and desires without setting necessary limits on what he may do and taking disciplinary measures to correct unacceptable behavior. It may involve letting the retarded child eat what he wants, not correcting rude behavior, and not disciplining disruptive behavior. Such overindulgence often stems from feelings of pity for the child. But such feelings of pity do not set realistic standards for behavior. Thus, the child may be spoiled and become unruly. Consequently, parents of retarded children need to get information from guidance counselors, teachers and social workers on what are realistic expectations for their child given his deficits in intelligence and/or adaptive behavior. According to Carr(1984) and Proctor(1983), parental instruction in setting realistic development goals, parental instruction in particular teaching techniques, parent counseling and support groups and good information and referral programs can all assist in these parenting tasks.

Sibling Stresses. A number of problems have been identified here including: (1)the shame some teenagers experience by having a retarded sibling; (2)the greater burden usually put on older siblings, particularly sisters, for the care of the retarded; and (3)the greater attention that the retarded may receive which may foster jealousy. Sibling attitudes often mirror those of their parents. They may range from shame and rejection, to realistic acceptance, to overindulgent catering to the wants of the retarded sibling. Sometimes siblings reflect the attitudes of their peer groups toward people who are different at a time when they are developing their sense of identify(Trevino, 1983). For example a person from Newark wrote Ann Landers(1970, 38-39) about a teenager's response to her mentally retarded brother:

> Some friends of ours have a retarded son. The boy is ten years old, but his mentality is at the four-or-five year old level. He is usually pleasant and well behaved, but it is apparent that the child is mentally deficient.
>
> The problem is the boy's 16-year old sister. She is ashamed of her brother and fearful that if her friends see him it will hurt her socially. She insists that the boy be in his room when she comes home from school--in case she brings a friend. When she has a date the retarded child must be kept out of sight.
>
> The parents want to be fair to the girl, but they want to be fair to the boy, too. They don't know what to do. Can you help?

Ann Landers responded that the parents, in allowing the child to be hidden as something shameful, were ignorant and were allowing their daughter to reflect their own attitudes. She advised them to put an end to this practice. The involvement of siblings in the diagnosis of the problem, behavior modification programs for the retarded youngster, and family counseling sessions can all be helpful in dealing with such stresses(Trevino, 1983; Carr, 1984; Vadasy, 1984).

Stigma. One of the things that both retarded individuals and family members have to live with is the stigma of retardation. But the research literature here is rather inconclusive as to what effects labeling has on a person's self-conception and treatment by others. While labeling may lead to stereotypes about behavior and explain why a person acts as he does, it may either benefit him in the sense of being the justification for the receipt of special services and help and increase tolerance and understanding or it may be disbeneficial by impairing effective treatment(Westling, 1986). Dudley(1983) maintains that many of the retarded are substantially aware of their condition and its negative value loading. At the same time they sometimes reject the attitudes others have towards them. Dudley found a variety of stereotyping instances of interaction between the retarded and normals primarily in a workshop situation. Dudley categorized the types of stereotyped interactions which promote stigma as follow:

1. Inappropriate Language References. This involved referring to persons with mental handicaps as "retardates," "stupid," "you look like a truck rolled over you," or as a "boy" or "girl" when the person was an adult.

2. Inappropriate Restrictions Imposed on Participants. These involved placing unwarranted limitations on clients which assumed their handicap was greater than it really was. Such restrictions may include being denied opportunities to do things, being punished for minor agency infractions, and having their freedom of movement unnecessarily restricted.

3. Violations of Confidentiality. This involved professionals sharing information with each other, outsiders and families that should have been held in confidence because that was promised to the client by the professional.

4. Deterring New Roles. This involved keeping clients in an agency from entering new roles such as starting a committee and limiting their freedom to do things they felt like doing and that would have harmed no one.

5. Physical Abuse. This involved physically restraining or slapping a client where such measures were uncalled for.

6. Involuntary Sterilization. One client was sterilized without his informed consent although he went along with his parents' request to have the operation done.

7. Excessively Loud or Scolding Tone of Voice. Such inappropriate yelling seemed to be based on the faulty assumptions clients were hard of hearing, wouldn't listen to unless yelled at, or were naughty.

8. Childlike Treatment. This type of treatment involved talking down to and/or touching, patting or pinching adult clients in a fashion that was appropriate for children but not adults.

9. Imitation of a Person's Limitations. This involved professional staff members using a voice like one of the clients, or using a slouching posture in a chair typical of one of the clients.

10. Denying a Participant an Opportunity to Present His View. Instances of staff members making a decision about a client in a way that directly affected the client but without consulting the person were witnessed. This type of decision making for others denied them participation in decisions where they could make a real contribution and have their dignity confirmed by being consulted.

11. A Pattern of Ignoring a Participant. Instances of not responding to questions by clients or acting like the client was not there were observed.

12. Open Ridicule. Some people moved away from unattractive clients on buses or at other locations, laughed at their behavior or talked in hushed tones-- apparently about the handicapped person.

13. Staring. "Staring was another form of blatant disregard of the participant's feelings that was reported by some of them"(Dudley, 1983, 60).

Care of the Retarded by Aging Parents. As parents age, particularly when they reach their 60s, 70s and beyond, they may find the care of an older son or daughter,

147

who is around 20 to 30 years younger, an increasing burden emotionally, physically and socially. Such parents may have earlier missed the sense of accomplishment that comes when a son or daughter graduates from high school, gets his first job, becomes independent, marries and has children(Konana & Warren, 1984). Prior to the onset of older age, such parents often worry about what will happen to an older retarded dependent, should they, the parents, become too sick or impaired to care for such a person. Or they worry about what will happen to their dependent when they die. At this transition point, they may plan ahead to (1)arrange for an out-of-home placement when it is needed, and (2)find a guardian, such as a sibling or family friend, who will look after the retarded person and his affairs. The appointment of a guardian occurs after a person has been found to be incompetent to look after his own person and affairs(Parry, 1985).

Factors Involved in Out-of-Home Placement. Nearly all the mildly retarded live with their families(Moroney, 1986). Only about one third of the more severely retarded are placed in institutions. What factors are involved in the process to seek a residential placement outside the home? A review of the literature(Risherman & Cocozza, 1984) reveals about three general factors are involved in this decision with the first one probably being the most critical: (1)severity of retardation and other handicaps; (2)the stress that caring for a handicapped person will generate in the family and the family's capacity to cope with this stress, and (3)the availability of services in a community and parental knowledge of these services. As the severity of the handicap increases and is accompanied by physical abnormalities that demand extensive and specialized care, a family is increasingly likely to seek institutional placement. The second factor is the stress that having a retarded member living at home generates in a family and the kinds of resources a family has for coping. In a sense we have several variables here that are interrelated. One is family resources or coping skills and these may be related to the experience of coping with handicaps. As presented in an earlier model in this chapter, these family resources include financial assets and income, number and ages of family members, number of parents working outside the home, and skills in dealing with strain and the perception of stigma. Placement in an

148

out-of-home residence appears to increase with family size but is inversely related to family economic assets. The parent's health, age and the quality of the marital relationship will also influence the perception of stress on the family(Westling, 1986).

The third factor is whether there are a variety of services and supports in the community and parents know about these in a timely way and can access them. If parents are confronted with no information and no referrals to parent support groups, parent counseling groups, pediatric care for the child, medical testing services, respite care, and educational testing and instructional programs, they are more likely to institutionalize a child who presents heavy demands on their time and behavior problems. However, having such services available better enables them to work through crises and maintain the child at home(Davidson & Dosser, 1983).

Over time the quality of advice given to parents about out-of-home placements appears to have improved. In the past, many parents were sometimes given confusing directions on what to do with a severely retarded child. Some physicians would say to send the child to an institution immediately, some would say keep the child at home and others would take a wait and see approach--that perhaps the child would outgrow the problem. In the past some families felt they were looked down upon by professionals in the field and treated as if they knew nothing about their child's needs(Scheerenberger, 1983). The new deinstitutionalization program and the ideology of normalization encourage home care and apparently more families are choosing home care. At the same time, some families choose some type of out-of-home placement where the range of alternative residential locations has been widened and the quality of such programs improved. The reasons that parents give for choosing an institutional or nonhome residence for their children include: (1)the high quality of care they believe is given in such institutions; (2)the belief that the 24-hour care their children need can better be provided by such specialized facilities than generic and uncoordinated services available in the community; (3)the belief that the children will be better off in a facility with their "own kind" where they will be shielded from a community that stigmatizes them and doesn't want them; (4)parents are able to relieve their feelings of guilt and inadequacy by placing the child in such a facility; and (5)the lesser cost of institutional placement than home care to the parents(Vitello & Soskin, 1985).

Institutional Releases to Home. Under the deinstitutionalization policy, some mentally retarded persons, who have spent time in an institution may be released. They may be released to a variety of residential placements most of which will be described in a later chapter. However, we will now look at those who are released to (1)either their natural family, or (2)to an adoptive home. In a 1978 national study it was found that 40% of those released from institutions were placed in their natural homes. However, there is some evidence that (1)the percentages of releasees placed in natural homes is declining over time, and, (2)that there is substantial regional variation in the percentage who are placed with their natural families. Willer and Intagliata(1984) report that only 12% of the retardates released from New York state institutions in the early 1980s were released to their homes. They found that the percentage released to their own homes was highest in the southern states where there are fewer residential alternatives available and lowest in the northern states where more residential alternatives are available. Another pattern, too, is that the earlier releasees in the 1970s were less severely retarded than those released in the 1980s. Generally, home placements are often less suitable for those who need extensive care--primarily those who have severe chronic medical problems, are profoundly retarded or have disturbing behavioral problems.

And what are the characteristics of those released to their natural homes? First of all, of those released to their natural homes, 43% had the request initiated by the family whereas only 9% placed in alternative residential settings had the request initiated by the family. In contrast, those released to alternative residential settings saw the institutional staff initiate the idea 84% of the time whereas the staff initiated the idea for natural home placement in only 34% of the cases. Natural homes receiving released retardates were not too much different from families that did not receive releasees home. But natural homes, on the average had lower socioeconomic status and the mothers of individuals placed in the natural home in New York state "were more likely to be separated or divorced without remarrying(21 percent) than mothers of individuals placed in alternate settings(6 percent)" (Willer & Intagliata, 1984). Secondly, those released in New York state to their natural homes were younger(average age of 26 compared to 48 for group homes and 46 for family care homes), more likely to be female(71% compared to 45% for alternative placements), severely or profoundly retarded(44% compared to 40% for alternative placements), and much more likely to have behavior problems before release from the institution. Furthermore, black and Hispanic retardates were much more likely to be placed with the natural family than were whites(Willer & Intagliata, 1984).

The activity patterns of those released from institutional placements were somewhat different than those released to alternate residences. Only 64% of those who returned home were involved in an outside-the-home day care program as compared to nearly all alternative residential placements. On the other hand, 84% of home releasees had routine home chores which helped structure their lives. Interviews with retardates showed this role function in the family gave meaning to their own sense of the quality of their lives. Most of them used generic community services like social events, barber and beauty shops, restaurants and attendance at worship services. A majority of them had friends visit them in their own homes. Many of those living at home had a pattern of using services that was similar to those living in alternative residences: 42% used available transportation, 49% used local recreational resources, 37% got speech therapy, 37% got individual counseling, 15% of the families got family counseling, and 5% of the retarded individuals got physical therapy. The family of such retardates felt their biggest unmet need was for family counseling(56%), companion(sitter) service so they could go out more often(42%), and individual counseling(Willer & Intagliata, 1984).

What impact did release to their natural home have upon the persons released? Most did not show gains in self-help care or in the control of maladaptive behavior such as disobedience displayed by 39% and destructiveness displayed by 20%. For every person who showed improvement in one of these areas there was another who showed losses. The majority of persons returned to their natural homes had deficits in community living skills such

151

as shopping, traveling alone, using the telephone, preparing meals, and money management. And few of them showed gains in improving these skills over time. And those living at home were most likely to exhibit periodic bouts of defiance, impatience and anger. Yet, interviews showed home is where they preferred to be in comparison to other placements(Willer & Intagliata, 1984).

What impact did the return of a retarded person to the natural family have? Willer and Intagliata(1984) suggest five outcomes. (1)The first occurs around the time of release when the family has fears and doubts that it can deal with the problems presented by the retardate, particularly behavioral outbursts and temper tantrums. But most families effectively coped with this anticipatory crisis once the retardate got home. (2)Second, the retardate gives companionship to other members of the family, particularly the mother who is responsible for most of the care. (3)Third, it did burden the family with long term care responsibilities which was handled three-quarters of the time by the mother. The need for supervision substantially increased her work load. This "affective burden" of inordinate time for supervision and "feeling trapped" was experienced by 28% of the mothers while 16% said they neglected other family members and 43% reported it was difficult to get free time. Many parents rarely went out. (4)Only about one family in seven felt that neighbors or relatives stigmatized them in some way and altered their behavior toward them and they in response to the stigmatizers. (5)The last impact was the financial burden where little information is available. Usually there are added costs for food, clothing, and especially medical care. There are also the costs associated with respite services so that parents can get away for periods of time. All individuals released to their homes get SSI(Supplemental Security Income) payments but not the state supplement to SSI available to those who go to other residential placements. In 1985, the SSI payment for disabled individuals was $357.40 a month. This offsets much of the costs of their care, particularly for poor families. Most natural parents do not see the financial burden as great and some fail to take advantage of free services because they have not been made aware of them.

An adoptive home is one where the mentally retarded are legally adopted and operate very much like a natural family. And some retardates also live in "foster homes" or "domiciliary care programs" where those who provide them room, board and supervisory services are reimbursed according to a rate schedule operating in their community and state. Such homes usually house only one or two retarded persons but sometimes as many as six. Many of these operate on principles much like a natural or adoptive home except for the fee-for-service arrangement with the state. Such "family care homes" are usually operated by couples or single women in their forties or fifties whose own children have left home. Most of them are low income families who depend on the reimbursement they receive for part of their income. In the early 1980s families in New York state were reimbursed $2970 annually for each person they cared for. We shall discuss alternative residential placements more fully in a later chapter.

PATTERNS OF FAMILY ADAPTATION

Although we know a substantial amount about the range of stresses that families with handicapped children are exposed to, not a lot of research has been done yet on family life styles that include retarded children. However, Mink, Meyers and Nihira(1984) have studied the families of 218 Trainable Mentally Retarded children. Their analysis of family life styles shows an extensive range of patterns of interaction and psychosocial orientation to the retarded children in such families. Their "cluster analysis" of the psychosocial home environment revealed seven family patterns as follow with the percentage of each type of family enclosed in parentheses after the cluster label name:

1. Child-oriented, cohesive(11.1%). This type of family had high parenting approaches to the TMR child and high father involvement. There was little stress reported in such families. Such families had rather low levels of educational expectation for their children and low levels of community involvement but positive attitudes toward the child's impact on the home. The children engaged in little maladaptive behavior and had high ratings on social adjustment.

153

2. Learning oriented, high residential qual-
ity(27.9%). Over one fourth of the families fell into this
pattern where the parents had high educational expectations
for the child and high expectations about harmonious family relations. Relatively low levels of family stress were
reported in these homes which had above average socioeconomic status. These children did better at school and
were relatively well adjusted at both home and school in
cohesive family environments where the needs of the children were well understood.

3. Low disclosure, unharmonious(9.1%). These
families tended to be tense, report high levels of stress and
have the poorest parent-child relations even though these
children were well adjusted at home and at school. The
children in these families had the highest academic
potential, but parental expectations often outran the
performance of the children at school. Consequently, these
parents tended to deny their children's retardation which
left them in a state of chronic disappointment over their
children's performance.

4. Disadvantaged, noncohesive(8.6%). These
families had the lowest involvement of fathers, tension
among siblings, low family cohesion, and low expectations
regarding the achievement of the children. These families
reported the highest stress levels. The children had high
levels of maladaptive behavior both at home and school in
these relatively low-income families where there was often
inadequate supervision.

5. Achievement-oriented, low residential qual-
ity(13.9%). These families were characterized by being
larger but with few problems among the siblings. Such
families had an above average achievement orientation for
the children and more interest in recreational activities.
There was a low stress level, average rates of maladaptive
behavior at home and school, and a relatively low quality
of home life. The children develop at their own pace with
little cognitive stimulation even though the parents voice
optimistic hopes for the achievement of their children.

6. Expression-oriented with few sociocultural
interests(12.9%). These families had low stress levels with
maladaptive behaviors at home and school about average
for the children. Mothers in this cluster were most likely to
work outside the home and have less time for the supervision of their children. While individual expressiveness was

verbalized, there was little interest in supervision or academic achievement.

7. Outerdirected, with little achievement ori-
entation(16.3%). These middle class homes reported relatively high levels of stress but also very high levels of
involvement in outside the home religious, recreational and
community activities. It appears that this outerdirected
community participation compensated for the lack of family cohesiveness and little supervision of and a lack of
interest in the educational achievement of the TMR child.

This review of a sample of families of Trainable
Mentally Retarded children reveals a diversity of lifestyles.
Some families show considerable stress, others little. Some
have high expectations for their children, others low ones.
Sibling relations are problematic in some families but not
in others. These families varied extensively in community
participation, child supervision, family harmony, and the
social and psychological adaptation of the children to their
home and school environments.

PUBLIC POLICY AND FAMILY HOME CARE

As we shall see in a later chapter, the nonnatural
home and the nonadoptive home alternatives for residential
care of the retarded can be quite expensive and come at the
expense to all taxpayers. It may range from around $1,000
to $3,000 a month or even more to provide residential and
habilitation services to retarded people. If the persons are
placed outside of the home the cost is borne by taxpayers--
primarily at the federal and state level. Because the home
environment is philosophically viewed as the most normalizing location for retardates and it is the least expensive
alternative, one would expect the states and the federal
governments to subsidize such care for both normative and
financial reasons. This, however, is not the case in some
states.

Relatively few states provide adequate services like
respite care or financial subsidies to parents who maintain
their children at home. Minnesota began a Mentally
Retarded Family Subsidy Program in 1976 to help control
the state's burgeoning costs for the care of the mentally
retarded. In that state the average monthly subsidy was
$245. Participating families reported that the money was

used principally to buy special items for the child, to purchase babysitter and respite care services for the parents, and to do more things outside the home for and with the retarded family member. However, one half of the families in the program said they would consider out-of-home placement if the child became more burdensome and appeared to be making no or little progress in developing self-help skills(Zimmerman, 1984). Vitello and Soskin(1985) report that Public Law 96-272, the Adoption Assistance and Child Welfare Act of 1980, provides a federal subsidy for either natural or adoptive families with a handicapped child. And P.L. 97-35, The Home and Community Medicaid Waiver under Title XIX of the Social Security Act, will allow states to provide services to families who have a retarded member considered at risk of institutionalization. However, one state does not provide a dollar subsidy if adoptive families will care for a retarded member. But, in that state, New York, if a family had earlier institutionalized a person and then took him back home they could receive a subsidy; whereas a family that had not institutionalized a child but always kept him or her at home could not collect the subsidy. After several court challenges in New York state, the only natural families to get a subsidy for home care were those who were involved in litigation to deinstitutionalize state institutions, while families who were not involved in litigation or had never institutionalized their child were denied state subsidy. Because of the low public cost of home care and its potential for quality care in instruction and services are provided to such families, one might expect the states to develop more of these policies to encourage the natural family to care for their retarded members. Vitello and Soskin(1985) argue that we need a better policy than the one we now have--one that would require a shared social responsibility by families and governments in assisting families with a disabled member. Vitello and Soskin(1985, 88) argue:

> Such a shift in social policy will require better communication between families and professionals than presently exists. Family members must be perceived and treated as equal partners in the planning and implementation of programs for their retarded member. Professionals must reori-

ent themselves to viewing the family, and not merely the retarded individual, as the unit of service. The family must be regarded as a valuable resource, and rather than professionals doing things **for** the family, they must being doing things **with** the family. On the other hand, if parents are to be given or to assume more control over the welfare of their retarded son or daughter, they must do so responsibly. This will require that they take the initiative to obtain the information and assistance needed to make the appropriate choices among the service options available to them.

THE FAMILY RIGHTS OF MENTALLY RE-TARDED PERSONS

A small number of Americans, the retarded, have had many of their rights questioned in the past including their right to marry, to have children, and to raise those children. Many still question whether they should have such rights in spite of the support for the normalization principle which would allow for the right to marriage, procreation and parenting among the retarded. With the development of thousands of community residential facilities in this country, many teenage and adult retarded persons live together with members of the opposite sex in such facilities. But in such facilities the question also arises as to what degree sex education ought to be provided and what degree of sexual freedom should be provided to such residents. Associated with these questions is the perception that retarded persons are at greater risk of being taken advantage of sexually or of unwittingly being sexually abused and possibly becoming pregnant(Vitello & Soskin, 1985). The profoundly and severely retarded usually have a suppressed sex drive. But the sex drive among the mildly and moderately retarded is relatively normal. However, when they live in various types of group facilities, which usually have a "no-locked doors" policy, they experience less privacy and much more supervision. Under such conditions their sexual outlets primarily involve masturbation. However, insofar as they have the opportunity, their sexual outlets would be expected to reflect the range of outlets open to nonretarded persons(Baroff, 1986).

Marriage

According to a survey, published in 1985, of the marriage laws of the states, some 23 states still have laws prohibiting the marriage of mentally retarded persons either with normals or each other. Many of these are antiquated laws that use a variety of archaic terms such as idiots, imbeciles, weak-minded, feeble-minded committed to institutions, those adjudicated mentally incompetent, and mental defectives. Eight states have exceptions to these laws for certain classes of the mentally retarded such as women over 45 or a man marrying a woman over 45 or if a judge approves the marriage, or two physicians approve of it. And only 10 of 23 states have any enforcement machinery, such as fines, to support the laws prohibiting such marriages. Generally, such laws have been ineffective, and are nearly impossible to enforce, and are disregarded by those issuing marriage licenses or those who marry people(Brakel, 1985). Still, their presence in the legal statutes present an affront to retarded persons. While it is unknown how many of the retarded ever marry, Bass(1973) estimated that about half of all mentally retarded people marry. The author presumes these are usually the mildly retarded.

The usual arguments forewarded to justify such legal prohibitions against marriage by persons with mental retardation is that they: (1)are mentally incompetent to understand marriage contracts and, thus, cannot give informed consent to them; (2)will not make suitable marriage partners; and (3)are more likely to bear or raise retarded children due to either genetic factors or inadequate parenting skills(Vitello & Soskin, 1985). The rebuttals to these three reasons, respectively, are: (1)that most mentally retarded persons are competent enough to give their consent and to deny all of them this right without due process would be unconstitutional; (2)there is no persuasive evidence regarding divorce rates or their blanket unsuitability for marriage to justify a prohibition against marriage; and (3)the assumption that all mentally retarded people are unfit to raise children is a legal presumption about a class of people that cannot be made on either constitutional grounds or on available evidence. There may be some retarded parents who are abusive to their children, cannot provide for their basic needs, neglect them, and cannot provide adequate care just as there are nonretarded parents who do these things. But, there are family laws in place which state child welfare agencies use to intervene in such families and gain custody of children in such families if there is good evidence that the child is being neglected or abused in some way. However, to presume that all mentally retarded parents are incapable of parenting is flawed logically, legally and by a lack of supporting evidence. The statutory law of custody today is based on the "best interests of the child" which requires a case by case hearing of the evidence before a judgment can be made that the state should take custody of a child(Brakel, 1985).

Sterilization and the Right to Procreation

Sterilization statutes go back to the eugenics movement around the turn of the century when it was believed that retarded people were more reproductive and always procreated retarded children. Many states passed laws approving of sterilization of the retarded and often without their consent. In 1971 there were still 26 states which had laws authorizing the sterilization of the mentally retarded with 21 states allowing it to be done without their consent. As of 1985 there are still 19 states which retain such laws, 14 of which permit sterilization without the subject's consent. However, there are wide state variations in the due process safeguards to protect either the interests of the individual and/or the interests of the state. Brakel(1985, 529) says that the performance of the procedure on nonconsenting persons confined to institutions is no longer a problem. Most sterilizations today, he believes, are performed "overwhelmingly, if not exclusively, with the consent of the subject." However, a few cases still occur where the person about to undergo the operation is mentally incapable of giving a valid informed consent. The laws of some states seek to elicit a valid "substituted consent" from parents or other parties and contain necessary standards or safeguards to help ensure that the final decision is both medically justified and done in the patient's best interest.

159

The President's Committee on Mental Retardation(1980, 8) investigated this issue and concluded, after reviewing relevant court cases:

> The right to procreate is a fundamental constitutional right encompassed within the constitutional right of privacy which applies equally to all United States . . . citizens, including incompetent and mentally retarded persons.

This committee points out that in cases of involuntary sterilization where the two tests of "substituted judgment"(or consent) and the "best interests" of the person are used, the following substantive standards should be applied so that no arbitrary or capricious judgments are made(President's Committee on Mental Retardation, 1980, 44-51):

1. That the person to be involuntarily sterilized is capable of procreation.
2. That the person engages in sexual activities at the present or will engage in such activities in the near future under circumstances likely to result in pregnancy.
3. That all less drastic contraceptive methods are unworkable, inapplicable, or medically contraindicated.
4. That the nature and extent of the person's disability renders him or her incapable of caring for a child, even with reasonable assistance.
5. That this is a medical necessity that the person be sterilized or that the person will suffer severe physical, psychological, or psychiatric harm if he or she parents a child.
6. That the person will not suffer psychological or psychiatric harm if he or she is sterilized.
7. That the guardians consents to the sterilization.
8. That the ward agrees with the proposed procedure or is incapable of indicating whether or not he or she wants to be sterilized.

9. That the person will not develop sufficiently in the foreseeable future to make an informed decision about sterilization.
10. That the person will not consent to sterilization if he or she were capable.
11. That the operative and long-term medical risks of the proposed method of sterilization are minimal and medically acceptable.
12. That the proposed method of sterilization is the least invasion of the person's body.
13. That the current state of scientific and medical knowledge suggests that no reversible sterilization procedure or other workable, less drastic contraceptive method will shortly be available.
14. That science is not on the threshold of an advance in the treatment of the individual's disability.

SUMMARY

Mental retardation originates in families which have the responsibility of making decisions about and caring for disabled persons. Two family care models of the processes involved in home care of disabled persons were presented to aid in pinpointing the key variables that affect the quality of care of the disabled and the quality of family life in such families. These models are then used to analyze decision-making and coping processes involved in considering abortion, euthanasia for highly defective infants, caring for the child, coping with a series of family stresses, and deciding whether to institutionalize a retarded person or to accept one back home who was earlier institutionalized. Patterns of how families adapt to a retarded member were inspected and revealed much variation.

The ideal of family home care was discussed with the point made that while pubic policy normatively supports home care, the state and federal governments have not adequately developed programs or subsidies to fully implement this ideal.

The rights of the mentally retarded persons to marry, procreate, and raise children are generally established in a majority of states. But even in those states where such rights are not assured, intervention in these matters is apparently quite rare.

Chapter 6

Services, Advocacy Services and Self-Advocacy in Normalization

This chapter will give an overview of services for the retarded as well as self-advocacy. In the chapters which follow a more detailed inspection will be given to residential services, educational and vocational training services, and employment services for the retarded. However, in this chapter we want to paint the larger picture of how services are developed over time to integrate the retarded into local communities. We want to look at the processes and key actors involved in the process of developing normalization programs and the nature of the service programs that come about as a result of citizen activities and state legislative action.

In the second part of the chapter we will distinguish between and describe advocacy services and self-advocacy. We will inspect the role that advocacy programs and self-advocacy can play in normalization.

HISTORICAL PERSPECTIVE ON THE DEVELOPMENT OF SERVICES

In Chapter 4 we noted that before 1850 nearly all the retarded lived at and were cared for in their own homes. At that time there were no specialized institutions for only the retarded although a few were put in lunatic asylums with the mentally disturbed. And a few ended up in jails if they got into trouble with the law or in almshouses if they were unable to care for themselves and had no family to care for them. Starting in the 1850s states began building small, family-like boarding schools which emphasized education during school age years. Over time these institutions grew in size, became more custodial in nature and segregated the retarded into large state hospitals, or institutions with other names, located in rural areas. While gains were made in the first half of this century in understanding the nature of retardation and offered more community-based services for the retarded, many of the retarded, especially those below the mild level, remained in large state institutions housing thousands of residents. Often the conditions in these large asylums were deplorable. Instead of habilitation services that trained and educated the residents for release, many of them deteriorated. Starting in the 1960s the idea of normalization developed. This concept led to programs to develop community-based services so that many retarded could live like normal people by using whatever services they needed in the local home community and living in normal homes if possible. The normalization movement included the deinstitutionalization program which involved keeping people in their own communities, improvement of institutional programs and the release of residents from state facilities back to their own communities where they would work, play and live. It also included the mainstreaming movement--to educate the educable and trainable mentally retarded in regular classrooms insofar as possible so they would not have to go to segregated institutions or classes.

Integration is seen as having a number of benefits; but to move from a program of segregation to integration involves the provision of a range of services that simply were not available in most communities. The benefits of integration include: (1)maintaining most children in their own communities and many in their own homes so that parents can have more contact with them; (2)educating retarded children locally so that their training for life can be overseen by and involve their parents; (3)maintaining retarded persons in normal communities so they can learn to use generic services and have the quality of life enhanced over what it would be in a remote and isolated institution; (4)having contact with a wide range of normal people daily so that the nonhandicapped will learn to be more tolerant and accepting of the handicapped and the handicapped will in turn have a wider range of persons to emulate as role models. However, because of nearly a century of segregation, to move from it to integration has not been an easy process. Change over to a full-blown program of integration involves (1)changing public awareness of and acceptance of the developmentally disabled living amongst them, and (2)developing a wide range of programs utilizing persons who need special training in thousands of communities. Special programs in housing, education, medical services, vocational training, and work supervision are needed and these need to be coordinated and sequenced to meet the needs of persons with wide ranges of deficits and abilities.

According to Grunewald(1972), the development of services for the mentally retarded usually go through four historical stages in any one nation following the sequence given below:

1.   Diagnosis. In this first stage the problems of mentally handicapped people are distinguished from those of others and their special problems identified. This stage includes formulating policies and plans to meet their special needs.

2.   Specialization.   This stage involves the development and centralization of services for the retarded. In many countries this involved the development of large state hospitals or asylums with various specialists present to meet client needs. However, because of the nature of large bureaucratic institutions and the low funding priority the mentally retarded have usually received historically, many of their needs are not met. Consequently, such large specialized hospitals become stagnant warehouses for mostly adults who have accumulated in them.

3.   Differentiation. This stage occurs when it is recognized that the diverse and complex needs of the retarded are not being met in large impersonal institutions. As the variability of the needs of the mentally handicapped are recognized, multi-disciplinary approaches are developed and new services begun, some of which are provided at the local level. This sets the process in motion to move to the next stage.

4.   Decentralization and Integration. This last stage occurs with the development of small, decentralized, community-based services organized for a defined geographical area and its populations. Integration occurs gradually as community services and facilities are developed so

that new cases of mental retardation can have their needs met locally and persons formerly in institutions are released to their home communities to use these emergent services and facilities.

We now turn to three case studies of decentralization and integration. Two of them occurred in small countries where the programs were national in scope and made administratively more feasible because one single national authority coordinated the move from differentiation to decentralization and integration. These case studies are those of Sweden and Denmark which have been world leaders in the normalization movement. The third case study occurred in the United States in eastern Nebraska. In the more heterogeneous United States, where the states or local communities are far more instrumental in developing human service programs, we find a much more spotty movement toward normalization with the various states moving at different paces and different ways toward decentralization and integration.

THREE CASE STUDIES OF DEINSTITUTIONAL-IZATION, NORMALIZATION AND INTEGRATION

The following three case studies are used to illustrate that different paths and different timetables and different "actors" are involved in the movement from specialization to differentiation and finally to decentralization and integration.

The Swedish Model

Dr. K. Grunewald(1974), Director of Mental Retardation Care Services for the Swedish Board of Health and Welfare, believes that Sweden is well into the fourth stage of decentralization and integration. Unlike the United States where the organizing of services for the handicapped is vested primarily in 50 different states with some federal financial assistance, in Sweden they are vested in one single authority--Mental Retardation Care Services which is part of the Swedish Board of Health and Welfare. This has enabled that country to move more swiftly and resolutely toward normalization.

Sweden has a population of eight million people. It provides a range of services for approximately 30,000 mentally handicapped children and adults--a little less than 4 persons per 1,000 population. Recognizing that there are many degrees of dependence associated with mentally handicapping conditions, the Mental Retardation Care Services has tried to develop a corresponding variation in the programs and facilities available that will allow progression of movement as retarded persons mature and/or develop skills. The usual progression is from a specialized mental hospital, to a large group home, then to a smaller group home, and finally to an individual home if the requisite skills are developed to make each of the moves. These moves also simultaneously involve movement from both specialized facilities to increasingly normal residences and moves from living in a larger group to a smaller group to one's own home(Grunewald, 1974).

In 1977 there were the following six major types of facilities with each having its own special programs oriented to the particular needs of its clients(Grunewald, 1974; Clarke, 1982):

1.   Special hospitals. Six special hospitals with a resident population of 1700 or 5.8% of the mentally retarded provide primarily short-term care to the antisocial and delinquent, the profoundly and multiply handicapped, and the medically fragile. Over time their resident population has been decreasing as more localized services develop, there are fewer admissions and more releases to other facilities.

2.   Larger county homes. There are 25 counties in Sweden with each one having one central residential home ranging in size from about 100 to 200 beds. Unlike the special hospitals which are organized on a medical model, these homes are based on a social model where behavior modification and training are carried out primarily for the moderately and profoundly retarded. Around 12% of the mentally retarded are in such facilities.

3.   Smaller county homes. These smaller residential units of under 100 beds, averaging about 40 beds, accommodate around 24% of the retarded. These types of homes, separated by age for children and adults, have their own training or occupational and industrial therapy programs.

4. <u>Boarding schools</u>. During the 1960s a number of boarding schools were built for school age children who live there 5 days a week and returned home on weekends. But, with the development of group homes and the integration of school age students into normal classrooms in the 1970s, these schools are being phased out now to avoid their nonnormalizing characteristics of isolation and segregation.

5. <u>Group homes</u>. Over 37% of the retarded in Sweden now live in one of several types of group homes depending upon their age and adaptive skills. Children are cared for by foster parents where the father typically works outside the home and the children go to regular schools. Usually there are 4 to 6 children in foster homes. Some older adolescents live in group homes under the supervision of caretakers. Group homes for adults usually involve one or two nonretardates living in their own flat but close to four or five retarded persons living in a "mother flat". To be eligible for group home residences, persons must be capable of using public transportation, go to either work or training during the day, and have need for relatively little supervision. Often the mildly and some moderately retarded persons live with their own families. Fifty one percent of the youth and 29% of the adults live in parental homes. Swedish philosophy is that such group home residences, other than parental homes, are the ideal and final step in normalization when the homes are small, scattered carefully throughout the community, and accompanied by training in social skills. The overall trend in Sweden is the growth in the percentage of persons resident in group homes which has helped shape more positive attitudes toward the mentally handicapped in that country.

The Danish Model

The Danish model of the development of the normalization principle is not dissimilar from that of Sweden. It began in 1959 when the National Service for the Mentally Retarded was first developed to be the single authority for administering services for these people. All services to the retarded are fully financed by the state. The board which administers this program includes representatives from a parents association for the retarded and officials from the Ministries of Housing and Health(Clarke, 1982).

168

Denmark, with a population of about 5 million, provides services to about 23,000 mentally handicapped persons. About 45 persons per 1000 receive a variety of services dependent on a diagnosis of the severity of their retardation and any associated handicapping conditions. About 45% of the clients in Denmark live in residential programs, usually full time, while the remaining 55% either get nonresidential institutional services(around 27% in kindergartens, schools, workshops, youth schools) or services provided to parents and their retarded children in their own homes(around 28%). Thirteen different types of residential institutions, boarding schools, group homes, special treatment homes, relief and holiday homes, and private care homes exist which provide residential or residential/training programs for about 9,500 retarded persons each year. About two thirds of the residential clients, however, live in one of 12 "central institutions" with one located in each of the 12 geographic regions of the country. These are primarily medically oriented facilities specializing in diagnosis, specialized treatment for the severer cases and operation of the mental retardation programs in the region. In 1959 Denmark inherited a pattern of specialized care--stage 2 in the Grunewald description and integration. Included in this is the pattern of extensive mainstreaming of mentally handicapped students into normal schools with school compulsory from age 7 to 21 for retarded students(Clarke, 1982).

The ENCOR Model

Beginning in the late 1960s, one of the earliest and also the most comprehensive normalization models developed in the United States was begun in the five easternmost counties of Nebraska. Although ENCOR, the East Nebraska Community Office of Retardation, was not organized until 1970, in the years immediately preceding that, steps were taken by a number of groups to initiate the normalization movement in that region. With good organization and strong leaders they were able to skip stage three(differentiation) and move rather rapidly from the stage of specialized institutions for the retarded(stage 2) to the final normalization stage that involves the decentralization of services and the integration of retarded persons more fully into community life styles. In this analysis we

169

will first look at the formation of groups to facilitate the move to normalization programs and then analyze the major components of that program.

Prior to 1968, most of the services for the retarded in eastern Nebraska were available at one large state hospital called Beatrice State Institution. It housed over 2400 retarded persons in an archaic, wasteful program that did very little to habilitate the persons living there. The facility was overcrowded, grossly understaffed, old and dangerous. Many parents were highly dissatisfied with the living conditions there and with the lack of habilitative programs for their offspring. Stark, McGee and Menolascino(1984, 68-9) describe the situation then:

> In the 1960s, parents of mentally retarded children in Nebraska, as in most communities around the world, had very limited program choices. They could decide to send their son or daughter away to the state institution for the mentally retarded or remain with their children at home. Local schools would provide some service. More severely retarded persons were not generally served at all. At the time, there was a waiting list to enter the institution. If parents had enough money, they could send their child away to a private institution. If parents rejected institutionalization altogether, they were left with virtually no supports in the community to assist them, limited access to education in the public schools, no services or programs such as vocational training, respite care, or residential services in the community.

Some of the parents became active in the Greater Omaha Association for Retarded Children(GOARC) which developed ideas about alternative service programs. At about the same time a group of concerned professionals also espoused the need for change. In 1968 members of the Nebraska Association for Retarded Children requested a study of the Beatrice State Institution. As a result of this lobbying effort, the Governor of the state appointed the Citizens Study Committee on Mental Retardation in 1968.

At about the same time in 1969 the Citizens Study Committee and GOARC made written proposals for a comprehensive service plan for retarded citizens. Some of the major points they made in their studies and reports were:

* Mental retardation services were under-financed. Local public zoos spent $7.00 a day to care for large animals and neighboring Kansas spent $12.00 a day for persons in public institutions for the retarded but Nebraska was only spending $4.50 for each retarded institutional resident daily.

* This underfinancing led to serious neglect of residents at Beatrice State Institution where residents lay in bed all day or crawled in their own excrement sometimes, rather than being taught self-care skills

* This inhumane, shameful and neglectful treatment should be replaced by a program that is based on the humanitarian rights of mentally retarded people.

* A comprehensive service program should be developed that includes residential, voca-tional, educational and family support ser-vices to be provided at the local community level.

* Mentally retarded persons should have maximal contact with their families and with their personal advocates.

* Services should be provided in an environ-ment that is conducive to personal develop-ment and happiness.

* Services should be as generic as possible to maximize normalization and integration principles.

In 1970 GOARC, essentially representing Douglas County, joined together with four surrounding rural counties to form ENCOR: the Eastern Nebraska Community Office of Retardation. This group was a quasi-govern-mental agency responsible for the development and man-agement of a community based service system for all mentally retarded children and adults in the service region.

Approximately 570,000 citizens live in this service region(Stark, McGee & Menolascino, 1984).

Beginning in 1970 ENCOR structured itself into four main service divisions: educational services, vocational services, residential services, and family guidance. We will look at ENCOR's services in each of these four areas. ENCOR also developed support divisions to service the four main service divisions: a planning department, a public education department, a staff development team responsible for staff training and a multidisciplinary team of professionals(Clarke, 1982).

Educational Services. For about seven years ENCOR provided some educational services for its younger clients. In 1970 it started a "developmental centre"(a special school) and by 1973 it had six such developmental centres catering to 225 children--between the ages of 2 and 12. However, in 1973 the State of Nebraska passed a "right to education bill" for all children and in 1977 another state law was passed mandating that local school districts provide a free public education to handicapped children from the date of diagnosis to age 21. Consequently, ENCOR has turned all education programs over to the local school districts since 1977 because they are mainstreaming students into regular schools under models of normalization and mainstreaming(Clarke, 1982; Stark, McGee and Menolascino, 1984).

Residential Services. ENCOR has flexibly developed a range of residential services to accommodate the various ages and types and levels of impairment of its clients while trying to locate these in their home communities to maximize family contacts and integration into local community service programs, work, and training. Over time a number of different types of residential units have evolved to serve a variety of training needs. Stark, McGee & Menolascino(1984) describe these functional types of residences:

1. Developmental Homes are foster homes providing a residence for one unrelated child where, however, the substitute parents have been carefully screened and trained by the ENCOR staff, the caretakers have backup staff to help them with training and administrative problems, and the placement is for a long period of time.

172

2.   Intensive Training Residences provide houseparent residential services for three age groups, children, adolescents and adults. The houseparents give attention to three to six persons who need special training according to their needs.

3.   Family Living Residences include houseparents and retarded persons of all age levels where the older and usually less impaired residents help with the care of younger residents. This mixing of ages is seen as a normalizing experience for persons without severe behavioral problems.

4.   Adult Minimum Supervision Residences are for persons over 18 who do not need intensive training and who spend their weekdays in sheltered workshops, competitive, or semi-competitive employment. Such homes give some supervision to residents as the need arises but where they are usually fairly independent.

5.   Board and Room Homes are for those adults who have graduated from intensive training residences or adult minimum supervision residences and who need only occasional backup support provided by a houseparent.

6.   Adult Developmental Homes are for adults who need special training and where only one or two live with a foster family who give them special training under support staff supervision with the goal that they may eventually move on to more independent type residences.

7.   Cluster Apartments are for adults who are relatively independent where they live in apartments in close proximity to one another. These apartments are supervised by a staff member who lives in one of the apartments and where the clustering makes supervision and peer integration more convenient.

8.   Counseled Apartments usually provide a residence for two to four retarded adults where only minimal supervision is given by a staff person who occasionally helps the residents with personal needs in the areas of hygiene, grooming, budgeting, home maintenance, and social skills. The staff person lives apart from them and makes contact with them as the need arises.

9.   Independent Living goes one step beyond counseled apartments where contact is made with residents only upon request by them.

10. <u>Five Day Residences</u> are for persons who are away from home during the week for specialized training but who return home on weekends. Such residential programs often serve rural residents who are receiving training in an urban area.

11. <u>Behavioral Shaping Specialized Residences</u> are transitional residential and intensive behavioral modification programs that are provided for severely and profoundly retarded persons with major behavior problems such as self-mutilation, autistic withdrawal, minimal self-help skills or aggressive behaviors. Such programs are often the first residential program for persons released from institutions or those unable to go to public schools because they display disruptive behaviors. Once the behaviors are corrected they return home or to other types of residential programs.

12. <u>Developmental Maximation Units</u> are only for severely and profoundly retarded individuals who are non-ambulatory, multiply handicapped and medically fragile. They have a series of high risk needs that essentially require specialized hospital treatment until their medical conditions can be stabilized, self-help skills developed and behaviors sufficiently stimulated and shaped so that they can move on to less medically supervised residential units.

13. <u>Crisis Assistance Units</u> provide short term residential care for retarded persons whose families are undergoing a crisis such as a death in the family, surgery requiring hospitalization of one of the family members, or because of some medical problem involving the retarded person.

Vocational Services. The ultimate goal of the vocational service program is to move as many retarded persons as possible into competitive employment or normal work environments. While some will never be capable of this, others will be. ENCOR operates 4 <u>Industrial Training Centers</u>, 1 <u>Advanced Industrial Training Center</u> and 5 <u>Work-Stations-in-Industry</u> programs. The purpose of the sheltered workshops which they call "industrialized training centers" is to help retarded persons acquire prevocational and vocational skills. In these training programs persons learn about job application procedures, interview techniques, personnel and employee benefit policies, production skills, quality control, industrial safety, employee and supervisor relationships and the operation of equip-

174

ment. In the sheltered workshop clients often do industrial subcontract work to learn basic production skills. At the Advanced Industrial Training Centers clients learn more particular production skills. At the Work-Stations-in-Industry locations in factories, motels, restaurants, and a variety of businesses, clients learn more specific skills under the direction of a supervisor. Higher skill levels are often needed here and emphasis is put on grooming, productivity, attendance, and a good range of self-help skills. Usually such employees must be able to use public transportation to get to such jobs. Some employees can move out of any of these training/production programs into competitive employment. By 1977 ENCOR had 217 clients in 4 industrial training centers, 42 clients in the advanced industrial training center, 73 clients located at industrial work stations, and 76 clients who had moved into competitive employment(Stark, McGee & Menolascino, 1984).

Family Guidance Services. ENCOR offers a number of services to families to guide them through the service bureaucracy to find the particular services they will need. These services include information and referral on services available, keeping detailed records on each client/family served and their progression through the program, social work counseling services to deal with the stresses and crises that occur in families with retarded members, and a variety of support services from arranging transportation and maintaining a toy library to coordinating voluntary services and arranging for respite care(Clarke, 1982).

While the ENCOR program has had to deal with budget cuts and other crises, it has successfully shown that most, if not all, retarded persons can be served in their own communities in normalizing ways. In the 1976-77 year ENCOR served 891 clients with a complement of 414 staff of whom 90% were full-time. In 7 years, 259 ENCOR region clients had been deinstitutionalized from Beatrice State Institution with 290 still remaining there and yet to be deinstitutionalized when the financial resources became available. In 1977 ENCOR had 40 residential units serving 90 children and 71 residential units serving 141 adults. In 1977 it provided crisis assistance to 125 families, served 71 clients in 9 preschool programs, aided 42 new clients and provided vocational services to 332 persons. In 1979 the range of needs of its 784 clients were quite diverse with

5.5% of them being profoundly retarded, 16.2% being severely retarded, 29.9% being moderately retarded, 36.2% mildly retarded, 7.1% in the borderline category, and 5.1% not listed. Those persons still residing at Beatrice were fairly similar to those already released except in self-help skills which were much more absent due to a lack of training and developmental opportunities(Clark, 1982; Stark, McGee & Menolascino, 1984). Stark, McGee and Menolascino(1984, 95) conclude:

>These data demonstrate that mentally retarded persons of all levels of disabling conditions can live in the mainstream of community life. There is no clinical reason for the institutionalization of any retarded person.

During the 1970s and the 1980s the different states developed a variety of deinstitutionalization and normalization programs that moved at different paces and variable ways to achieve integration. We will look at some of these programs in more detail in later chapters. Next we turn to a brief review of services that could be or are available for the prevention of mental retardation. After that we will look at advocacy dynamics and self-advocacy efforts.

SERVICE PROGRAMS FOR PREVENTION

In Chapter 3 we looked at the causes of and prevention of mental retardation. While an early national goal of the President's Committee on Mental Retardation was to reduce the prevalence of retardation by 50% by the year 2000, this may be a difficult goal to achieve unless a wide range of preventive service programs are developed and used by parents and prospective parents. Such programs include: (1)further research on the biological and environmental origins of mental retardation; (2)education programs to make both professionals and the public aware of the causes of retardation and preventive strategies that work; (3)prenatal genetic diagnosis and genetic counseling and family planning programs; (4)prenatal care and maternal nutrition programs; (5)newborn screening programs; (6)immunization programs; (7)early postnatal screening, diagnosis and treatment programs; (8)infectious disease control programs; (9)programs oriented at the removal of toxic origins of retardation; and (10)a variety of early intervention and educational stimulation programs(Milunsky, 1983). Since these topics provide more than enough material for a book, we will selectively look at preventive service programs that have been developed nationally or in some states.

The 1963 Title I of Public Law 88-164 financed the construction of 12 Mental Retardation Research Centers(MRRC) across the country. The primary goals of MRRC are the promotion of research and the prevention of mental retardation with a secondary goal of training people in both of these areas. The 12 MRRCs receive substantial federal funding from a variety of National Institutes of Health but primarily from the National Institute of Child Health and Development. The 1963 Mental Retardation Facilities and Community Mental Health Centers Construction Act(P.L. 88-164) also created University Affiliated Facilities for the Developmentally Disturbed(UAF). As of 1980 there were 47 UAFs in 34 different states. The interdisciplinary programs operated by UAFs provide research, training and prevention services to a wide audience of professionals and citizens. UAFs provide particular prevention services through preventive screening programs for a number of diseases linked with mental retardation such as PKU, lead-base paint poisoning and Tay Sachs disease. UAFs link parents of high-risk children with medical clinics and counsel pregnant teenagers at risk for bearing developmentally delayed children. UAFs also educate the public about the danger of fetal alcoholism and drug taking during pregnancy, the uses and benefits of amniocentesis, as well as the critical importance of immunization. The UAFs also directly offer genetic and metabolic screening programs and act as advocates for parents in getting medical services for the prevention of retardation(President's Committee on Mental Retardation, 1980).

Another federal program that substantially assists in prevention of retardation is the National Child Health and Crippled Children's Program. Funds from this program are allocated to the states on a formula basis to provide a range of services to mothers, children and the handicapped. These funds are used by the states to run immunization clinics, family planning programs, maternity and infant care services for high risk pregnancies, maternal and infant nutrition programs for low income families, newborn metabolic screening programs through which 97% of all newborns are now screened for metabolic disorders, Child Developmental Clinics for children suspected of retardation and a variety of other programs(President's Committee on Mental Retardation, 1980).

Some states offer service programs designed to prevent retardation. These programs fall into the following four categories, the last three of which may be simultaneously offered: (1)comprehensive statewide prevention programs, (2)statewide genetic screening and counseling programs, (3)states having high risk intervention programs, and (4)states with early case finding activities. Each of these four types of programs will be briefly illustrated inasmuch as a full description would require a book-length chapter. California is one of the states with a fairly comprehensive prevention program administered through 21 regional centers for the developmentally disturbed spread across the state. These centers offer genetic screening and counseling, early case finding of the disturbed, a high-risk infant follow-up service and early intervention services for the developmentally delayed or disabled. South Carolina offers a statewide genetic screening and counseling program through two state centers and nine satellite clinics. Services include clinical evaluations, parent counseling, diagnostic laboratory testing, treatment planning and long-term follow-up. Missouri runs a program that is limited to a high risk intervention program that is designed to reduce the incidence of perinatal mortality and mental retardation by providing medical and surgical intervention only to mothers and infants with high-risk conditions. A few states offer some type of early casefinding care which is sometimes followed up by limited intervention programs. Delaware, for example, provides a Community Nursing and Developmental Program to about 900 families a year. This program utilizes three nurses and two child developmental counselors to: locate cases of developmental disabilities throughout the state, provide a home-based self-help program for the developmentally delayed, refer people to appropriate agencies for follow-up care, and offer up to three months of respite care annually for delayed children to reduce the stress to parents of such care(President's Committee on Mental Retardation, 1980).

There are a variety of prevention programs at work in this country. As we have seen they range from genetic screening and counseling of parents, to genetic and metabolic prenatal and postnatal screening, perinatal intensive care, immunization and environmental intervention programs that are oriented to multifactorial causes of mental retardation. While such programs have spread and received increased federal and state fiscal support over time, there are still problems in having an adequate supply of the full range of these programs and being able to access the needed services by both professionals and parents who are inadequately aware of them.

The Changing Rights of the Retarded

The "rights" of retarded people to be treated as other citizens and to receive the growing range of services available to them and their families needs to be put in the context of social change. Human rights are not embedded as givens in the nature of things. Rather "human rights" are products of change that are invented by individuals and groups and often put into law as was the "Bill of Rights" in our constitution. Rights and responsibilities are human inventions that define the prerogatives and obligations citizens owe to one another in a nation state. As we saw in Chapter 4, a variety of social forces began coalescing after World War II which changed attitudes toward the retarded and led to many court cases and legislative enactments to extend new rights and new services to the mentally retarded in the four decades following the war.

In this section we will briefly discuss the rights of the retarded and then in the last part of the chapter look at the roles that advocacy and self-advocacy play in gaining rights and in developing and improving services for the retarded.

Rights can be classified as human rights or legal rights. Human rights are those that some groups of people, say many citizens in our country, ideologically believe should exist. Human rights are assertions about what prerogatives and opportunities persons should have. Legal rights are those that have been enacted by legislators into law or in which precedents have been established by court interpretations of existing laws. However, it is possible for there to be legal rights which technically exist but for which there has been no implementation by executive bodies. For example, a state law may say the retarded ought to be educated and housed in the least restrictive environment. However, if the money, personnel and other implementation measures have not been provided by the state to achieve these rights, then the legal right is rather meaningless and empty. Statements about human rights often evolve from individual humanitarian writers or from advocacy groups. For example, in Chapter 4 we quoted the 1971 United Nations Declaration of Rights of the Mentally Retarded. This statement of rights recognizes both individual differences in claims to such rights and such contingencies as the resources available to a society to implement such rights. Issam B. Amary(1980) argues that the mentally retarded/developmentally disabled should have seventeen rights to: (1)freedom, (2)freedom of choice, (3)due process of law, (4)human dignity and respect, (5)a family, (6)marry, (7)treatment, (8)comprehensive education, (9)vocational rehabilitation services, (10)worship, (11)live in the least restrictive environment, (12)self-expression and speech without fear of reprisal, (13)prosperous employment, (14)protection, (15)protection from experimentation and research, (16)a guardian or advocate, (17)refuse services. The President's Committee on Mental Retardation(1975) says that rights can be classified under three general principles: (1)<u>positive presumption rights</u> are rights presumed to exist for all people and which may not be denied to an individual without proof that society's needs require that this be done; (2)<u>due process rights</u> are those that require if a person is to be denied some right or to regain some right once denied to him it can only be done through a formal legal process that safeguards that person's rights from arbitrary standards; and (3)<u>instrumental protection rights</u> which are rights obligating society to provide to its citizens the special assistance and services they might need to exercise their other rights. Table 6.1 lists some of the rights of the mentally retarded under these three general principles.

During the civil rights era of the 1960's and 1970's the rights of the retarded were proclaimed and fought for by advocates as never before. Advocates come in a variety of forms and use a variety of techniques to gain rights for individually mentally retarded persons or whole categories of people. We now turn to the role of advocacy in helping

Table 6.1
Rights of the Mentally Retarded Conceptualized
Under Three Principles

Positive Presumption Rights	Due Process Rights	Instrumental Protection Rights
Right to:	Right to:	Right to:
*education	*not be labeled	*treatment
*manage one's	for exclusion-	*a development
own affairs	ary or discrim-	opportunity
*vote	atory reasons	including
*worship	*legal access to	early inter-
*develop	the courts to	vention and
one's sexual	sue and form	family or
and social	contracts	family-like
identity	*the least re-	home
*marry	strictive or	*physical acc-
*be paid for	drastic alter-	ess to all
work	native(in any	facilities
*dignity	setting)	*have an advo-
*fail		cate when
		needed
		*reasonable
		protection
		from harm

Source: President's Committee on Mental
Retardation, 1978, 76.

to gain the rights of developmentally disabled people.
Some of these rights can be clumped together under the
goal of normalization and others under the right to treatment.

ADVOCACY FOR THE RETARDED

The word advocacy has legal roots in the sense that
British lawyers were persons who were to plead in
another's behalf. Advocates today certainly need not be

lawyers. They can be any person or group that speaks in favor of some cause or person. Neufeld(1979, 45) defines advocacy as a "set of beliefs that result in action aimed at defending, maintaining, or promoting a cause." The cause may be a person's unmet needs, the denial of their rights, or the change of administrative practices which hamper the development of skills in the least restrictive environment. The cause may be improved mainstreaming practices in educational settings, deinstitutionalization, better case finding of mental retardation in a community, or improved information and referral services for getting genetic counseling services from qualified professionals. The cause may be a single person who needs a particular vocational rehabilitation service or a class of people residing within the boundaries of a state or state institution for the mentally retarded who need a wider range of residential alternatives.

Dimensions of Advocacy

Advocacy is the process of doing something for or speaking in behalf of some person, group or cause. Advocates are people, conceptualized as individuals, informal groups of individuals, or formal groups such as the Association for Retarded Citizens. Briar(1968, 90) describes an advocate as "his client's supporter, his adviser, his champion, and, if need be, his representative in his dealings with the court, the police, the social agency and other organizations that affect his well being."

One dimension of advocacy then is who is doing the advocating. A second dimension of advocacy is the advocate's relationship to the advocatee(the person or group being advocated). The advocate may be a parent where the social and/or blood bond is the critical factor precipitating the helping response. The advocate may be a friend or a community volunteer who wants to help a particular person or a "cause." The advocate may be some professional who advocates for "clients" which means that there is some implicit contractual arrangement between the client and the professional or the organization which employs him. Thus, the Association for Children with Retarded Mental Development has 5000 members and 400 staff. While it is primarily a provider of residential educational and social services in New York City, its staff also sometimes engages in advocate roles for clients(Gruber, 1986). Its primary function is to provide services while a minor role is to advocate for the clients it serves. In contrast to this type of organization is the Association for Retarded Citizens with 160,000 members, a staff of 35 and 47 state affiliates and 1500 local community affiliates. This is a relatively pure advocacy organization which carries out a wide range of research, publication, organizing activities, and related service activities to promote the well being and rights of all retarded citizens(Gruber, 1986). While the ARC may advocate for the needs of individual persons who are retarded, it is primarily what Federico(1980, 259) would call a "policy making advocate." Here "advocacy is interpreting the unmet needs to persons and groups who have the resources to help them meet them and then attempting to influence decision making on behalf of people in need." Federico goes on to point out that "advocacy is closely tied to policy making, the process of deciding how societal or agency resources will be used."

Neufeld(1979) points out that the relationship between advocates and advocatees is a critical one. He suggests there are two types of advocates relative to organizational financial support. Internal advocates are those who work within the system that employees them. For example, some agencies employ ombudspersons who are to look for and investigate complaints about deficient services in their employing organization. They are to be advocates for the aggrieved parties in trying to correct oversights or deficiencies which are harming the advocatees. In contrast, external advocates are those who are not members or employees of the agency whose alleged deficiencies need to be altered. They have an independence that internal advocates lack. As Neufeld(1979, 47) points out, the internal advocate is always susceptible to being coopted or brought off by his employing agency under the quip "whose bread I eat, his song I sing." At the same time, while external advocates have greater independence, they may have less access than internal advocates to agency information and their accountability may be less defined. External advocates often have to take on an adversarial role in helping their clients or cause. And if they are unpaid volunteers, their advocacy roles may be more transient and less stable(Neufeld, 1979).

A third dimension of advocacy is the nature of the role or activity that the advocate engages in. Zastrow(1981) points out that social workers(or others, for that matter) who help individuals, families, organizations or communities may engage in four types of role models. (1)The enabler role essentially involves helping people help themselves. In this role the helper assists individuals articulate their needs, identify their problems, explore alternative resolution strategies, and then select and implement a particular strategy. In this way the helped individual is developing his own coping skills with the assistance of another person. (2)The broker role involves the helper linking an individual or group of people who need some form of assistance but are unaware of how or where to get the help they need. Thus, a broker might locate families who have an adult retarded member who stays at home all day and take that person to a sheltered workshop to become eligible for training and work. (3)The advocate role is seen as more active and more directive in getting a service or getting better services for a person who had been denied a service or given a poor treatment in the past. In the advocate role the helper is ideally serving the exclusive interests of the client. (4)The activist role involves seeking more fundamental institutional change at the policy or program operation level and because of some perceived social injustice or widespread deprivation. Thus, the view that the segregation of the retarded in large, understaffed, nonhabilitative, state institutions was inhumane has been the precursor of attempts to develop alternative programs in residential settings. The activist role usually involves the selection and use of tactics seen as more effective for bringing about widespread social change: research on and exposure of inhumane conditions, lobbying efforts at local, state, or national levels, confrontational strikes and boycotts, assertive publicity campaigns, and negotiations with adversaries. While these distinctions are helpful in identifying different kinds of helping activity, the advocate role, as we conceive it may substantially overlap the enabler and broker role and especially the activist role as developed by Zastrow.

A fourth and last dimension of advocacy is the target of change. This target may be variously conceived as being of local, regional, state, or national in scope. It may be some program that is totally absent or one defective in some way. This and the other three dimensions of advocacy should become clearer as we illustrate the roles that advocates have played in changing policies and services for the mentally retarded.

Levels and Type of Advocacy

The advocacy efforts by those concerned with the plight of the retarded of America could easily fill many volumes. The purpose here is to illustrate the various levels and types of advocacy on behalf of the retarded and to evaluate their significance.

In Chapter 4 we noted that a number of reformers like Dorothy Dix and early leaders in the development of boarding schools were external and internal advocates respectively for developing services for the mentally retarded in the mid 1800's.

Undoubtedly the most important advocates for the retarded have been their parents and the groups they formed. Working in some 1500 local chapters, 47 state chapters and the National Association for Retarded Citizens, they have lobbied for the expansion and alteration of services for the retarded. As individual parents or in conjunction with local, state, and national ARC chapters they have gone to court over several hundred times in the last two decades and won many significant gains for their own children or all retarded citizens. In the view of Halpern, Sackett, Binner and Mohr(1980) the deinstitutionalization movement for the mentally retarded has significantly come about because of the activist advocacy roles of parents and their local, state and national ARC organizations. In turn this deinstitutionalization effort has spawned increased citizen involvement and the development of numerous volunteer citizen service programs to provide needed social support for the mentally disabled who were attempting to adjust to community life after release from institutions.

Halpern, Sackett, Binner and Mohr(1980, 99) point out that while deinstitutionalization programs have been developed for both the mentally ill and the mentally retarded, those for the latter have been more fully developed and better funded because the mentally retarded have had many and strong advocacy groups working for them while the mentally ill have not had such support. The mentally retarded advocacy groups have included lobbyists, state ARC's and citizen advocacy committees which "have demonstrated their effectiveness in making the system respond to the client's views of his or her interests and needs." Such "advocacy groups have also been very influential in demanding and monitoring the provision of community based services and the rights of individuals residing in institutions." Parents and the three levels of the ARC are examples of external advocates.

According to Stark, McGee and Menolascino(1984), parental advocacy groups, such as the Greater Omaha Association for Retarded Citizens(GOARC), usually go through a number of stages as they engage in advocacy for improving and expanding services for the retarded. Stage 1 involves a dissatisfaction with current services and then a consequent development of a vision of services that could be offered. However, parental advocacy groups usually lack the resources to develop a comprehensive services plan. So in stage 2 they develop a small scale demonstration program to show the feasibility and worth of such a program. This may involve a special preschool program, parent counseling groups, or several community residential facilities or other programs. When parents and professionals see that such programs in the community work well and are accepted by the residents, they are ready for the next stage. Stage 3 occurs when the advocate group lobbies and wins governmental support for the expansion of the program for all such persons. At this point the demonstration pilot program is usually absorbed into the generic service system operated by some level of government by itself or through contractual arrangements with private providers. In this stage also the advocate group may initiate new demonstration programs for more difficult clients or for more additional services. In stage 4 the parental advocacy group develops a monitoring program to evaluate the quality of services provided and to act as a change agent to rectify inadequacies in the services provided. In this stage it offers services to parents who have difficulty with the service system. As a result of these activities, and usually coincident with the fourth stage, the parent association gives birth to self-advocacy where the mentally retarded advocate for themselves. Some parent groups have developed monitoring instruments to assist individual parents or groups of parents to systematically evaluate the quality of community based residential programs or other services(Lensink, 1980).

One of the things the parents of the retarded often do is develop self-help groups, sometimes under the auspices of formal organizations such as local ARC chapters. Willer and Intagliata(1984) point out that such groups enable parents to share factual information about their children's disabilities, about community services available, and skills in child management problems. Equally important, they allow parents to share both their sad and joyous experiences and work out informal respite care systems to deal with the burdens of demanding care. The Greater Omaha Association for Retarded Citizens(President's Committee on Mental Retardation, 1978) has developed a "Pilot Parents" program. In this program a parent with a developmentally disabled child can call for assistance from another parent who has successfully adjusted to the same problem. Before a parent can become a peer counselor for a one year period, they must go through a training and information adoption program operated by GOARC which matches requests for services with those trained to give them. For example, one 18-year old mother who had been advised by her physician to put her newborn Down's Syndrome child in an institution decided to take the child home after talking to a "pilot parent".

A number of specific organizations offer both peer counseling and advocate services. For example, the National Association for Down Syndrome and the National Down Syndrome Congress bring together families and professionals to offer counseling and advocacy services. The Mental Retardation Association of America, with 22 state groups, lobbies for comprehensive services while providing support groups for families with retarded youngsters(Gruber, 1986).

The monitoring and advocacy functions of parents is well illustrated by "The Troubleshooters" in Seattle, Washington. Many parental groups have found that agencies are often unresponsive to their needs and delay providing services to their children by giving them a bureaucratic runaround. By 1978 there were 40 "troubleshooters" operating out of 24 offices in the state of Washington. This advocacy service had its beginning when two parents, in 1972, found problems in getting services for their retarded adult offspring. They made an agreement with Seattle's Northwest Center for the Retarded, which their adult child attended, to write a manual on how to get benefits for dis-

187

abled adults. They received a small grant from the HEW Developmental Disabilities Office to fund the preparation of the manual. The President's Committee on Mental Retardation(1978, 18) reports:

> Their plan was simple. First, they would attempt to move through some of the service getting processes as parents of adult mentally retarded children. Then, they planned to write out guidelines and steps that other parents could follow. However, after one month of attempting to move through the system, they were overwhelmed by the obstacles and degradation they encountered. "We found we were caught up in systems never designed for us and they simply didn't work," says one of the parents. "So we decided to help families individually and work on the systems at the same time."
>
> During the next three years, a system for helping individual families who called on a special Troubleshooters telephone line was developed by the two parents and their office manager. At the same time, they joined with the state Developmental Disabilities Planning Council in building a variety of coalitions which began to provoke changes in all of the public assistance delivery systems for developmentally disabled persons.
>
> In 1976, the Troubleshooters became an independent family advocacy agency, and the governor called for the setting up of four Troubleshooter offices in other areas of the state. The new Troubleshooters were salaried by the Comprehensive Employment and Training Act(CETA) and their training was supplied free of charge by the veteran Troubleshooters of Seattle.
>
> In 1977, the governor ordered that the Troubleshooters be "the designated Protection and Advocacy Agency throughout the state for all persons with developmental disabilities and other handicaps."

Today, the agencies are powered by $40,000 Protection and Advocacy funds, $440,000 CETA funding, $160,000 worth of Vista Volunteer service and $400,000 of "in kind" and other volunteer services from 45 agencies who have established formal and informal alliances.

All those preparing to become "troubleshooters" must now go through a 30-day training program on how to fill out agency forms, knowing the rights of disabled persons, how to assess the unique needs of families, and how to secure agency services.

The Developmental Disabilities Act of 1975 legislated the development of an advocacy system in every state for the developmentally disabled many of whom are mentally retarded. This is a clear example of an internal advocacy system. Each state was to develop a "Developmental Disabilities Council" composed of representatives from all state agencies serving the disabled as well as one-third of the members being developmentally disabled persons or their parents or guardians. These DD Councils were to help plan and coordinate state services for the developmentally disabled, monitor services, and be an advocate for client(Breen & Richman, 1979; Flynn & Nitsch, 1980).

Although state DD Councils are to establish a "protection and advocacy agency" independent of any state agency that provides services to the developmentally disabled, such advocacy agencies are not ideally suited to initiate litigation against other state agencies because they are all part of the state government. At the same time, such advocacy agencies do have the potential to assist clients in achieving their rights under the law(Mayer, 1979). One of the biggest achievements of the Developmental Disability movement and its organizational base, the state Developmental Disabilities Council, is its enhancement of public awareness of the needs and rights of disabled persons(Wiegerink, 1979). The Vermont DD Council, for example, implemented a "Project Awareness" program to publicize the needs and rights of disabled persons. This program included the preparation and distribution of a "press kit" on the needs and rights of disabled persons, getting speakers to talk about the DD movement on talk shows, a legislative information kit, and a toll-free hotline to allow ease of inquiries about services for the disabled(Knox, 1979). Various state DD Councils have set up a number of advocacy and "benefactor" services. For example, the states have advocacy services which: (1)provide legal aid attorneys with specialized knowledge of handicap law to aid clients, (2)work with state consumer protection groups to formulate training programs for lay-citizen advocates, (3)maintain liaison with state agencies, bar association, and state legislators, and (4)help evaluate legislative and administrative proposals for their impact on the services and rights of the disabled(Mayer, 1979).

Nebraska has developed a benefactor/advocate program for persons discharged from state institutions. In this program an unpaid "live-in friend" stays with an institutional releasee to assist him in shopping, money management, personal care, use of telephones, banks and public transportation, cooking and other things like use of leisure time. This benefactor program involves both teaching and advocacy responsibilities that is modeled after Edgerton's research findings in California. Edgerton found that a most critical factor in an institutional releasee's adjustment to community life was having a benefactor or friend help them cope with their new experiences and responsibilities. Such benefactors not only aided them in developing coping skills but also strengthened their self respect and their ability to "pass" as normal people because they were associated with a normal person(Neufeld, 1979). Another example of a combined advocacy and service program is Project Impact operated in three southeastern states by the Association for Retarded Citizens with funding coming from the Community Services Administration of the federal government. This program uses indigenous outreach paraprofessionals to go into low-income Black and Hispanic neighborhoods to: counsel women on family planning, engage in case finding of the developmentally disabled, assist families in locating and using services for the disabled, negotiate with service agencies, set up peer counseling groups on how to prevent and ameliorate retardation, and provide literature to families at risk for retardation(President's Committee on Mental Retardation, 1980).

One additional form of advocacy is coalition building. This is where two or more formal groups who have a common cause join forces to advocate jointly. By joining together to lobby for changes they enlarge the population base they represent and have more financial and people resources available to make their cause known. A number of groups with specific disabilities, such as the blind, deaf, physically disabled, and mentally retarded sometimes join together to pool their resources to push for common legislative objectives or programs that serve any one of these disability groups or those with multiple disabilities. One form that coalition building has taken is the formation of the American Coalition of Citizens with Disabilities, formally organized in 1975(Birenbaum & Cohen, 1985). The ACCD linked together several existing groups concerned with disablement while retaining the autonomy of each constituent association. This group has effectively lobbied for implementation of Section 504 of the Rehabilitation Act of 1973. Section 504 of this act prohibits recipients of federal funds from discriminating on the basis of mental and physical handicaps. Scotch(1984) argues that the implementation of this act has transformed federal disability policy from one of good will to one of confirmed legal civil rights.

SELF-ADVOCACY BY THE RETARDED

The most recent form of advocacy to emerge for the retarded is self-advocacy. Perhaps its late emergence is explained by the belief of many persons that the retarded are incapable of self-advocacy including the views of some professionals who in the past have sometimes been their advocates assuming they could not advocate for themselves. Gunnar Bybwad, President of the International League of Societies for the Mentally Handicapped, wrote in 1980(quoted in Williams & Shoultz, 1982, 51):

A new voice can be heard in our movement. As yet it is hesitant, unsure, but it is steadily gaining in strength. It is the voice of those we once thought incapable of speaking, hence our battle cry used to be: 'We speak for them'. It is the voice of those once considered ineducable, who are now attending schools. It is the voice of those once deemed unemployable, indeed deemed 'incapable of sustained effort', who now bring a pay cheque for a full weeks' work.

I have been privileged to attend some conferences managed largely by people with mental handicap themselves. Thus, I was not surprised when I learned a few days ago that a recent major policy meeting to discuss the future of the Canadian Association for the Mentally Retarded, no less than ten persons with mental handicap, one from each province, participated in the deliberations.

I am aware that many of our readers will comment: 'This may be possible for those who are only mildly handicapped, but surely for the majority this is just a fantasy, an impossible dream.' No more impossible than the dream that all persons with a mental handicap can go to school, can gain acceptance in the community, can learn to move about, can learn to make responsible choices.

Let us not argue how soon or how many of our young people will be able to express themselves. Let us instead ask ourselves: Are we ready to listen to their new voice?

Self-advocacy is speaking for oneself, making one's needs known, and asserting one's rights. Not all mentally retarded persons have the skills or can develop the skills to do this. But many can if given some help to learn the necessary skills to engage in self-advocacy and if provided the opportunities to assert themselves.

In 1978 the President's Committee on Mental Retardation noted the emergence of this movement(53):

A gentle protest can now be heard throughout the nation from mentally retarded persons who are tired of being overprotected. They have begun to object when professionals and nonprofessionals make decisions for them and speak for them, when, with a little time and patience they could have decided

192

and spoken for themselves. These first protests are, perhaps, the latest step in a natural evolution: they have come out of groups of handicapped persons in community settings where new styles of organization have enabled individuals to speak more genuinely about themselves than ever before.

In *We Can Speak for Ourselves*, Paul Williams and Bonnie Shoultz(1982) describe the origins of self-advocacy in Omaha, Nebraska, and discuss its independent start in Oregon with the "People First" program and the growth of the movement both nationally and internationally. They say the idea for a self advocacy group began with Ray Loomis in 1975, seven years after he left Beatrice State Institution where he lived for 15 years and whose superintendent had predicted he wouldn't succeed in the outside world for more than three days. Loomis chose the name "Project Two" for the group of handicapped people which got together to discuss their needs and do things together. The first meeting was only attended by three people but by the end of the year they had 40 people attending. At first the members deferred to the professionals who were there and were often hesitant to speak. But over time an organizational structure began to emerge as they developed goals and activities to achieve their goals. Leaders emerged, committees were formed, committee tasks developed and group processes regularized even though such things came about more slowly and hesitantly than with some new groups because the people lacked experience in being self-directing in group processes. In the first year they elected officers and talked about ways of getting more people involved. In the second year they planned and carried out a camping trip and then planned a statewide convention modeled after the convention held in Oregon. In that year some of the Project Two members testified at public forums by ENCOR as it held public hearings to gauge public opinion in the planning process for deinstitutionalization.

Planning the convention called "People First of Nebraska," took a substantial amount of time as they first had to find out what is necessary to hold a convention. They developed committees to carry out these tasks. They also made a number of other decisions: (1)that mentally handicapped people would run at least this first convention even though they would invite people with other disabilities; (2)that the convention would be financially self-supporting so they would establish their independence from "helpers"; and (3)that the convention, including general sessions and seminars, would be led by mentally handicapped people and not professionals. Sometimes they got help from professionals and parents working in the field of mental retardation, but they did the decision making, made the arrangements, provided the publicity and carried out this first state convention which 160 people attended in 1978. A general euphoria came over those who attended this convention where 37 resolutions were passed. Some of the resolutions were statements of value, some were assertions of rights, some were statements about how to improve services and some stated action goals like the resolutions to start such groups in many cities and towns and to hold another convention the next year. The first seven resolutions which state their philosophical values are(Williams & Shoultz, 1982, 223-4):

1. We believe that we are people first, and our handicaps are second. We wish people would recognize this and not give us a tag like 'handicapped' or 'retarded.'
2. We believe that we have the right to fight for our own rights and that unless we do we won't get them.
3. We believe that people shouldn't just stay at home and feel sorry for themselves and ask for pity; there's a beautiful world out there, and we want to be part of it.
4. We believe that we should work to destroy the physical and mental restrictions on **everybody** and not just ourselves.
5. We believe that it is important to get people out on their own.
6. We believe that it is wrong for the public to run us down and treat us badly.
7. We believe we can win this fight, if we work together.

The people who attended this and subsequent annual conventions went to discussion groups, elected state officers, prepared resolutions, had a dance, shared their feelings and, according to the hotel manager, had less breakage and noise than most conventions. Williams and Shoultz(1982, 29-30) summarize these events as follow:

> The people who have accomplished all of the things described above are mildly, moderately and severely mentally handicapped. Most cannot read or write. Even more have not yet learned to follow a budget or live independently, although all are moving towards independence at their own speeds. It is true that non-handicapped advisers have been present to provide many kinds of supports, but the people in Project Two and the other self-advocacy groups in Nebraska have found that they are able to support each other and complement each other's skills and thus overcome each other's deficits. A person who reads can help a non-reader to follow an agenda; an ablebodied person can hold a page or a microphone for a person with cerebral palsy; a person who speaks can translate for a person who uses signs; and a person who is hard to understand can teach other members to listen more carefully. The support and teaching that they provide for each other had led to the continued growth and diversification of members' skills and understanding.

The origins of self-advocacy of the mentally handicapped have been traced to Sweden where a network of leisure clubs for the mentally handicapped were established in the 1960's. A tradition grew in Sweden that the mentally handicapped selected their own officers and ran their own clubs after some initial assistance by the non-handicapped. Courses were provided in Sweden to teach members the decision making skills to enable them to run their own clubs. Officers and members of clubs began writing other clubs and exchanging ideas. Out of this grew regional conferences and finally a national convention in

1968. A similar but later program like this developed in Great Britain with the first national conference being held in 1972. In 1973 a group of professionals developed a conference for the mentally handicapped in British Columbia which was visited by some people from Oregon. At that time in Oregon there were already twenty some "support groups" operating and made up of a social worker and releasees from the state hospital for the mentally retarded. The two professionals and three handicapped people who attended the 1973 British Columbia conference came back enthused about the idea of a self-advocacy group. They shared their experiences with the Oregon support groups and got a representative from each group plus some representatives from the state institution(Fairview Hospital and Training Center) to assist in planning a convention for the state. After many months of organizing and planning, the first convention was held under the title "People First," and the theme, "We Have Something to Offer" in 1974 in Otter Crest, Oregon. There was some confusion at the first convention of handicapped people in the United States as 200 persons were expected but 560 showed up. During the planning stage the committee members were looking for a name for their new organization. One member said, "'We are tired of being seen first as handicapped or retarded or disabled. We want to be seen as people first'"(Williams & Shoultz, 1982, 54). "People First" was the name that won the vote.

The People First self-advocacy movement has grown rapidly. The second convention was held in 1975 in Oregon with 750 attending. By 1978, statewide conventions had been held in six other states and provinces and then a People First International convention was held in Portland, Oregon in 1980 with over 1,000 attendees from the United States and Canada. By 1982 there were "at least 70 local or state groups that have a predominant membership of mentally handicapped people, and they all have a slightly different history"(Williams & Shoultz, 1982, 56). By 1986 there were 20 state chapters of People First International. This organization provides training and advocacy consultation and workshops to local groups of developmentally disabled persons(Gruber, 1987).

A number of gains have been made by the self-advocacy movement that are viewed by many as beneficial not only for those with handicaps but for other citizens as well(President's Committee on Mental Retardation, 1978; Birenbaum & Cohen, 1985; Williams & Shoultz, 1982):

1.   An organizational mechanism was developed that allows and encourages handicapped people to speak for themselves in all types and sizes of assemblies. One professional who works with the handicapped describes this great breakthrough as follows(quoted in President's Committee on Mental Retardation, 1978, 55):

> Many of these people have been participants in conventions held by professionals and voluntary organizations, and when they tried to speak out in their unsophisticated manner, they were often smiled at and ignored, or they were politely quieted. At Otter Crest, they had a chance to speak out unashamedly. They were unpolished at first, but the very chance to speak out without others putting a damper on them was like breaking out of prison.

2.   These organizational mechanisms have given opportunities to growing numbers of the handicapped to develop social skills, organizational skills, support skills, self-confidence and self-esteem. They have developed immeasurably to make them happier people who are involved in tasks that improve the quality of their lives. And along the way both the recognition of their rights and the opportunities to exercise their rights have improved.
3.   The development of the self-advocacy movement has opened up organizational channels for the retarded to be representatives on state Developmental Disability Councils and in a variety of other organizations such as local, state and national chapters of the Association for Retarded Citizens. This means their voices are being heard and can have an influence on the policies and programs which affect them so directly.
4.   Their public image is improving as a result of the self-advocacy movement. Many citizens are beginning to understand that the mentally handicapped hate to be called "retarded" and wish to be recognized as people first whose identities are much more than the particular limita-

tion they have. A new tolerance and respect for their rights and abilities will result from the power of self-advocacy.

> And so a new consumer force has been born that preaches "self advocacy" and "the power of peer group education." Already, many professionals in the field of mental retardation have been moved by the activities emerging from this group of people who, a few years ago, would never have been expected to represent their own interests(President's Committee on Mental Retardation, 1978, 55).

Williams and Shoultz(1982) trace the social origins of the self-advocacy movement of the retarded in the United States to: (1)advocacy efforts by parents and ARC chapters; (2)the civil rights movement of the 1960s; (3)the growth of consumer advocacy groups which argue for the rights of consumers to have some say in the quality of services or products that they buy or receive; (4)the growth of self-help groups where people with the same problem join together to share their experiences such as with bereaved widows, heart attack survivors, and drug addicts, and (5)the social movement of deinstitutionalization and normalization.

SUMMARY

Historically, the development of services for the retarded in industrial nations has gone through four stages: diagnosis, specialization, differentiation, and then decentralization and integration. Many nations and states within the United States are in the process of moving into the fourth stage wherein community based services are being developed for retarded people which permits them to live in their home communities.

An inspection of the services for the retarded in Sweden, Denmark and the service area of the East Nebraska Community Office of Retardation show different service and administrative patterns for deinstitutionalization and normalization. The ENCOR model shows that a wide range of medical, residential, educational, training, work and support services can be developed in the local community to avoid the higher costs and less developmentally oriented programs associated with large, remote, state institutions for the mentally retarded.

A wide range of prevention programs were reviewed that could reduce the amount and severity of retardation. We noted that different states have attacked the problem of prevention with various degrees of vigor and comprehensiveness.

The rights of the retarded have evolved over time and been expanded substantially in the last three decades. The United Nations Declaration of the Rights of the Mentally Retarded and the moral and legal rights of the retarded as developed through legislation and court cases in this country indicates that the rights of the retarded can be classified into three types: positive presumption rights, due process rights, and instrumental protection rights.

The rights of the retarded have been promoted first and primarily by advocates, but more recently, starting in the 1970s, by self-advocates. Types and levels of advocacy are defined. Parental advocacy, often through formal organizations like chapters of the Association for Retarded Citizens, has been the most important external advocacy for bringing about change. But internal advocacy groups such as state Developmental Disability Councils have also been important in promoting the rights of the mentally retarded. Self-advocacy has spread rather rapidly in the last decade. It has opened up organization mechanisms for the developmentally disabled to develop a variety of organizational and social skills, to develop their self-confidence, have their views seriously heard, and improve their social image.

Chapter 7

Deinstitutionalization and the Residential Lives of the Retarded

The deinstitutionalization process has been going on for over two decades now. One of the sizable effects it has had is to change the place of residence of those formerly living in institutions or who would have been living there were it not for this movement. In this chapter we want to first define deinstitutionalization, then look at the factors which brought it about. After that we will look at the forms that residential care may take, the changing patterns of residential care and the various funding streams for such care. Finally, we will look at the patterns of life in community residential facilities including assessments of their quality.

THE MEANING AND GOAL OF DEINSTITUTIONALIZATION

Earlier we defined deinstitutionalization as including three related processes: (1)releasing people from institutions, (2)keeping people from going to them in the first place, and (3)modifying institutional practices to make them less "institutional" in character. The first two processes also require the development of community based services for the mentally retarded such as special residences, educational programs, habilitation and training programs, medical services, and family support services. Without such services deinstitutionalization would have little effect on the lives of people except to alter their place of residences. The goal of deinstitutionalization is more than changing the place of residence of about 5% of the retarded population.

The goal of deinstitutionalization is to make as normal as possible the lives of retarded people by integrating them with other people residentially, educationally, socially and economically. This goal has been captured under the term "normalization" which we discussed earlier. "Deinstitutionalization" particularly refers to altering their place of residence although it is not limited to that. "Mainstreaming" gives particular emphasis to integrating the retarded into regular classroom settings and schools although it has implications also for integrating the retarded into regular patterns of recreation and social life in a community. The concept of the "least restrictive alternative" can be applied to residential, educational and work settings. It recognizes that sometimes the mentally retarded need special care and services. But that such services should be as close to what most people use as the clinical and medical conditions of the retarded person will allow(Bruininks et al, 1980).

The goal of deinstitutionalization, then, is not only to change the place of residence of thousands of persons living in large institutions. More importantly, it is to remove them from environments which stifled their development to environments which are believed to more fully stimulate their human potential--those that other people live in. The concept of "institutionalization" captures the idea that periods of long residence in a specialized care facility may be debilitating whether for prison inmates, nursing home residents or residents in a large mental institution. Such persons are found to develop dependency on others and daily routines. They are cut off from exposure to a variety of people, social changes going on outside the institution, and the development of skills necessary to live life normally for few demands are made upon them in such total institutions. They may develop an institutional syndrome of low morale, negative self-image, preoccupation with minor things, intellectual ineffectiveness, docility, anxiety, and a lack of spontaneity. They lose or do not develop the capacity to be self-directing, autonomous human beings(Zastrow, 1982; Ward, 1984; Cockerham, 1981).

202

Thus, the deinstitutionalization movement is a sociopolitical movement based on assumptions and evidence that institutional care often stifles human development, undermines human dignity and deprives people of freedom. The goal of deinstitutionalization is to enhance the development and functioning of retarded people by providing them high quality services and normal social stimulation so that their lives will have as much quality in them as possible.

FORCES PROMOTING DEINSTITUTIONALIZATION

Beginning in the 1960's a number of social and economic developments interacted to lead to the deinstitutionalization movement. These forces accumulated during the 1970's when the rate of deinstitutionalization increased. The six social and political forces we will look at are (1)the emergence of the advocacy movement, (2)the indictment of large public institutions for the mentally retarded, (3)the acceptance of the normalization principle, (4)judicial activism, (5)legislative and executive actions for the retarded, and (6)the escalating costs of care.

Emergence of the Advocacy Movement

In the last chapter and in Chapter 4 we noted one of the forces for change has been the dissatisfaction that many parents have had with the system for services for the retarded.

Parents and parental groups in the Association for Retarded Citizens found waiting lists to place children in institutions, deplorable care in many instances within those institutions, and a lack of support services in their home communities if they decided to keep their children at home. While local and state ARC associations have sometimes tried to provide services to clients, they have usually lacked the resources to offer the full range of educational, residential, and support services needed. Consequently, the major thrust of the ARC has been advocacy. In the early 1970's the major thrust of advocacy by the ARC was on reforming state hospitals to provide more and better services in such cases as *Wyatt v. Stickney* in Alabama in 1972 and *New*

York State Association for Retarded Inc. v. Rockefeller in New York in 1974. These cases helped establish the right of institutional residents to habilitation. Starting at about the same time but culminating in a later thrust were parent-initiated cases whose focus was on habilitation in the least restrictive environment. Thus, in *Pennsylvania Association for Retarded Children v. Pennsylvania* in 1970 and *Mills v. Board of Education of the District of Columbia* in 1972, courts ordered the integration of mentally retarded children into the least restrictive educational environment. In the *Pennhusrt State School and Hospital v. Halderman* case in Pennsylvania in 1977 the court found that habilitation should occur in the least restrictive environment. This was the beginning of the legislative thrust to close down state schools/hospitals for the mentally retarded and relocate their residents to community residential and habilitation programs(Kindred, 1984; Vitello & Soskin, 1985).

In addition to litigation, ARC has developed policy statements and been an effective lobbyist at state and national levels to allocate more resources for the care of the retarded. In 1976 the National Association for Retarded Citizens adopted a position statement on residential services. This statement included 13 principles. We include the following three to illustrate the association's emphasis on deinstitutionalization(Patterson, 1980, 139, 147, 148):

> *Principle 2.* Residential facilities of all varieties are particularly vulnerable to conditions or situations that can impair the quality of life for the residents whom they serve. Facilities become dehumanizing when they become developmentally counterproductive by violating the dignity of the resident and limiting his or her opportunity to gain "useful knowledge." Dehumanization is a denial of the individual's basic rights to liberty and the pursuit of happiness guaranteed by the United States Constitution.
> *Principle 11.* Programs for mentally retarded persons should utilize the community's existing services to the fullest extent. Utilization of community services provides opportunities for the retarded person to

experience a broader array of social situations which can contribute to learning new skills and increasing independence.

Utilization of general community services also provides opportunities to sensitize community agencies to the service needs of retarded individuals and their families.

Principle 13. Community services should be strategically located throughout the state, region, or county to promote maximum social integration of disabled citizens into the community.

Institutional Indictment

The indictment of the quality of care in many facilities for the mentally retarded has come from many sources: scholars writing about the deficiencies of such places; testimony given by clients, parents, friends and professionals in court cases; and mass media exposes of the living conditions in such places. This is not to say that the quality of care in all places is or was uniformly bad. But there appears to be a tendency for large institutional organizations, even those with the best of intentions, to provide routinized, depersonalized care that stifles rather than stimulates individual growth(Raynes, Pratt & Roses, 1979).

Research findings in the 1960s and 1970s generally found that negative effects occurred in clients housed in large retardation facilities. A number of studies of particular institutions, while perhaps not generalizable to all such facilities, have shown some of these negative effects to be: (1)the intellectual functioning of clients living in institutions often deteriorated over time; (2)institutionalization, rather than promoting personality growth and the development of social skills, sometimes produced maladaptive and disruptive behaviors; and (3)mortality rates in such institutions were abnormally high--particularly among the youngest(Gilhool, 1980; Meazzini, 1984; Vitello & Soskin, 1985).

Between 1966 and 1969 a major study of 134 public facilities for the mentally retarded was supported by the American Association of Mental Deficiency. Helsel(1971) reports some of the damaging findings in this study were that 50% of the institutions were below the minimum standards for safety, 60% were judged overcrowded, 83% were below staffing requirements set by the profession, 60% had inadequate space for educational and recreational programming, and only 23% compensated residents for maintenance work in the facility even though 65% used residents for such work.

But perhaps the most critical part of the indictment came from mass media exposes when sizable segments of the public were shown and told of the horrible conditions in some facilities. The most notorious of these was the Willowbrook State School expose. This New York state institution on Staten Island had over 6000 residents when Senator Robert Kennedy visited its snake pit conditions with a television camera crew in 1965. In 1972, when Geraldo Rivera did an ABC eyewitness news series on Willowbrook's conditions showing half-naked people in their own excrement, over 300 people called in their grief and outrage on the first night. By the end of the second night there had been a total of 700 calls. This series of broadcasts also showed alternative living programs so that it could be publicly known that not all the mentally retarded lived as did Willowbrook's 5300 residents in 1972(Shearer, 1976). It is hard to gauge the effect of such exposes; but they seem to stir public outrage, precipitate congressional inquiries, and often result in reforms at the institutional level or legislative reforms down the road.

The Emergence of the Principle of Normalization

At about the same time that the parental advocacy movement was gaining strength and institutional conditions were being exposed by the media, scholars and lengthy court cases, the principle of normalization was being articulated by Nirje(1980) and Wolfensberger(1976). As we discussed earlier, the normalization principle involves making clients as normal as possible by having them live in residences, attend schools, and be involved in programming and work as normal as possible. This normalization principle variously involves humane treatment which respects the dignity of all people, integration into expanded social opportunities for persons in their home communities, and raising our expectations of how much they grow if given the right opportunities.

Some have justified the existence of large state custodial institutions for the lowest performing levels of retardates by arguing they are subtrainable and cannot benefit from community residential programs(Ellis, et al, 1978). However, Stark, McGee and Menolascino(1984) argue that such classifications and labeling are unsubstantiated by sound research and become "self-fulfilling prophecies of client failure." They argue that such labeling and treatment of the severely and profoundly retarded leads to blaming the victim, lack of individualized programming, and ignores the developmental model which is the basis for normalization.

In 1976 the National Association for Retarded Citizens adopted four principles to support the developmental model for community residential programming(Patterson, 1980, 143-4):

Principle 7: Retarded children and adults are capable of learning and development. Each individual has potential for progress, no matter how severely handicapped he or she might be.

Principle 8: The basic goal of programming for retarded persons consists of maximizing the individual's personal, social, and vocational development, and as such is identical with the goal of educating and socializing all other citizens. The adequacy of programs, as well as of physical and psychological environments, can be evaluated in terms of the degree to which they fulfill this goal.

In general this goal is more rapidly met by including the retarded individual within the mainstream of society or by replicating the patterns and physical characteristics of the prevailing culture when it is necessary for a retarded person to live away from his or her natural home.

Principle 9: Specific program objectives must be tailored to meet the needs of each individual, and will vary for different degrees of impairment. The most feasible and constructive approach, in view of current limitations of knowledge, is to assume that most retarded persons have the potential for greater mental, physical, and social development and for eventually leading an independent life-style. This approach must dominate program planning until the individual's response to appropriate programs clearly reveals his or her inability to obtain this goal.

Principle 10: All programs for retarded persons must meet the three basic criteria of the developmental model:

1. Contribute to increasing the complexity of the individual's behavior.
2. Contribute to increasing the individual's ability to control his or her environment.
3. Contribute to maximizing those qualities that have been designated as "normal" or human.

These developmental principles became part of the ideological credo of spokespersons for the retarded.

Judicial Activism

The civil rights movement of the 1960's flowed into the disability rights movement of the 1970's. Public interest attorneys often became the champions of the mentally retarded as they pressed many court cases for the rights of retarded for habilitation and then habilitation in the least restrictive environment. According to Vitello and Soskin(1985, 35), "these court decisions had a significant impact on the deinstitutionalization of mentally retarded persons."

As more group homes for the mentally retarded opened in urban and suburban communities, the deinstitutionalization movement faced a new challenge of exclusionary zoning or the threat that such "artificial families" as existed in group homes did not constitute a "single family" as defined by local zoning ordinances. However, nearly all court cases have found that group homes were single family residences(Vitello & Soskin, 1985). Behind this legal resistance to allowing group homes opening up in single family neighborhoods has been three fears of residents. These fears were: (1)group homes would lower property values in the neighborhood, (2)that crime would increase in such neighborhoods, and (3)that they would undermine the good characteristics of such neighborhoods. Of forty studies of the effects of group homes on such neighborhoods, only one found such effects to occur(Community Residences Information Services Program, 1986).

Legislative and Executive Action for the Retarded

Both the executive and legislative branches of the federal government have responded to the needs of the retarded. In 1961 the President, John F. Kennedy, appointed the President's Committee on Mental Retardation which has had an impressive record in an advisory role in recommending research and action programs to combat the causes of retardation and better serve the retarded. A year later this committee recommended a national program to deal with the problem and President Kennedy addressed Congress on the first phase of an implementation program. Major legislation was passed in 1963 when Public Laws 88-156 and 88-164 were signed into law that led to state planning programs and implementation programs. In 1971 President Nixon pledged to expand federal efforts in order to reach two goals: (1)reduce by half the occurrence of retardation in the U.S. by the year 2000, and (2)enable one third of more than 200,000 retarded persons in public institutions to return to useful lives in the community. Over the years the President's Committee on Mental Retardation has supported a substantial amount of research, held many conferences to explore the issues, and published over 60 documents on its work(President's Committee on Mental Retardation, 1986). Much of the work of this committee, particularly in the 1970's, was oriented to deinstitutionalization efforts.

Much of the legislation passed by Congress with regard to the mentally retarded has had an important impact on the normalization principle of deinstitutionalization. What follows is a chronological list of federal legislation which has had an impact on the deinstitutionalization process.

1963: Maternal and Child Health and Mental Retardation Amendments(P.L. 88-156). This law made grants to the states to develop comprehensive plans for mental retardation services.

1963: Mental Retardation Facilities and Community Mental Health Center Act(P.L. 88-164). This legislation has funded the improvement of institutional residential facilities and blanketed the country with Mental Health/Mental Retardation offices which, in addition to providing a wide range of services, helps to coordinate and implement residential programs.

1970: The Developmental Disabilities Services and Facilities Act(P.L. 91-517) made federal funds available for the construction of group homes.

1971: In 1971 Title XIX of the Social Security Act(Medicaid) was amended by P.L. 92-233 to authorize Medicaid funds being used by the states to ensure that institutions for the retarded provide an appropriate range of services to assist residents in developing independence skills to maximize their return to communities at the earliest possible time. Since this money had been earmarked for "medical" institutions, the money had to be used by these institutions in compliance with strict federal standards. These federal standards include adherence to (1)requirements for medical staffing and operation; (2)strict fire and safety codes; (3)requirements for developing and periodically reviewing individual treatment plans; (4)recognition of the rights of residents, and (5)certain minimum operating standards with regard to space for programming and sleeping quarters and the number of residents allowed per bedroom. Institutions or group homes funded under Medicaid are called Intermediate Care Facilities/Mentally Retarded or ICFs/MR. Since the Medicaid program requires the state to nearly match federal dollars(this match is variable by the income level of the state), this has been an attractive program to the states. Rather than having to pay all of the costs of residential care, the states can have around 50% of the costs of care borne by federal funds if they meet the eligibility requirements listed above. This financial incentive to develop ICFs/MR has enabled the states to engage in "cost-shifting"--transferring formerly state costs to the federal government. At the same time ICF/MR facilities generally allow a medical model of treatment.

1972: Title XVI of the Social Security Act was passed(P.L. 92-603) which created Supplementary Security

Income for the aged, blind and disabled. Commonly called "SSI"(Supplemental Security Income), this program provided a minimum monthly income to the aged, blind and disabled who are also poor by federal income guidelines. Many states also supplement the federal SSI monthly payment with a smaller state SSI payment. The income from SSI can be used by retarded/disabled persons to pay for room and board costs. SSI payments can also be paid to federally defined poor families for home care for a severely retarded child who lives with them. In nearly all states, retarded people who are receiving SSI payments are also eligible for free health services(under Medicaid), food stamps, and social services like "day treatment" under Title XX of the Social Security Act.

1973: The Vocational Rehabilitation Act(P.L. 93-112) provided grants to the states to assist in developing educational, vocational, employment and independent living services for the disabled in their communities.

1974: The Social Service Amendment(P.L. 92-603) altered Title XX so that the federal government could reimburse states up to 75% of the expenditures for certain services for needy citizens. Some of the services provided under this legislation for the needy retarded included day care programs for children and adults, protective services, transportation and other appropriate services to reduce the need for institutionalization.

1974: Section 8 of the Housing and Community Development Act provides a rent subsidy for needy persons(a few of whom may be retarded) to rent apartments or homes. In this program a fair market rental price is set for each housing unit used by eligible renters. The eligible renter then pays 30% of his income toward the rent(originally 25%). The federal government then pays the difference between the fair market rental charge and 30% of the person's income.

1975: The Education for All Handicapped Children Act(P.L. 94-142) provides grants to the states for the education of developmentally disabled persons. This act will be discussed more fully later. But it made community education services much more available to all levels of retarded persons than had existed prior to its passage.

1975: The Developmentally Disabled Assistance and Bill of Rights Act(P.L. 94-103) required states to prepare deinstitutionalization plans for the mentally retarded and develop the necessary services and housing to implement these plans. It also required the states to develop advocacy and protection services for all such persons.

1977: Revisions were made to Title XIX of the Social Security Act(Medicaid) which allowed the states to develop smaller ICF/MR facilities to serve 15 or fewer persons. This allowed the states to relocate some retarded persons from larger facilities to smaller facilities and shift some of the costs of residential care to the federal government.

1978: The Rehabilitation, Comprehensive Services, and Developmental Disabilities Amendments Act adopted a functional definition of developmental disabilities, merged developmental disabilities into the Rehabilitation Act, and encouraged states to develop comprehensive agencies to support the growth of independent living.

1979: The Health Planning Resources Development Act required states to develop community-based health services for the mentally retarded.

1981: The Community Development Block Grant Program provided financial support to local governments if they wanted to develop services or community housing for the retarded.

1981: Section 2176 of the Omnibus Reconciliation Act was passed which authorized a waiver of certain Medicaid requirements to allow states to cover home and community based long-term care under Medicaid. As we shall see later in this chapter, this allowed for expanding the movement of retarded persons from larger institutions to smaller ones.

The Escalating Costs of Care

There are many types of governmental costs associated with mental retardation. Braddock(1986a) lists six such types of costs: (1)services, (2)training, (3)research, (4)income maintenance, (5)construction activities, and (6)information and coordination activities. These will be discussed in greater detail later. By far the largest two of these six costs is for services and income maintenance. Of the total 1985 federal expenditures for MR/DD, 38.5% of it or $2.99 billion was spent for income maintenance and 60.2% of it or $4.68 billion was spent for services of four types: (1)vocational rehabilitation services, (2)human

212

development services, (3)educational services, and (4)residential/medical services. This fourth category comprises 82.3% of the services budget.

There are three critical factors here: (1)one is the rapid escalation of total federal costs for MR/DD care, (2)second is the increasing proportion of MR/DD costs borne by the federal government, and (3)third, while the costs of large institutional care have been and remain high, the costs of small group home care has risen rapidly especially when these homes are converted to ICF/MR status so they can get federal Medicaid funding.

In 1985 total federal MR/DD costs were $7.773 billion. This is nearly one-half of total public(federal-state-local) outlays for mental retardation in this country(Braddock, 1986a). These expenditures have risen rapidly from less than .1% of the total federal budget in 1950 to .4% of the federal budget in 1970, and then to over .8% of the budget in 1985. As a percentage of the Gross National Product, MR/DD expenditures increased at an annual average rate of 35% between 1950 and 1956, 25% between 1956 and 1967, and 9% a year from 1967 to 1981. Since 1981, while total expenditures have increased, the percentage of the GNP going to MR/DD expenditures has declined slightly.

One of the reasons for deinstitutionalization has been that it is more economical to house and service retarded persons in the local community. Thus, in addition to the humanitarian reasons for deinstitutionalization captured under the theme of normalization, there has been the drive by federal and state governments to lower total care costs by moving retarded persons to smaller residential settings for care. Table 7.1 shows the comparative daily costs of operating different types of residential programs in 1982 in the United States. Public group residences with over 63 residents averaged $85.94 per day in comparison to about $41 per day for group residences caring for one to 63 residents and $49.33 for private group residences with over 63 residents(Braddock, 1986). While it is true that the large public residence have lower functioning clients on the average, other factors are also involved in explaining why it costs twice as much per year to provide care for mentally retarded persons in such facilities--$31,368 annually in comparison to about $15,000 annually in smaller group residences. The larger public facilities use more expensive

Table 7.1

Number of Residents and Average Per Day Reimbursement by Type of Facility: United States, 1982

Type of Facility	Facilities N	Facilities %	Mean $ per day per Resident	Retarded Residents N	Retarded Residents %
Foster Homes	6,587	42.1	16.15	17,147	7.0
Group Residences					
1-5 Residents	2,448	15.7	40.29	8,456	3.5
6-15 Residents	4,117	26.3	37.88	34,646	14.2
16-63 Residents	655	4.2	45.06	19,814	8.1
Group Residences*					
Private**	231	1.5	49.33	22,522	9.2
Public**	216	1.4	85.94	119,898	49.2
Semi-Independent Living	306	2.0	27.40	2,870	1.2
Boarding Homes	185	1.2	15.97	1,264	.5
Personal Care Homes	383	3.7	17.05	4,070	1.7
Nursing Homes	303	1.9	49.81	12,292	5.3
Totals	15,633		63.04	243,669	

*Sixty-four or more residents

**Numbers for facilities and residents estimated by interpolation

Source: Hauber et al, 1984.

214

staffing and facilities. Thus, one of the reasons for dein-stitutionalization has been the attempt to control rapidly escalating costs.

THE CLASSIFICATION OF RESIDENTIAL SET-TINGS

One of the difficult things to deal with in putting different types of residential settings into categories is that the states or subregions thereof, have not adopted a uniform nomenclature for residences for the retarded. Neither have researchers agreed on a common nomenclature or typology. Furthermore, residences can be classified according to a number of significant factors:

1. Ownership
   a) Public--state/county owned and operated
   b) Private
      (1)Non Profit
      (2)For Profit
2. Size--number of residents
3. Location--urban, suburban, rural; clustered or scattered
4. Cost of operation
5. Length in operation
6. Operational Model: Medical Model vs. Educational/Behavioral Shaping Model
7. Characteristics of residents as measured by IQ and/or adaptive behavior scales including presence of medical/physical problems affecting ambulation and self-care skills.
8. Modes of funding: many mixes of multiple legislation funding sources from three levels of government(federal, state, local) and pri-vate funding is possible.

Furthermore, these classification devices can be crosstabu-lated in many ways. Publicly operated homes may be large, medium, or small, have a variety of ecological loca-tions, be operated on primarily a medical or education model, and show wide variation in operating costs, length in existence and in the mix of characteristics their clients exhibit. Private facilities may be operated by either small

215

or large non-profit organizations or by small for-profit groups operating one or two homes to large interstate corporations who operate a mix of residential and other services. The student of residential programs should be aware that there are wide ranges in the quality and types of residential programs. Classification devices are often arbitrary and may hide characteristics that are overlapping in other areas.

In Chapter 6 we looked at the types of residential alternatives that existed in Sweden, Denmark, and the ENCOR program in Nebraska. They exhibit one type of classification system. Vitello and Soskin(1985) classify residential services into two major groups with subclassifications as follows:

    I.   *Individual Placements:*
          A.   Adoptive Homes
          B.   Foster Families
          C.   Apartment Living
    II. *Group Placement:*
          A.   Small Groups:
               1.   Group Homes
               2.   Boarding Homes
          B.   Large Groups:
               1.   Nursing Homes
               2.   Institutions

There is no uniform agreement as to the numerical cut-off point when a small group becomes a large group. But most professionals in the field believe there should be a continuum of both residential and other services to match the complex and changing needs of retarded persons. Ideally, a range of residential services should be available to meet the needs of retarded persons as they mature from infancy to adulthood, develop skills and sometimes regress. Ideally, as they become more independent they ought to move from more to less restrictive residential environments(Copeland & Iversen, 1985).

We will now look at the range of housing arrangements of those mentally retarded people who do not live with their own natural families or in their own homes or apartments. About 95% of all retarded people live in these two types of housing units. Therefore, the following description of residential programs covers no more than 5% of the mentally retarded.

The types of residential programs listed below generally move from the least restrictive to the most restrictive and from the most integrated to the least integrated.

1. *Adoptive homes* are those in which the adoptive parents legally adopt a retarded child and the biological parents relinquish their legal responsibilities for caring for the child. Adoptive homes are a most suitable form of deinstitutionalization if the parents can give adequate care for the child. Adopting is an alternative when the natural family either believes they can't or don't want to take care of such a child. ·It has been undertaken by some families who are infertile and who can't find a normal baby since there is a shortage of adoptable young children and who enjoy the sense of accomplishment and satisfaction such a child may bring. Adoption has been encouraged as a residential alternative because of its low cost relative to other residential programs and the assumed quality of care it will yield. It has been encouraged by child welfare agencies, the 1980 Adoption Assistance and Child Welfare Act which can provide a federal subsidy for either adoptive or natural families with a disabled child, and the 1983 Home and Community Medicaid Waiver which enables states to provide some services to families who have a handicapped child judged to be at risk for institutionalization. From 1954 on the federal tax code has also allowed deductions for the care of a disabled spouse or dependent. The number of all types of families claiming such deductions increased from 100,000 in 1971 to 300,000 in 1978(Perlman, 1983; Moroney, 1986; Vitello & Soskin, 1985).

2. *Foster homes* are those in which foster parents are reimbursed for the care they offer each child or adult. In the 1982 national census by Hauber et al(1984) 6,587 foster homes provided care for 17,147 retarded residents. While these constituted 42.1% of the facilities, they contained only 7% of the retarded living outside their own homes and families. The average number of residents per home was 2.6. There is substantial variation among the states with regard to subsidy levels and support services available to foster families. In 1982 the average national cost for foster home care was $16 per person per day($5,840 annually), compared to $42.77 per day for community group residences($15,611 annually), and com-

217

pared to $86.25 per day for institutional care($31,481 annually)(Birenbaum & Cohen, 1985).

Various investigations have been made into the quality of care offered in foster homes. The research findings often show both benefits and limitations or drawbacks in such care. But it is important to recognize that the quality of care and the outcomes for foster family care may depend upon a number of factors: (1)the reimbursement level for care, (2)the motives of those who become foster families, (3)the characteristics of the clients which are placed, (4)the number of clients placed in a given home, and (5)the kind of training and ongoing supervision and support services that are given to such families. Some of the positive findings with regard to foster family care for some residents are: (1)their lower costs, (2)improvements in adaptive behavior, (3)improvements in skills and interpersonal relations, (4)later release to less restrictive settings. But problems that sometimes occur include: (1)shifting of residents from one foster home to another, (2)readmission back to more restrictive residences when the placement didn't work out, (3)community opposition to the program, (4)the lack of supervision or overprotectiveness in some placements, and (5)the stress that this induced in some families because of the intensive demands for care it made(Willer & Intagliata, 1984; Birenbaum & Cohen, 1985; Vitello & Soskin, 1985).

Foster family care may receive greater emphasis in the future because of its lower cost compared to other placement alternatives and its potential for offering normalizing family care setting for all levels of retardation. California, New Jersey, and New York states are putting a heavy emphasis on home care. Pennsylvania experimented with several "family living programs" beginning in 1984 with good successes. Starting in 1987 this program is being expanded statewide. While each provider agency works out its own reimbursement levels for foster families in 1986 one provider was paying a family $21 a day for care which was going to be increased to $25 a day in 1987. In addition to these costs were costs borne by the provider agency in screening families, giving them extensive training and supervision and backup services such as respite care.

3. *Supervised independent living arrangements* is where retarded persons live in their own homes or apart-

218

ments but are periodically visited by a supervisory staff to see how well they are doing on such things as personal care, hygiene, work attendance, nutritional standards, and budgeting. These types of residences were not included in the 1982 national survey.

4. _Supervised semi-independent living arrangements_ are those in which staff live in the same building but do not share the same housing unit as those they supervise. In the 1982 national survey there were 306 such programs housing 2,870 residents or 1.2% of all residents. There are variations in different programs whether the supervisors are volunteers or paid-staff and the frequency and kinds of supervision given. These residential programs are usually seen as permitting substantial independence for relatively high functioning clients.

5. _Boarding homes_ are those which provide sleeping rooms and meals but not regular care or supervision of clients. Boarding homes are licensed by the states. While some retarded people may live in integrated boarding homes with non-retarded clients, only those that were exclusively for the mentally retarded were included in the 1982 national survey. In 1982 only 185 facilities housing 1,264 clients(average of 6.8 clients per home) were in existence. These constituted just 1.2% of the facilities and .5% of the residents surveyed. Boarding home care ranges from good to bad with some places housing up to 30 residents in dreary homes. Such boarding homes have often been pictured in the mass media as deinstitutionalization dumping grounds primarily for the mentally ill rather than for the mentally retarded.

6. _Personal care homes_ are boarding homes in which staff provide a range of personal services such as helping residents dress, bathe, and transporting them to medical appointments. They too are licensed by the state but must meet somewhat more rigorous standards than boarding homes. In 1982, 583 personal care homes(3.7% of all residential facilities) provided residences for 4,070 clients or 1.7% of the total. Much like boarding homes, they range from small bright places to larger dreary homes that offer relatively few integrating experiences.

7. _Group residences_ is a broad category that ranges from 1 or 2 residents living with a supervisory staff member up to 2000 persons in a state institution. Often these are divided up by size into small and large. In the

1982 national survey carried out by Hauber et al(1984), there were 7,260 small facilities(N under 64) which made up 46.2% of all facilities and housed 25.8% of all persons in any type of facility included in the survey. The large group residences, that is those with over 63 residents, constituted only 2.9% of the facilities but housed 58.4% of all the residents included in the survey. And most of these persons were in large public institutions as opposed to large private facilities.

The smaller group homes, that is those with 10 or fewer residents, have generally been the most popular type of home ideologically since it approximates a more normal family size that allows for more individual attention. In group homes there is 24-hour supervision by paid staff. However, the regulations governing the operation of such group homes varies substantially by whether they are funded by Medicaid as ICF/MRs or by other funding streams and whether the residents are judged capable of self-preservation and by other client characteristics.

One of the debates that continues is whether all residents in the larger institutions should be moved to smaller institutions. Those against such moves cite one or more of these arguments: (1)larger institutions can provide more intensive and specialized care for the medically fragile and profoundly retarded; (2)it would be a costly waste of facilities to close down such places; (3)the staff at such places would lose their jobs or have to be transferred to community based programs(that often pay less); and (4)larger institutions have gotten a bad press from a few with deplorable conditions, while many are doing an excellent job of caring for some with low levels of potential and preparing others for release to less restrictive institutions. In contrast, those in favor of closing large facilities argue: (1)large institutions are inherently depersonalizing and stigmatizing, (2)the costs of care can usually be reduced by moving to smaller facilities, and (3)smaller facilities provide more normalizing environments for growth. Clearly the process of deinstitutionalization requires the availability of a greater range of community services than have often been available(Willer & Intagliata, 1984; Halpern, Sackett, Binner & Mohr, 1980; Lakin & Bruininks, 1985; Copeland & Iversen, 1985).

8. _Nursing homes_ are state licensed facilities that offer either IMF(intermediate facility nursing care services)

or SNF(skilled nursing facilities). These facilities offer care primarily to the aged retarded and profoundly retarded of all ages who lack many self care skills. In the early deinstitutionalization movement, in the 1970's, such places were often a dumping ground for institutional releasees. Such medically oriented facilities are needed by some retarded persons(Vitello & Soskin, 1985). In the 1982 national survey, 303 nursing homes provided care to 12,982 retarded residents for 5.3% of all residential programming included in the survey.

Under the concept of a "continuum of care," a wide range of facilities are needed to serve the variable mix of needs that retarded persons have. We now turn to an analysis of the changing patterns of residential care for the retarded.

LONG TERM TRENDS IN PUBLIC RESIDENTIAL FACILITIES

Public residential facilities(PRFs) are those state operated large institutions for the mentally retarded. Over the course of their 130 year existence in the United States and up to about 1960, they essentially became long-term care custodial facilities. Starting in the 1960's and accelerating in the 1970's there has been a movement to try to improve the programs and facilities of these large institutions while simultaneously developing more community based residential and services programs for releasees from these places and to lower the admission rates to keep as many mentally retarded in the community as possible.

Five trends are clearly noticeable as regards to Public Residential Facilities.

1. The number of residents in PRFs has declined sharply since 1967. Table 7.2 shows that the number of residents in PRFs climbed steadily from 1950 to 1967, the peak year when 193,188 persons were in PRFs. From 1967 to 1976, the population of PRFs declined 39,604 from 193,188 to 153,584--a decline of over 20% in nine years. And in the 6 year period from 1976 to 1982 the resident population declined 22% to 119,335.

2. While the number of PRFs has increased, the average size of the resident populations has decreased. The average size of the resident population has decreased for

two reasons--fewer residents in more PRFs. The large size of state institutions has been one of their most criticized as-

Table 7.2
Number of Residents in U.S. Public Residential Facilities for the Mentally Retarded, 1950-1982

Year	Number of Residents	Year	Number of Residents
1950	128,145	1974	166,247
1955	143,548	1976	159,058
1960	161,900*	1978	139,410
1967	193,188	1981	125,799
1971	189,546	1982	119,335
1972	181,035	1983	114,020
1973	173,775	1984	109,827

*Number estimated from a graph.
Sources: Butterfield(1976), Scheerenberger (1983) and Braddock(1986b).

pects for it has been associated with depersonalization and lack of habilitative programs. In 1970 there were 190 PRFs containing 189,546 persons with an average of 998 residents in each. By 1981 there were 279 PRFs serving 119,335 persons for an average size of 428 residents. By 1982 there were 117 private facilities serving over 100 residents each with 18,915 persons housed in them for an average size of 162. In 1982 there were 224 public institutions housing 117,239 residents for an average size of 523. In 1982, 48 public institutions still had over 751 residents each with 4 containing over 2000 residents(Hauber, et al, 1984).

3. Staff ratios and public expenditures for PRFs have increased rapidly. In an effort to reform institutions, their staffs have been enlarged which has resulted in increased public outlays for institutional expenditures. In the 1930s there were around seven clients for every staff member in public institutions. By 1950 there were about 5 clients per staff, 3 clients per staff in 1960, 1.7 in 1970 and around 1.4 by 1980. This high and costly labor intensive

222

service industry is required in large institutions where three shifts of attendants must be maintained in addition to social workers, physicians and dentists, kitchen and custodial help and a range of other therapists. In fiscal year 1980-81, the cost of maintaining a resident in a public institution had increased 615% from 1970-71 and had increased 117% over 1975-76. The average cost of maintaining a person in a public facility in 1980-81 was $77.99 a day per person($28,466 a year) but ranged from a low of $25.61 a day to $213 a day(Westling, 1986). By 1986 the daily average per diem in the U.S. had reached $121.24 in public institutions. This figure represented a 75% increase over 1980(Braddock, 1986c).

Table 7.4 later in this chapter also indicates that the ICF/MR program, which includes both small and large facilities, has shown similar trends. Between 1977 and 1982, the ICF/MR program has witnessed (1)a much faster growth in small rather than large programs, (2)a more rapid increase in the number of clients served by small institutions, and (3)a much faster decline in the number of beds in large institutions as compared to small institutions. And ICF/MR Medicaid expenditures have risen rapidly--304% between 1977 and 1982.

4. Admission rates to PRFs have decreased. Admission rates include both new admissions and readmissions. During the 1961 to 1971 period, first admissions declined slowly while readmissions were relatively stable but began picking up slowly after the rapid deinstitutionalization phase was begun in 1967. But new admissions during this time period exceeded readmissions about 13 to 1(Butterfield, 1976). With the advent of more community residential services in the 1970s, the admissions rates fell more sharply. In 1970 there were around 16,000 new admissions annually to PRFs. But by 1980-81 the admission rate had declined 66% to around 5500 per year(Vitello & Soskin, 1985).

5. PRFs are increasingly serving the most severely retarded. The overall trend for the last twenty years is that releasees from institutions and new potential admissions who have been kept at home and never admitted to PRFs have been the less severely retarded. Or conversely, those admitted and/or maintained at public institutions have been (1)the profoundly and severely retarded, (2)those with complex medical problems associated with

223

Table 7.3

Adaptive Behaviors in Percent by Type of Facility, U.S. 1982

Type of Facility	Cannot walk without assistance	Cannot dress without assistance	Cannot eat without assistance	Cannot understand spoken word	Cannot communicate verbally	Are not toilet trained
Foster Home	9.3	29.9	11.9	10.4	24.9	13.1
Group Residence (1-5)	7.5	18.9	7.3	6.6	21.3	9.1
Group Residence (6-15)	4.8	14.9	5.7	4.3	16.2	6.0
Group Residence (15-63)	13.5	25.7	15.0	9.8	22.7	15.1
Group Residence (64+)	23.9	50.3	32.3	23.0	45.4	34.6
Semi-Independent Living	3.6	2.3	.5	1.5	3.7	.1
Boarding Homes	2.7	9.7	3.5	2.1	4.8	3.9
Personal Care Homes	5.4	19.0	6.6	6.8	16.1	6.5
Nursing Homes	4.8	67.7	50.3	36.2	54.0	49.0
U.S. Total	18.9	39.1	23.8	16.9	35.4	25.3

Source: Hauber, et al, 1984, 243.

224

Table 7.4

National Data on ICF/MR Programs

	Year		% Change
	1977	1982	1977-1982
Number of Institutions by Size			
--Under 15 beds	188	1,202	+539
--15 beds or over	389	652	+93
Beneficiaries Served by Size			
--Under 15 beds	1,710	9,714	+468
--15 beds or over	105,207	130,970	+24
Average Bed Size of ICF/MR			
--Under 15 beds	9.1	8.1	-11
--15 beds or over	270.5	200.9	-26
Average N of Beds per ICF/MR	186	76	-59
Proportion of Population			
Under age 22	35.6	22.6	-37
% Severely/Profoundly Retarded in			
--under 16 bed facilities	30	44	
--16-75 bed facilities	48	57	
--76+ bed facilities	66	76	

Table 7.4

National Data on ICF/MR Programs
(continued)

| | Year | | % Change |
	1977	1982	1977-1982
% Mildly/Moderately Retarded in			
--under 16 bed facilities	70	56	
--16-75 bed facilities	52	43	
--76+ bed facilities	34	24	
Federal ICF/MR Expenditures	$520 Million	$2.1 Billion	+304

Source: Adapted from Tompkins(1986).

retardation, and (3)those with the most serious behavior problems. In the 1982 national survey of residential facilities, 78.3% of the public facility residents were severely or profoundly retarded in comparison to only 40.2% in the private facilities which have a substantially smaller average size(Hauber, et al, 1984).

Table 7.4 illustrates trends between 1977 and 1982 of the characteristics of persons in ICFs/MR. While all sizes of ICFs/MR were treating larger proportions of the severely and profoundly retarded in 1982 than in 1977, the largest proportion of the more severely retarded were in the larger facilities. Thus, in 1982, 76% of the residents in the largest institutions were severely and profoundly retarded compared to 57% of those serving 16 to 75 residents and 44% of those serving under 16 residents. Over time, the average age of residents in ICFs/MR is going up suggesting a tendency for them to accumulate in larger facilities.

Table 7.3 shows that in 1982 large group residences(64+ beds) and nursing homes are the kinds of facilities that are most likely serving those without six kinds of adaptive behaviors. Around half of their residents or more cannot dress without assistance, cannot communicate verbally, and are not toilet trained.

While there has been remarkable progress in moving retarded persons to smaller, more normalizing settings, in 1982 over 58% of the residents included in the Hauber et al(1984) national survey still resided in institutions of 64 or more residents. And only 28% were in settings of 15 or fewer residents.

TRENDS IN COMMUNITY RESIDENTIAL FACILITIES

Community Residential Facilities(CRFs) are residential facilities and programs that are located in normal residential environments rather than large institutions usually located in remote rural locations on sizable tracts of lands. CRFs are usually conceptualized as including foster homes, boarding homes, personal care homes, semi-independent living arrangements and particularly group homes of limited size. They may be public or private facilities. Private facilities tend to dominate CRF programs.

Table 7.5
Number of Community Residential Facilities
Opened From 1962 to 1976

Year	Number Opened	Year	Number Opened
1960	35	1969	171
1961	39	1970	238
1962	44	1971	260
1963	54	1972	306
1964	71	1973	439
1965	86	1974	490
1966	79	1975	605
1967	98	1976	559
1968	177	Total	3,751

Source: Westling, 1986, 210.

Time Of Opening. An inspection of the date when CRFs opened is one way to chart the progress toward deinstitutionalization.   Before 1960, only 222 CRFs had opened. As shown in Table 7.5, CRFs were opened in a slowly increasing rate from 1960 to 1967. Beginning in 1968, the number of openings of CRFs increased rapidly up to 1975 when 605 were opened in a single year. The rate of opening has continued at a high level since then. In the six year period from January 1, 1977 to June of 1982, 8,065 new facilities opened(a rate of 1,466 a year). Most of these were small CRFs(Hauber et al, 1984).

Number.   In 1982, there were 15,633 facilities serving 243,669 retarded residents. If we exclude 303 nursing homes and 449 institutions serving 64 or more residents, we find that 95% of the residences(14,881) were serving under 64 residents. However, these 95% of the facilities were serving just 36.2% of the residents. This means that nursing homes and large residences were still serving 63.8% of all the residents(Hauber, et al, 1984).

Size. The trend in ICF/MR programs has also been toward small institutions as shown in Table 7.4. Between 1977 and 1982, of the 1,277 new ICFs/MR opened, 79.4% of them were smaller facilities--those serving under 15 residents. During this same time period, the number of residents served by small facilities increased 468% while the number served by large ones increased only 24%. On

228

the other hand, of the 140,684 residents in ICFs/MR in 1982, 93.1% were in facilities serving 15 or more clients. ICFs/MR make up only 11% of all facilities but care for 57% of all retarded residents. Of the 1,854 ICFs/MR, about 76% are privately operated while 24% are publicly operated. Many of the larger state institutions for the mentally retarded have been converted to ICF/MR programs.

CRFs serve a variety of clients. Boarding homes, personal care homes and semi-independent living arrangements as well as some group homes, serve primarily higher functioning clients. But over time some of the group homes, adoptive and foster homes have increasingly accepted lower functioning clients.

METHODS OF EVALUATING DEINSTITUTIONAL-IZATION

There are several ways to evaluate the effects of deinstitutionalization. One of these is on cost effectiveness. We have already looked at some data which suggests that it is less expensive to society to move clients from larger facilities to less restrictive or more normalizing residential placement. A second way, and the focus of this section of the chapter, is to evaluate the quality of the living environment and the social processes that go in residential settings to see what effect they have on clients.

Evaluation of residential facilities, the social processes that go on within them, and their outcomes on clients is a complex undertaking inasmuch as it tries to relate a person's residential life to the total quality of his or her life. The critical questions in evaluating the quality of residential life are those generic questions that hold true for all evaluation measures:

1. What is to be evaluated?
2. Why is it to be evaluated?
3. Who will do the evaluation?
4. How will the evaluation be done?
5. When is the evaluation done?

Let us look at each of these questions in somewhat greater detail as they apply to community residential programs.

1.   What is to be evaluated can include the qualities of the house they live in, the neighborhood's quality,
the availability and use of services, the quality and skills of
the staff that provide services, the system of management
that operates the program, staff-client interpersonal processes, and a variety of outcomes measures which attempt
to assess the growth of clients in literally dozens of skill
areas as well as their life satisfaction.

2.   Why the evaluation is done may be for multiple
reasons such as (1)state licensing to determine if licensing
standards are being met, (2)academic evaluation so the
quality of life can be described, assessed and perhaps compared to other programs, and (3)the use of evaluative
information to maintain and enhance effective parts of the
program and to alter the program in areas where it is
believed to be deficient.

3.   Who does the evaluation is usually closely tied
to the other four questions of evaluation. The kinds of
evaluations may include self-assessment by the providers
of services, or outside evaluation by a state or federal
licensing board, a peer review team of similar professional
providers, a state-funded advocacy group, a locally funded
advocacy group, independent academic investigators, or
single citizens or parents.

4.   How will the evaluation be done question
includes a wide variety of answers including methods that
vary by what is being evaluated, who is doing it and for
what purpose the evaluation is being carried out as well as
the resources and sophistication of the evaluators. A number of evaluative instruments, rating scales and ethnographic observation and interview techniques have been
developed to assess the quality of life in various residential
settings. We will look at several of these out of the dozens
that have been developed.

The *Revised Child Management Scale* developed by
King, Raynes and Tizard(1971) contains 30 items to
measure: (1)rigidity of routine, (2)block treatment,
(3)depersonalization, and (4)social distance practices in the
management of residential programs. Each of the 30 items
has three scale scores that can be summed for the four sub-
areas of the test as well as for the whole test. Each question can be scored in one of three ways: 0 indicating a

child-orientation, 2 indicating an institution-orientation, and 1 indicating a mixed pattern between the two.

Rigidity of routine in management practices are institutionally oriented when they are inflexible from one person to another, from one day to the next, or individuals are treated alike even though they are different. In contrast, management practices are seen as child-oriented when they are flexible by taking into account differences in circumstances or persons. Six questions make up the measurement of rigidity. One of the items is "are there set times when visitors can come into the unit?" The scores for the three possible answers are: 0--any time(except during specified times), 1--any day, but set times, and 2--certain days only. The other five items have similarly scored response sets and have to do with: (2)getting up and (3)going to bed at the same time on weekends as weekdays, (4)whether there are set times for being in the garden or yard or in (5)their own bedrooms, and (6)whether children are routinely toileted at night.

Block Treatment has been a useful concept in measuring normalization. Block treatment involves regimenting people for certain services or activities as groups-- such as all showering at the same time, being lined up for toileting, all waiting in line for a bus or meal. Block treatment is avoided when the organization of activities include voluntary participation and residents being allowed to do things at their own pace. Block treatment is measured by 8 questions dealing with blocked group activities for (1)doing nothing after getting dressed, (2)waiting in line for breakfast, (3)waiting for bathing, (4)waiting after bathing, (5)whether they move in groups or as individuals after toileting, (6)waiting at tables for meals to be served, and (7)afterwards, and (8)the amount of organization involved in walks.

Depersonalization occurs when child management practices are so institutionally oriented that residents have no personal possessions, privacy or opportunities for self-expression and initiative. They are child-oriented when they have these things. Nine questions are used to measure this and ask about: (1)private clothing, (2)private toys, (3)extent of personal clothing, (4)private storage for clothes, (5)private storage for books and toys, (6)presence of their own pictures in their rooms, (7)amount of time allotted for play, (8)whether individual birthday parties

231

with presents are allowed, and (9)how the tables are laid out for meals.

Social distances measures the distance between staff and clients. A high social distance or an institutional orientation would occur when communication is formal, functionally specific and the staff have exclusive territories. Management practices are child oriented where the staff and clients share the same living space in informal and functionally different ways. Seven questions dealing with access to the kitchen and other areas, methods of assisting in toileting and bathing, eating meals and watching TV together, and frequency of going on outings with the staff are how social distance is measured.

Another type of measurement involves using various adaptive behavior scales to measure if clients have learned new skills or been able to reduce the amount, intensity and kinds of disruptive behavior over time. These longitudinal and repeated measurements allow the evaluator to assess the rate of development or regression in behaviors related to program impact.

A frequently cited instrument is one developed by ENCOR(East Nebraska Community Office of Retardation) called "PASS"(Programme Analysis of Service Systems). While it is a fairly long and detailed instrument that can be scored, Clarke(1982, 251-55) summarizes its major components by a series of principles and questions:

INTEGRATION--to take part in the mainstream. To be accepted by peers.

Size or Dispersal
1.   Are there so many handicapped persons being served that the surrounding community is not able to accept them?
2.   Is the number of people served in a residence so large that the people don't go outside for their personal relationships?

Program and Facility Labels
1.   Does the sign outside tell that the people inside are "different?"
2.   Would the labels produce a negative or hopeless feeling among most people?

232

Social Opportunities
1.   Does the handicapped person interact with non-handicapped persons where he lives? Where he works or goes to school? In his free time? When he shops, attends church, and the like?

AGE APPROPRIATE STRUCTURES--to be valued by others as a true peer.

Facilities Design and Decorations
1.   Is the facility, the design of the facility and wall decorations appropriate for the age of the persons being served? Are adults living or working in child-like settings?

Possessions
1.   Are the possessions owned by the handicapped person appropriate to his age? Does what an adult own make him appear child-like?
2.   Are attempts being made by staff to encourage their clients to own age appropriate possessions?
3.   Is there appropriate space where a person lives for the possessions he owns?

Labels and Forms of Address
1.   Are handicapped adults addressed as though they were children? Is a child-like nickname used, such as Tommy or Bobby?
2.   Are labels such as kid, child, youngster used when referring to a handicapped child?
3.   Does the staff use a tone of voice with handicapped adults that would be used with children?

Activities and Routines
1.   Are handicapped persons engaged in activities that are appropriate for their age? Do adults work during the day? Is a child's school session limited to two hours?
2.   Are the daily routines of handicapped persons typical and age appropriate? Is an

adult given a coffee break--or is it a recess? Is a nap scheduled during a child's school day?

Autonomy (self direction) and Rights

1. Are handicapped persons given a chance to make input into decisions regarding their lives? Who makes the decisions in a person's life?

2. Are handicapped persons assisted in becoming independent rather than dependent? Will he need just as much support six months from now?

3. Do handicapped persons exercise more rights as they grow older?

4. Are handicapped persons encouraged to exercise their rights, such as voting or privacy?

5. Are rights removed only when there has been a determination of reduced competency in the area to be limited? Is the restricting of a person's right used only as a last resort? Are there other alternatives?

Sex Behavior

1. Do handicapped interact with the opposite sex? Are they given time alone?

2. Are handicapped persons given support to understand their sexual identity? Does it begin at an early age?

3. Is counseling available to handicapped adults who may need assistance about dating, marriage, and birth control?

Personal Appearance

1. How typical of his age is a handicapped person's hair style and clothing? Are there subtle mannerisms that make him look different than his peers?

CULTURE APPROPRIATE STRUCTURES--to know and respond to local customs.

Labels and Forms of Address
1.   Are labels or forms of address used for handicapped persons which are demeaning, devaluing and implying inferiority? Does the form of address show the person to be valued as an equal?
2.   Are handicapped persons labeled by their diagnosis, such as "he is an epileptic" or "he is a retardate"?
3.   Are courtesy and respect towards handicapped persons lacking when staff talk to them?
4.   In his presence, is a handicapped person talked about as a third party? Does the conversation go on as if he were not there?

Personal Appearance
1.   Are staff committed to correct physical defects which make a person look different?
2.   What is being done to help handicapped persons and bizarre mannerisms such as self-mutilation, extreme destructiveness, and repetitive behaviors? Do these measures work? Is there a persistent and creative effort to try again?

SPECIALIZATION--to meet the needs of each person at his particular stage of growth.
1.   Is the program designed to meet the specific needs of every handicapped person?
2.   As needs change, how does the program change?
3.   Is a person regressing because he does not fit into the group by reason of his age, ability, or behavior?
4.   Is the activity being done in an appropriate setting under the right need?
5.   Does the staff have what it takes in skills and attitudes to meet the specific needs?

DEVELOPMENTAL GROWTH--to enable a person to learn at his own pace.

Physical Overprotection
    1.   Are physical features built into the facility to prevent handicapped persons' movement?
    2.   How are situations involving risk used to prompt growth?

Social Overprotection
    1.   Is control so emphasized or challenging opportunities so lacking that an individual's growth is restricted?
    2.   Are there some rules in the program that non-handicapped people would not tolerate?
    3.   Are handicapped persons denied new experience because "they are unable to handle them"?

Intensity of Programming
    1.   Is there a conviction among the staff that handicapped people are growing? Do their records prove that growth is taking place?
    2.   Is the teaching effort reorganized? Does it push people to their potential?
    3.   When growth is stalled, where is the responsibility placed--on the person's handicap or the staff's lack of creativity?

QUALITY OF SETTING--to create an atmosphere where a person feels comfortable and accepted.

Physical Comfort
    1.   Is the furniture and physical environment comfortable?
    2.   Is the temperature controlled? Is it quiet? Do the people like the food?
    3.   If a home, does it have a "lived-in" quality?
    4.   "Would I feel comfortable if I worked or lived in this place"?

Environmental Beauty

1. Has attention been paid to the appearance of the surroundings? Do the efforts show good taste? What about details?
2. "Is this place pleasing enough to have my family live there"?

Individualization

1. What evidence is there that people are encouraged to express themselves in their own way?
2. Is there a place where a person can be alone?
3. Do people usually do things as a group?
4. Do the individualized program plans reflect the differences in people?
5. Is it evident that staff appreciate individuals as having their own rich personality?

Interactions

1. What interaction is going on between clients, staff and the public? Is it warm, or cold and distant?
2. Are there individual friends among staff and clients? Are people listened to?
3. Who seems left out?
4. "Would I be happy here?"

The various states use "inspection instruments" to license facilities serving the mentally retarded. Pennsylvania, for example, has a 236-item licensing instrument for group residents serving under 9 persons with an additional 23 questions if it serves 9 or more. The use of these instruments helps to ensure that the facility is physically safe, that the staff is qualified by ongoing training programs, that treatment programs are being undertaken, that any use of restraints is justified, that the residents and staff are receiving proper medical care and that the clients are well fed, their rights protected and records kept on everything pertinent to their habilitation and welfare. These licensing requirements are highly detailed and cover such fine points as the maximum temperature allowed for tap water, lockup for all prescription medications and the necessity of maintaining a log of each medication taken, a

237

log on the exit time of monthly fire drills, the use of individual soap cakes, the minimum size requirements for bedrooms, and written records of progress on individual habilitation plans.

Another kind of evaluation that has been done uses multiple tools to gather data. Typically such evaluations are done by academic investigators who are attempting to gather data to comprehensively assess the processes and impacts of residential programs. Such evaluations usually use a mix of the following data gathering techniques: (I)questionnaires and/or interviews of (a)residents, (b)immediate services staff, (c)administrators running the program, and (d)parents; (II)the review of existing records on clients such as IQ and adaptive behavior test scores, client medical records, case notes and histories, and (III)a variety of observations about the facility, its setting, its staff, and staff-client interactions in a number of settings. Many dozens of such studies have been carried out and reported in journal articles and book length monographs. Some of these ethnographic evaluation studies have been short, focused studies which report on a few dozen residents or a few residences in one state. Others have been more comprehensive, used larger and more representative samples, and involved more qualitative analysis. Rather than try to review all the studies done, we will look at several major studies and at several points in time. Using different time frames also makes us aware that the operation of residential facilities is evolving and ever changing.
    5. The question of when evaluation is done relates to its purpose, methodology and who is doing the evaluation. It may be a cross-sectional study done in a relatively short period of time and completed 6 months, 2 years or 5 years after persons have been released to or lived in community residential settings. Or it may have a longitudinal focus where releasees are comparatively studied one and three years later or using some other time frame.

THE OUTCOMES OF DEINSTITUTIONALIZATION

As already indicated measuring the outcomes of desinstitionalization is a complex process. We will look at several studies.

The *Coming Back* Study

One important evaluation was done by ABT Associates under contract with the U.S. Office of Education. This research was reported by Ellinor Gollay, Ruth Freedman, Marty Wyngaarden, and Norman Kurtz under the title *Coming Back: The Community Experience of Deinstitutionalized Mentally Retarded People*(1978). It involved studying a sample of 414 residents(and their parents or group home staffs) who had been released from 9 different institutions between 1972 and 1974. The characteristics of these releasees were as follows:

-   54% were male, 46% were female
-   18% were children, 82% were adults
-   79% to 85% received "good ratings" on five indicators of grooming, dress, and appearance while only 1-3% got "poor ratings" on these things.
-   42% had no additional disabilities while 58% had one or more.
-   Most of the releasees had been in an institution an average of 10 years although most had also lived at home prior to going to the institution.
-   Of the sample, 41% were mildly retarded, 33% moderately retarded, and 26% severely retarded.
-   About 66% of the persons released had participated in some type of prerelease preparation such as training in self-care skills, or in a sheltered workshop at the institution.

Where did the releasees live? Fourteen percent lived in their natural home, 17% lived with foster parents where there was an average of 7 residents, 49% lived in group homes where the average number of residents was 12, 10% were in semi-independent apartments and 10% lived independently. Most lived in residential neighborhoods although over 33% had no access to public transportation. The facilities where they lived were well maintained, clean and homelike with only a few exceptions. And how did the community respond to these mentally retarded persons? Family views of their acceptance in the

239

community was much better for the children than the adults. Community acceptance of the adults was rated "very friendly" or "friendly" by 42% of the families, "neutral" by 38% and "unfriendly" or "very unfriendly" by 20%. In the first two years of living in the community the adjustment to the new residences and people living there went smoothly for most retarded persons. However, while 45% liked some of the people they lived with, 81% also said they didn't like some of the new residents. While about one-third of the families reported some stress in dealing with family relations, nearly all of the retarded preferred living outside of the institution.

What were their weekday activities? All, but 11% who stayed at home, were either in school or work or a day program of some type. Of those who worked, 25% were in competitive employment, while the other 75% were in a sheltered workshop, rehabilitation, or job training centers. This varied by level of retardation: 30% of the mildly retarded, 24% of the moderately retarded, but only 5% of the severely retarded were in competitive or regular employment. Those who worked averaged about 30 hours a week in unskilled and semi-skilled jobs. Most of them found satisfaction in their work but some didn't like their low pay or difficulties in the job with other workers and there was a shortage of jobs outside of sheltered workshops where many would have preferred to work.

What of their social and leisure activities? As Gollay et al(1978, 93) observe, "It is hard to determine which standards should be used to assess the quality of mentally retarded people's social experiences. Should we compare their experiences to those of the so called normal population?" The leisure activities of the study group are quite similar to those of normal people. The vast majority of them watch TV and listened to radio(98%), went shopping or did errands(85%), attended movies (83%), took vacations(81%), went to parties(75%), visited friends(72%), went to church(71%), played sports(70%), engaged in hobbies(63%), and attended sporting events(58%). However, some of these events were engaged in less frequently than we might expect. Their families or supervisory staff felt that 21% of them did not manage romantic relationships very well, 14% and 24% respectively felt social relationships were a "big problem" or "somewhat a problem," while 11% and 27% respectively felt loneliness was a "big problem" or "somewhat a problem." There was much variation in the social-recreational lives of the persons studied. Some had rich social lives and had adjusted well while others were lonely and isolated from many activities. Gollay et al(1984, 94) conclude in this regard that "the opportunities for social experiences and for establishing social relationships appear to be inadequate for many retarded people living in the community."

Another question the study authors asked was what services they got. Forty percent did not receive an institutional follow-up but 97% had case managers who helped them secure needed services while 74% had relatives and friends who aided in adjustment to the outside world. About three quarters of them got nearly all of the services they needed but 17% did not receive the speech therapy they needed, 26% of their families did not get the training and support services they needed and wanted prior to release, and around 7% of the released persons experienced difficulty in getting other services they needed. All but a few percent of them were getting training in a variety of daily living skills. Overall, the released persons adjusted well to community life. The biggest problems they faced, in they and their parents' views, were finding and keeping jobs, loneliness, behavior problems and getting some services. But the "biggest problems" were so for only around 10 to 20% of the mentally retarded.

Of the 440 persons studied in this research, 58 or 13% returned to the institution. While there were many variations in the characteristics of those who returned to institutional life, the authors found six characteristics that were tendencies among those who returned: (1)they tended to have more behavioral or psychological problems such as getting along with other people at work and where they lived, being lonely, engaging in socially unacceptable behavior and getting into trouble with the law; (2)they were more likely to live with foster families than other residential settings; (3)they participated in fewer community activities such as structured day programs or organized leisure activities; (4)they tended to have more unmet needs for services and training, especially unmet medical needs; (5)they tended to rely more on continued institutional support such as receiving medical treatment and case management services from the institution where they had been;

241

and (6)they expressed less satisfaction with living in the community and in the residence where they lived and both they and their families rated themselves as adjusting less well than those who remained in the community.

The Bercovici Study of Barriers to Normalization

In *Barriers to Normalization: The Restrictive Management of Retarded Persons*, Sylvia Bercovici(1983) reports on a research project that had two phases. In the first, exploratory, phase carried out in 1973 to 1975, 40 California residential facilities for the retarded were studied using ethnographic and qualitative research methods. In this phase, 24 group homes, 13 family foster care homes, 2 nursing facilities and one independent living arrangement program were analyzed to see to what extent they provided normalizing living arrangements. Particular attention was given to (1)the physical site and its relation to the community, (2)the practices and attitudes of the private operators of the facilities, and (3)the behavior of the residents with regard to supervisory practices involving rigidity of routine, block treatment, depersonalization, and social distance. Of the 40 facilities, 8(20%) were evaluated as providing "normalized" environments, 22(55%) were described as having "custodial" environments, and 10(25%) as falling between these two extremes or having "maintaining" environments.

In the second phase of the study, lasting from 1976 to 1979, seven residential facilities were studied more intensely in order to "describe and analyze management practices found in residential settings and to determine how they affect clients' adaptation to the larger community"(Bercovici, 1983, 59). The researchers used in-depth interviews with staff, family, and clients, extensive observation, videotapes, and letters and diaries to put together an ethnographic picture of privately operated group homes. California is one of the states that has opted for private care, largely for profit, rather than public or a mix of private and public providers. The facilities ranged in size from 8 residents to 120 residents whose retarded occupants had a mean age of 36 with a range from 21 to 68. Most had been in state hospitals, some more than 20 years, and now averaged 5 years in a CRF. While 20% of the residential programs had normalizing management practices, 55% did not but rather had custodial practices which acted as barriers to normalization.

In the next few paragraphs we will emphasize and give attention to the practices Bercovici found in some of the facilities that act as barriers to normalization in community residential facilities. At some points we will contrast this with normalizing practices found in a minority of facilities.

1. Physical characteristics of the houses and neighborhoods that act as barriers to normalization. Some of the facilities had an "institutional appearance" with signs on them, fences surrounding them and were rather shabbily furnished and maintained. Some of the occupants shared rooms with others and had little space they could personally call theirs where they could keep things of significance to them. Some were located in predominantly commercial areas which had better access to shopping and restaurants but which were seen as "bad neighborhoods" that were perceived by many as dangerous to venture into. Some of the facilities were isolated from normal residential neighborhoods because of zoning prohibitions against residences containing more than six persons. But for-profit operators sometimes went to lower cost housing in low rent, high minority-concentration, commercial neighborhoods in order to maximize profits. This isolation was also contributed to by neighborhood residents who stigmatized the residents as a "surplus" or unwanted population.

2. Facility management and staff practices of rigid routines block treatment, depersonalization, social distancing, and mortification practices were barriers to normalization and integration. These practices did not occur at all facilities but were common practices. Some programs had rigid rules that said a resident could not leave the grounds of a home alone or with other residents if unaccompanied by a staff member although some were capable of doing so without danger to themselves or others. Some programs barred residents from kitchens or staff rooms. Block treatment in the forms of queuing up for baths, meals, and organized group walks was not an uncommon practice. Depersonalization was a common practice in some facilities. Most residents lacked privacy because they had no locks on their doors and staff members entered their rooms at will without knocking. In some places, residents could not speak to the staff or manager unless spoken to

first, could not make private calls, had their mail censored, and were not allowed to speak to the research investigator unless the manager was present to monitor and clarify anything that they said. Social distance was observed in some settings where the staff and residents ate apart, did not engage in common activities such as watching TV, and where the residents had to address the staff as "Miss," "Mr." or "Mrs." but in turn were referred to by their first or last names or nicknames.

Mortification or social degradation practices were observed at some facilities. For example, the researcher reports that one manager not only talked about one of the residents in his presence but reported his limitations and bad behavior, such as the theft of books from a library, to the investigator. It was not unusual for this residence manager to berate clients in front of other clients or visitors. He would chide them on their "childish" purchases, evaluate their work as of poor quality, or denigrate their limitations in front of others.

3. A barrier to normalization existed in certain management practices to reduce the risk of losing clients. Private facility operators, especially those operating for profit, wanted to have a stable client population. To lose a client, either back to an institution or to a less restrictive residential program, was a threat to income and possibly a threat to the routinization of work if a new client had to be trained to be compliant with the facility's daily routines and require minimal staff time in management.

Facility managers generally wanted to do several things simultaneously--present a "front" to the public or outside case managers that the clients were being habilitated at the same time that they wanted to maximize profits. Generally they used a cost efficiency model to maximize return. This involved (1)hiring around minimum wage staff who, with few skills, were less likely to be occupationally mobile, (2)minimizing the number of staff needed by using custodial practices which minimize individual attention by utilizing block treatment, rigid routines and authoritative commands, (3)closely monitoring client behavior in order to prevent time-consuming problem solving processes when clients didn't behave, (4)using client labor for many tasks to be done around the facility, which is peonage unless the work is part of their habilitation plan, (5)carefully controlling expenditures for food, fringe benefits, household supplies and equipment, and recreational outings, and (6) trying to minimize client contacts with outsiders in order to control the flow of information and observations which might jeopardize their license. But at the same time, they try to manage impressions about residents to outsiders to show they are doing things for clients or that the clients are making progress. This often involved using two different themes. First, for lower functioning clients, they often emphasize how much progress has been made by saying, "you should have seen him when he first came out of the hospital." But second, for higher functioning clients who might be lost to a less restrictive facility, they usually emphasized their disabilities and character defects. "He is not really as competent as he appears" is a way to maintain the client in the same environment. Another way to manage a CRF efficiently is to minimize contacts between residents and/or managers and "outsiders" whether they be friends, families or agency personnel. Some managers restricted phone calls and visiting hours and intimidated clients to the effect that if they complained about the conditions they lived under their freedoms could be even more circumscribed and their life conditions worsened. Under these conditions client dependency rather than autonomy is fostered because residents often learn that if they squeal on bad staff practices some form of retaliation may follow. Thus, one way to reduce the risks of losing clients is not to allow them to have much freedom to learn independence skills. At the same time, by controlling their behavior closely they minimize staff efforts which also maximizes profits.

4. Isolating factors existed in the system of services provided to retarded residents. Although normalization and integration are ideals, Bercovici argues that the "system" or total program has practices built into it which act as barriers to normalization. Some evidence for this comes in the following forms: (1)Retarded persons living in CRFs have few meaningful contacts in the community outside of their family. Their daytime activities and residential lives are spent with other retarded people. (2)Most of the clients know they are retarded and know they live somewhat differently than others for most of their contacts are with people like themselves. Bercovici(1983, 150) reports that many of the residents wanted to live in the "outside" world of "normal people" but,

were either not permitted to, were discouraged from, or were not shown how to go out into the community beyond the facility to make use of the resources available to ordinary persons to establish relationships with anyone outside of their residence or workshop.

(3)The subjects of the study had been conditioned to be studied, managed, and treated differently. The assessment practices used in the mental retardation system of services turns persons into objects by removing the personal views of both the assessor and the client in Bercovici's view. It focuses on checklist deficiencies rather than in trying to make situational assessments of why clients act the way they do. The subjects lead "fishbowl lives" who are subject to constant surveillance and control by a collaborative network of nonretarded service providers. Clients know feedback occurs among caregivers and they must be careful in what they say and do. Thus, even in smaller CRFs, clients can become passive people whose lives are managed by a system with custodial practices. Bercovici(1983, 157) says,

> Although the deinstitutionalized mentally retarded persons in the study were ostensibly in the community, the research discovered that, in fact, they were quite isolated from the larger society and had very little familiarity with it. As a result of this isolation and lack of experience, many of these individuals exhibited institutional behaviors years after hospital release and lacked the adaptive skills necessary for a more independent existence. Furthermore, a number of the more communicative informants spontaneously expressed their realization of this situation, perceiving themselves to be on the "inside" while "normal" people were on the "outside." These individuals in community placement came to be seen as a hidden population.

246

The *On My Own* Study

Andere Halpern, Daniel Close, and Debra Nelson in *On My Own: The Impact of Semi-Independent Living Programs for Adults with Mental Retardation*(1986) focused their study solely on persons who were living in "semi-independent living programs"(SILPs). They interviewed 339 clients in 34 different residential programs in 4 states(California, Colorado, Oregon, and Washington) in the first round of interviews in 1981 and 1982. In the second round of interviews about 8 months later they reinterviewed 257 of the same clients in SILPs. They also interviewed SILP administrators, gathered other data about the clients, and carried out a number of observations.

The SILP program is for relatively high functioning clients. Only 17% of their respondents had IQs below 55, while 52% had IQs between 56 and 70 and 31% over 70. As a group the 339 clients had an average 68% score in independent function while only a few scored low on an inappropriate behavior scale. Sixty-four percent of the clients had chronic health problems. Forty-eight percent of the clients were male. Two-thirds of the clients were between 21 and 30 years of age but ranged from 18 to 59.

In the Halpern, Close and Nelson study in 4 western states, the quality of the housing varied substantially, but ranged from very good to poor. Most of it was good. Ninety percent lived in apartments. A total of 76% lived in an apartment in an integrated facility while 14% lived in apartments with a subsection or cluster of apartments for people with disabilities. Seven percent lived in homes or duplexes, 3% in mobile homes and none in boarding homes. Only 24% lived alone while 76% had roommates. Most of those with roommates had only one(56%), while 18% had two or more roommates. While a majority of SILP clients were satisfied with their housing, one-half lived with roommates they did not choose but were assigned to them by SILP program administrators due to economic necessity or the lack of SILP residences when they were needed. Some SILP residents didn't like their assigned roommates and preferred either living alone or with a roommate of their choice.

In the Halpern study three-fourths of the residents lived in housing units that were relatively clean and free of food odors by interviewer estimates; and 90% of the clients

247

were satisfied with the furniture and decoration of their apartments. At the same time one-fourth had poor housekeeping skills that resulted in dirty, smelly apartments. In some studies the quality of the neighborhoods has not been very high for some people in semi-independent living programs. But the research staff for the Halpern study found nearly all the residents living in neighborhoods where the buildings and yards were well maintained and clean, building vacancy was low in the area, and the neighborhoods were primarily zoned residential rather than commercial.

An important factor in housing and community satisfaction is access to services. In the Halpern study only 8% of the clients in SILP programs in 4 states were licensed to drive. Thus an urban environment close to generic services is important for community life satisfaction. Over 80% of the SILP clients said they had easy access to stores, laundries, restaurants and drugstores. Only 54% had easy access to a doctor or medical facility. Thirty percent of the residents said it usually took too long to get to places they wanted to visit and 65% wished they had other modes of travel than the ones they used most frequently--walking or riding a bus.

Another factor in neighborhood quality of life is clients' safety from physical, social and economic abuse. The Halpern interviewers asked clients if they had experienced three major abuses(robbery, beating, sexual assault) in the last six months in both rounds of interviews six months apart. Twelve percent of the clients reported being robbed in round 1 interviews and 11% in round 2. Six percent and 4% reported beatings at the two interviews. Alleged sexual assaults dropped from 21% in round 1 interviews to 5% in round 2 interviews. Three forms of "minor abuse" were more prevalent at both rounds of interviews. Embarrassment/teasing was reported by 56% and 21% of the clients in the two interviews, followed by 32% and 17% reporting loss of money through unpaid loans at two points in time, and 31% and later 15% reported threats and harassment.

One of the interesting findings in this study was the low rates of deviant behavior found in the SILP residents. Only 1.7% of them had been arrested in comparison to 5% of the general population. Only 3.5% had been involved in crime compared to 6% for the general population. And in

248

comparison to the general population, they had lower use rates of alcohol, cigarettes, and marijuana.

During the study period, 5% of the clients moved out of SILP to more restrictive residential environments including a group home and foster home. Most of these moves were triggered by a decline in their health due to poor nutrition or poor medication management or behavior problems.

Family and friend contacts were made with 95% of the SILP residents. Sixty-five percent reported at least weekly phone contacts with their mother while weekly family visits were reported by 27% and another 32% saw their parents or relatives at least monthly with the remaining 41% seeing their parents or siblings less frequently. Over three-quarters of the SILP residents reported getting some type of assistance from their parents. Generally, contacts with the family were supportive of normalizing experiences. About half of the SILP clients had "benefactors," that is persons who gave them help on an ongoing basis and when needed without paying them. About one-half of the benefactors for these people were their friends and the other half were parents.

Friendships play a critical role in social support for all people including the mentally retarded. While 81% of the SILP residents had two or more close friends and 71% reported they had enough friends, 77% reported they would like to have more contacts with their friends inasmuch as 65% reported visiting their friends weekly with 35% only seeing them monthly or less. Their friends were often their benefactors who gave them advice, spent leisure time with them, assisted them financially or in finding jobs or in moving. SILP residents engaged in a variety of leisure activities which Halpern, Close and Nelson(1986, 114) describe as "virtually no different from those of most individuals in this country." Eighty-six percent of their sample experienced satisfaction with their leisure lives.

Only 12% of the sample was married and less than half of these people had children. But the majority of the SILP clients had some type of romantic relationship and most of these persons had been exposed to sex education. About one-quarter had been sterilized(41% involuntarily) and another quarter of them used some type of birth control. Only 5% appeared to be sexually active without some means of protection.

Community integration is one measure of normalization for it indicates the amount of time handicapped people spend with nonhandicapped people. In this study the investigators found that SILP clients spent around 54% of their waking hours with other handicapped clients, about 22% with nonhandicapped people, about 20% alone and about 6% with their family. Perhaps this is not surprising given the facts of their residential living program and that 37% of them worked in workshops for the handicapped.

SILPs offer a variety of services to clients, although in the 34 resident programs covered in this research there was substantial variability in the services offered. In many instances other agencies offered services that were needed. The services offered by either SILP or other agencies included skill training, nutrition counseling, sex education, crisis intervention, transportation, advocacy services, case management, sheltered work, industrial work stations, medical care, mental health, behavior management, job placement, specialized therapies, dental care, and community college classes.

Client satisfaction with the 16 services listed above was fairly high. Client dissatisfaction over 20% of the time was found in only three areas: 33% wanted improvement in mental health services, 37% in sheltered work, and 59% in job placement.

Problems in SILP programs do appear to exist although client satisfaction and various outcome measures indicate they are working fairly well given their newness. Semi-independent living programs have evolved rather recently. Only 17% of the SILPs in existence nationally in 1982 were open in 1973. One of the serious problems that many SILP programs experience is high staff turnover ranging from 50% to 100% annually and averaging 80% nationally.   The deleterious consequences of high staff turnover include: (1)a lack of continuity, (2)instability in the services rendered, and (3)higher costs associated with the constant need to recruit and train new staff. The reasons for high staff turnover in SILPs and other CRF programs are (1)low pay--often around the minimum wage, (2)demanding jobs that receive little training, (3)poor job screening, and (4)little opportunity for upward mobility. The SILP programs studied by Halpern, Close, and Nelson(1986), however, experienced only a 42% annual turnover rate in spite of low wages and only about 5 days of training for direct service staff.

This review of three major studies on the impact of deinstitutionalization shows a variety of outcomes and patterns of adjustment. Other studies(Willer & Intagliata, 1984; Bell, Schoenrock & Bensberg, 1981; Mayeda & Sutter, 1981; Lei, Nihira, Sheehy & Meyers, 1981; Schalock & Lilley, 1986) also show a variety of benefits and gains as well as deficiencies in how different types of residential programs impact on heterogeneous retarded people. It is impossible at this time to get a comprehensive picture of residential programming inasmuch as several hundred thousand retarded residents live in around 15,000 community residential programs operated under variable standards by the fifty states. Under these conditions we might expect substantial variation in the quality of the programs and the quality of lives of people in them.

The Oregon Study of Deinstitutionalization

A study was carried out in Oregon in 1988 to determine the effect of deinstitutionalization upon the lives of 327 persons released from its largest institution for the mentally retarded--Fairview Training Center(Horner, et al, 1988). The releases took place between 1983 and 1986. The average age of releasees was 34 while their average length of stay had been 13 years. About 47% of those released were either severely or profoundly retarded. Three effects studied were (1)changes in lifestyle of releasees, (2)changes in family reactions to their release, and (3)residual changes in Fairview Training Center's operation.

First, several changes in the lifestyles of those released compared to those who remained in the institution were that (1)while releasees had about the same number of activities as those at the institution, the releasees had more activities in the community; (2)releasees had more variety in the kinds of activities they engaged in, and (3)they had a network of about 12 people they regularly interacted with compared to only 6 for those at Fairview Training Center.

Second, before release, over half of the parents were afraid the release would not benefit their children. However, after release, over 90% of the parents were "pretty satisfied" or "very happy" with the results and 75%

felt their children were happier in community residential facilities.

A third effect was that the reduction of residents at Fairview Training Center allowed it to intensify staffing for the remaining residents and close down undesirable residential units(Horner, et al, 1988).

FUNDING STREAMS FOR RESIDENTIAL CARE

Understanding the funding streams for MR/DD persons is not an easy task. At the same time it is an important task if people working in the system know how it operates and why it often contains disincentives for deinstitutionalizing retarded persons to the least restrictive environment. Copeland and Iversen(1985, 291) contend,

> Current planning and financing services for developmentally disabled persons in the United States is fragmented, it tends to keep important parts of the funding for services "invisible" to planners at federal and state levels of government, it promotes fiscal incentives diametrically opposed to program theory and court decision, and it includes no coherent budget and program strategy. The result is a large, incoherent "nonsystem" of public and private bureaucracies, budgets, and services that is highly resistant to change.

To understand funding streams, we will first review some types and levels of funding for MR/DD persons. First is a distinction between individual and program funding. In individual funding the money goes from some level of government to an individual consumer who meets the criteria for it such as being disabled, poor or sick--often complex and overlapping criteria that may be means tested. Some examples of federal individual funding are transfer payments to individuals entitled to receive them such as Supplemental Security Income, Social Security Disability Insurance, food stamps, regular medical services under Medicaid, and section 8 housing subsidies. States may offer individual funding too such as in state supplements to

252

SSI payments. In contrast, program funding is where the money goes to the provider of some service such as an ICF/MR facility or an adult day care program or a sheltered workshop. Federal monies for such programs usually go to the states which have established a series of state agencies to disburse the funds when the provider agencies have met the various administrative and program requirements to be eligible for funding. In some cases the state may operate the facility itself or funnel the money to independent profit or nonprofit agencies either under contracts to reimburse them for operating the program or on some per diem or per service cost basis.

Secondly, some types of federal program funding require either a percentage or dollar match of state funds, or local funds, or both state and local funds. For example, in Pennsylvania, the federal government pays for about 57% of the costs of operating an institutional ICF/MR and the state pays 43% of this Title XIX(Medicaid) program.

Funding for residential service programs comes from a variety of federal, state and local services through program funding and individual transfer payments. The complex web of funding sources and methods has contained funding disincentives to deinstitutionalization to the least restrictive environment in the past. While these have been reduced with the Medicaid waiver program, they still exist.

One of the assumed operating principles here is that each level of government wants to minimize taxes for the costs of operating MR/DD programs by shifting them to a higher level of government. Thus, local governments want to shift such costs to the state or federal governments while the states usually try to shift them to the federal government because it has greater taxing power. In Pennsylvania, for example, local governments pay virtually no part of the costs of residential care for the mentally retarded.

Table 7.6 estimates sources of funding for Public Residential Facilities and Community Residential Facilities in terms of program and individual funding streams. Before the Medicaid waiver program was introduced in 1981, it was far more cost efficient for the states to operate ICFs/MR than CRFs even though ICFs/MR are both more expensive and more restrictive as a rule. The Medicaid waiver program has reduced the financial disincentives against the more cost efficient and less restrictive CRFs. It

Table 7.6

Sources of Funding for PRFs and CRFs in Pennsylvania

Type of Program	Program Funding		Individual Funding
	Federal	State	(Federal)
Medicaid ICF/MR (PRF or CRF)	57%	43%	---
Medicaid Waiver CRF	57%	43%	SSI, Food Stamps, Section 8 Housing Subsidy, Domicilary Care
Estimated Total Cost Distribution	47%	33%	20%
CRF without Medicaid Waiver	---	100%	SSI, Food Stamps, Section 8 Housing Subsidy, Domicilary Care
Estimated Total Cost Distribution	---	80%	20%

is most cost efficient for the state to operate ICFs/MR, than ICFs/MR under the Medicaid Waiver program and least cost efficient to operate totally state funded CRFs. Furthermore, certain costs here are not quite comparable. Under the last two types of programs, that is CRFs with and without Medicaid Waiver, residents in these types of facilities are still eligible for individual Medicaid medical and dental services. The size of these costs is unknown, but may average about 10% of the total residential costs from which they are excluded in Table 7.6. Individual Medicaid costs are based on a formula reimbursement schedule so that in Pennsylvania about 57% of these costs are borne by the federal government and the remainder by the state.

Table 7.6 covers only the costs associated with residential care. The costs of other services rendered to MR/DD persons include education costs, adult partial hospitalization programs, and the costs associated with vocational training, sheltered employment, and medical care. As Copeland and Iversen(1985) point out, many of these programs have costs that are hidden to legislators and very often people operating different types of service programs. Thus, all the costs associated with services to a particular MR/DD person would be very difficult to assemble and sum because they are hidden in a complex web of multiple program and individual funding streams.

The cost of providing residential care in different types of programs is both substantial and variable. Table 7.7 shows the mean cost per diem per client, as well as other data, for three types of private providers in Pennsylvania. Table 7.7 gives only the average costs of per diem per client for each provider type. However, within each of these provider types there is substantial variation. While the mean per diem costs in Pennsylvania for CLAs was $60.98 in 1982-83, they ranged from $29.30 to $143.80. The mean per diem costs of PLRs(an older term for certain residential facilities serving more youthful and severely retarded clients) was $51.28 but varied from a low of $24.97 a day to $91.30 a day. And the mean per diem in ICFs/MR was $86.49 but varied from $42.67 a day($15,575 annually) to $142.79 a day($52,118 annually)(Poister Associates, 1985).

Why do costs within one state vary so much? In their analysis, Poister Associates(1985) found that about

Table 7.7

Selected Characteristics of Private Providers in Pennsylvania*

Provider Type	N of Programs	Clients per site	Mean Cost per diem per client	% 18 or Younger	% Severe or Profound	% Non-Profit	Mean Staff Per Client
CLA(1)	127	2.8	$60.98	10	28	88	1.1
PLF(2)	34	46.6	51.28	46	59	54	1.1
ICF/MR(3)	29	29.7	86.49	24	75	95	1.5

(1) CLA stands for Community Living Arrangements more popularly known as group homes.

(2) PLF stands for Private Licensed Facility.

(3) ICF/MR stands for Intermediate Care Facilities for the Mentally Retarded.

*Based on self-selected sample of 104 private providers out of 190 operating in Pennsylvania in the 1982-83 Fiscal Year.

Source: Poister Associates(1985).

90% of the cost variation in PLFs, 80% in CLAs, and 66% in ICFs/MR could be explained by a number of variables. The most important was staff/client ratios. That is, as staffing per client increased, so did the per diem costs. Closely related to staff/client ratios were client characteristics. Thus, increasing levels of retardation, young age, and the need for special medical and behavior-shaping treatments correlated positively with both higher costs and higher staff/client ratios. Two less important factors associated with cost were whether employees were unionized and the location of the program. Generally, unionized employees got better pay which raised per diem costs and those programs located in the Philadelphia area where wage rates were apparently higher also had higher per diem costs.

SUMMARY

Deinstitutionalization began in the 1960s and gained momentum in the 1970s and is continuing on into the 1980s. Its goals of integrating retarded persons into more normal residential, educational, and work environments are being slowly achieved as community services are developed. The deinstitutionalization movement is the result of six sociopolitical forces that include the advocacy movement, the critical indictment of large state institutions for the retarded by the media and others, the acceptance of the normalization principle for the retarded in parental, professional and legislative groups, judicial activism by the U.S. court system, legislative and executive actions on behalf of the retarded, and the escalating costs of caring for the retarded in large institutional programs.

We inspect a number of ways to classify residential programs. One classification device looks primarily at their mode of operation and list eight types other than their own natural families and independent living. These following eight types provide residential programs for less than 5% of all mentally retarded people: (1)adoptive homes, (2)foster homes, (3)supervised independent living arrangement, (4)supervised semi-independent living arrangements, (5)boarding homes, (6)personal care homes, (7)group homes, which may vary greatly in size, sponsorship and funding, and (8)nursing homes.

An analysis of the long term trends in large public residential facilities shows the number of persons in them is declining, the number of such facilities has increased but their average size has decreased, staff ratios and public expenditures for them have increased, admission rates to them have gone down, and they are increasingly serving the more severely retarded. An analysis of community residential facilities shows their numbers have increased greatly over the last two decades, that they are serving a greater number and proportion of all retarded people, and their size is decreasing.

The methods and purposes of evaluating the residential settings for retarded persons is reviewed. Particular attention is given to the Revised Child Management Scale, Programme Analysis of Service Systems(PASS), state licensing instruments, and comprehensive evaluations using both quantitative and qualitative techniques. Three comprehensive studies, using somewhat different methods, reveal a variety of outcomes in different types of residential programs. They point to the need for matching client characteristics with residential facilities and the need for monitoring and evaluating programs to assure quality in residential programming.

The complex funding streams for residential care for the mentally retarded is reviewed and distinctions made between program and individual funding. Some funding streams in the past had disincentives for moving mentally retarded persons to the least restrictive environments even though they were often less costly to operate.

Chapter 8

Education of the Mentally Retarded

One of the areas where the greatest change has occurred with regard to the treatment of the mentally retarded
is in the area of education--especially public education.
One of the great benefits of our society is a free public
school education. However, for a long period of time many
of the developmentally disabled, including many who are
mentally retarded, were excluded from this benefit. However, the 1975 passage of Public Law 94-142, The Education for All Handicapped Children Act, has opened up the
right of developmentally disabled persons to a "free and
appropriate" public education that was long denied to many
of them. The law went beyond simply saying they had a
right to education. The education was also to be
"appropriate". And the law specified that one part of this
appropriateness is one that occurs in the "least restrictive
environment" possible. Section 612(5)(B) of Public Law
94-142, according to the U.S. Department of Educa-
tion(1980, 33),

> requires that to the extent appropriate,
> handicapped children be placed with chil-
> dren who are not handicapped. Any special
> classes or other separation should be under-
> taken only when the nature or the severity of
> the handicap renders regular classes unsatis-
> factory even when supplementary services
> are provided.

The implementation of this law has generated
extensive controversy not only as to where and what kind

of education is "appropriate" for various types and levels of handicapping conditions but also as to whom should bear its costs and how it should be implemented given the skills and education that teachers have.

In this chapter the issues surrounding the education of the mentally retarded, particularly the implementation of P.L. 94-142, will be inspected. However, it is important to understand why P.L. 94-142 involved a radical change in the education of the mentally retarded. Thus, we turn first to a brief history of the education of the retarded before the passage of The Education for All Handicapped Children Act.

HISTORICAL PERSPECTIVES ON THE EDUCATION OF THE RETARDED

A quick overview of the history of the education of the mentally retarded shows these developments in sequence: (1)the development of special residential schools for the retarded beginning in 1848 with expansion of the number and size of such special schools among the states continuing up until the mid 1960s; (2)the development and slow expansion of special classes for the Educable Mentally Retarded(EMR) from about 1900 to 1950; (3)the development of some special schools for the Trainable Mentally Retarded(TMR) in the 1950s and 1960s along with a rather rapid expansion of special classes for the EMR in the same period; and (4)the mainstreaming or integration of EMR and some TMR students into regular classrooms and/or "appropriate" educational settings in the 1970s and 1980s.

The Development of Special Residential Schools

The early history of the United States before 1848 records no formal program of education for the mentally retarded. They stayed at home or became residents in almshouses for the poor and incompetent. As late as 1850 it is estimated that 60 percent of the residents of poorhouses were the blind, deaf, insane and mentally retarded(Kirk & Gallagher, 1983).

The first residential schools for the blind, deaf and retarded were begun by a physician, Samuel Gridly Howe,

260

in Massachusetts. The Massachusetts legislature granted Howe $2,500 to open a school for ten mentally retarded students in 1848. As we saw in Chapter 4, the next fifty years was a period of institution building in the United States. Separate but quite similar facilities were built and located primarily in rural areas during this era for both the mentally retarded and insane. The facilities for the retarded provided about the only educational programs available to them. These residential institutions provided for two different needs of American society during this time of heavy immigration and urbanization. First, they provided a viable source of treatment, education and support for persons in need by locating them in largely agricultural colonies where they could be partially self-supporting. Second, they removed deviant persons from sight where they might be a nuisance, neglected, or taken advantage of in an urbanizing society.

The early residential institutions were begun as schools primarily for the mildly but also for some moderately retarded persons. The goal of their founders was to prepare these students for return to their families and communities after the schooling years were over. However, over time the schools were flooded with the more severely retarded whom families and communities felt least capable of handling and providing for. The goal of educating them for self-sufficiency and returning them to their home communities was undermined. Thus, residents accumulated in these institutions and gradually, over time, such schools expanded and their custodial functions predominated over rehabilitative or educational functions. Also, such institutions catering to deviants have historically been underfinanced which subsequently led to understaffing, deprivation and neglect, reaching scandalous levels at times(Kirk & Gallagher, 1983).

The Development of Special Classes for the Mentally Retarded

The second development to affect the educationof the mentally retarded was the initiation and expansion of special classes for them in public schools. The first such class appears to have been started in Rhode Island in 1896. The impetus for such classes appears to have three sources: compulsory school attendance requirements, pressures by parents to place their more mildly retarded children in school since state institutions would or could not accept them, and the development and acceptance of such classes in Germany beginning in 1867. These classes often contained not only the mentally retarded but other "troublemakers" who disrupted normal classes(Westling, 1986).

After the turn of the century the spread of special education classes occurred acrross the country. The development and use of intelligence tests in the first several decades of this century swelled the numbers of students for which special education classes were seen as approrpriate. By 1922 23,252 students were enrolled in special classes. These numbers increased to 75,099 in 1932, 98,416 in 1940 and 113,565 in 1952. Through this time period the persons served in special education classes were almost exclusively the Educable Mentally Retarded(Kirk & Gallagher, 1983).

The Development of Special Schools and the Expansion of Special Classes

In the period from 1950 to 1970 several developments occurred. The first of these was the development of special schools for the Trainable Mentally Retarded and other handicapped persons. Public school programs for TMR students had been quite limited up to 1950. But several events conspired to promote the development of special schools and programs for the handicapped after World War II. These included the return of handicapped veterans from the War, the organization of parents into chapters of the Association of Retarded Children and the growing importance of education in an affluent industrialized society. Federal resources were first used to help rehabilitate handicapped veterans and some of this technology and concern had a spillover effect for the education of handicapped children.

Secondly, many retarded citizens or other handicapped youth were kept at home because they were not sufficiently retarded to be placed in state institutions yet they were sufficiently retarded or multiply handicapped so as to be excluded from many EMR classes. The private sector responded by developing some special classes and special schools for such students. But public pressures mounted for the development of special schools and additional public school classes to educate and train not only EMR but also TMR students. Thus, between 1952 and 1958, the number of mentally retarded in public special schools and classes nearly doubled from 113,565 in 1952 to 213,402 in 1958. A number of new federal financial supports were initiated for special education beginning in 1958 and continuing on so that the number of mentally retarded in public schools and classes increased 230% between 1958 and 1969 when their number reached 703,800(Kirk & Gallagher, 1983; Westling, 1986).

Prior to 1958 there had been no federal financial support for the training of special education teachers or for the support of special education programs in the some 20,000 school districts in the United States. However, beginning in 1958 Congress authorized the first program to train teachers who served mentally retarded children. In 1960, $985,000 was distributed to 16 institutions of higher education and 23 state education agencies for teacher training programs in this area. This funding was continued and expanded under Title III of the Mental Retardation Facilities and Community Mental Health Centers Construction Act of 1963(P.L. 88-164). The passage of the Elementary and Secondary Education Act of 1965, as amended in 1966 and 1967, not only started the Bureau of Education for the Handicapped in the Department of Education, but also required that 15% of the funds under Title III of this act be earmarked for projects involving handicapped children. In 1967 the federal funding for special education state grants for all handicapped children was only $2,425,000 but rose to $11,700,000 in 1968 and $24,500,000 in 1969. And in 1966 the federal government began supporting funding of the education of children located in state institutions for the mentally retarded. In 1966 the size of this funding was $8,400,000 which rose to $13,800,000 in 1969(Braddock, 1987).

Mainstreaming in the 1970s and 1980s

The civil rights movement of the 1960s had a sizable spillover effect on the handicapped rights movement which blossomed in the 1970s. By the late 1960s, special education was receiving heightened attention. The federal government had begun funding teacher training programs and local school district financial support would rapidly accelerate during the 1970s. And both local school districts and state education agencies were adding monies to special education programs for the mentally retarded and developmentally disabled.

In the late 1960s and early 1970s there was considerable controversy over the appropriateness of special education classes. The research evidence was quite mixed as to whether mildly retarded youngsters did better in segregated special education classes or in integrated classes. Some studies, for example Guskin and Spicker(1968), argued the mildly retarded did no better academically in special classes than regular classes. But other studies, Kolstoe(1976) for example, argued that special classes could give more individualized instruction, use special education materials, and utilize teachers specifically trained for teaching the handicapped. Such classes, it was argued, did more than train the students academically, they helped students adjust better. But critics of such classes pointed out that they negatively labeled students and this was harmful to their self-concepts and social adjustment. Furthermore, critics of such classes also pointed out that certain racial and ethnic minorities, principally black and Hispanic students, were disproportionately enrolled in such classes which hinted at discrimination(Kirk & Gallagher, 1983).

However, in addition to research on the academic and social merits of special education for EMR students, two other social forces were at work which were propelling the reconsideration and redirection of the education of the mentally retarded in the 1970s. One of these was the activities of parents in the National Association of Retarded Children(now National Association for Retarded Citizens) which found a strong ally in the federal courts(under the concept of judicial activism). A number of significant court cases were related to the education of the severely and profoundly retarded who had largely been neglected up to this time. In 1971 a federal court ruled in *Wyatt v. Stickney* that institutionalized persons have a right to treatment. In 1972, a federal court ruled in *Pennsylvania Association for Retarded Citizens v. The Commonwealth of Pennsylvania* that a public school education was the right of all citizens including severely and profoundly retarded citizens. Such court test cases followed in a number of states and helped prompt the enactment of state and federal legislation to deal with the education of all handicapped children.

The second force was the passage of federal legislation related to the education of the developmentally disabled. This legislation not only constitutionally defined the right of <u>all</u> developmentally disabled persons to an education but also began some and expanded other funding streams to assist the states in such an endeavor.

Kirk and Gallagher(1983) argue that there were four main reasons why special education classes came under increasing indictment in the 1950s and 1960s which led to an impetus for mainstreaming starting in the 1960s and which subsequently led to congressional and state action in the 1960s and 1970s to support mainstreaming. These four reasons were that: (1)"<u>many children were misclassified as mentally retarded</u>." Some states had vague definitions of mental retardation while others used an IQ score below 80 rather than the AAMD definition of retardation of an IQ score below 70 as the cutoff point for special education. Thus enrollment in special education soared from 87,000 in 1948 to 1,350,000 in 1975. (2)"<u>Many minority children were misclassified as mentally retarded</u>." Minority group children were often given IQ tests in English rather than in their native language. This inappropriate use of intelligence testing was seen as a precursor to dumping disproportionate numbers of "troublesome" minority students in stigmatizing special education programs. (3)"<u>Research on the efficacy of special classes showed few beneficial results</u>." This eroded confidence in the assumption that special teachers and special classes were educationally helpful or appropriate. (4)"<u>Special classes for the mentally retarded became classes for problem children</u>." Because of the changing entrance requirements for admission to special education classes, it was theoretically possible that up to 10% of all students could be admitted to such classes. However, since most schools did not want more than about 2% of their students in such classes, educational politics prevailed where special classes became dumping grounds for the most troublesome students.

We noted earlier in this chapter that in 1958 Congress began funding teacher training programs for special education teachers. In 1966 it began funding the states to carry out education programs in state institutions for the retarded and in 1967 Congress began funding state grants to assist in the education of handicapped children. In 1968

265

Congress amended the Vocational Education Act stipulating that 10% of the funds expended under this state grant program be allocated to programs serving handicapped children. In 1970 Congress passed the Developmental Disabilities and Facilities Construction Act(P.L. 91-517) the key feature of which was that each state would receive a formula grant if it established a coordinated service planning council to include public and private agencies offering welfare, education, public health, mental health and rehabilitation services in the state. In 1972 Congress modified the Economic Opportunity Act by requiring that at least 10% of Head Start's enrollment be composed of handicapped children. The Rehabilitation Act of 1973(P.L. 93-112) contained two things which bolstered support for the retarded: (1)it required that state rehabilitation agencies give priority treatment to the more severely handicapped, and (2)it contained a civil rights provision requiring that qualified handicapped individuals could not be discriminated against by any program receiving federal assistance or by any employer who had contracts with the federal government involving $2,500 or more. But undoubtedly the most important piece of federal legislation came in 1975 with the passage of P.L. 94-142, The Education for All Handicapped Children Act. This act required (1)an appropriate education in the "least restrictive environment," and (2)greatly expanded the federal funding levels made available to the states to assist in the higher costs associated with educating the developmentally disabled. The framers of this legislation intended that by 1982 it would fund 40% of the "excess costs" of educating handicapped children but critics argued that it has only funded about 10% of such costs. In the next ten years, from 1976 to 1985, the federal government's funding for handicapped education greatly expanded. The largest expansion came during the Carter presidency while funding remained relatively stationary during the Reagan presidency beginning in 1981(Braddock, 1987).

Braddock(1987) has provided researchers a valuable service by identifying some 53 federal activities currently operating in the field of mental retardation. In Fiscal Year 1985 the federal government spent an estimated $7,773 billion on all programs for the mentally retarded. Of this total, approximately 6.1% or $476,583,000 went to a variety of education and rehabilitation programs. There

Table 8.1

Estimated Federal Aid to the Education of the Mentally Retarded (in thousands)

Year	Aid to State Schools (1)	Title VIB & pre-school Incentive Grants of PL 94-142 (2)	Title VI, C & F of PL 91-230 (3)	Voca-tion Education Act as Amended	Voca-tional Rehabil-itation Act as Amended	Impact Aid as Amended (4)	Total
1966	8,354		715	463	13,399		22,931
1968	13,865	7,207	1,300	1,542	29,569		53,483
1970	21,664	11,357	5,290	10,704	51,590		100,605
1972	32,929	13,888	8,494	18,950	62,014		136,275
1974	52,500	18,055	14,071	21,152	82,090		187,868
1976	57,633	35,098	17,260	16,025	87,696	4,210	217,922
1978	61,377	87,169	18,125	14,774	94,425	6,482	282,352
1980	60,147	234,696	18,015	20,800	95,891	6,256	439,805
1982	62,147	233,997	13,549	23,426	106,932	6,629	447,139
1985	59,166	242,222	16,682	24,311	124,536	9,666	476,583

267

Table 8.1

Estimated Federal Aid to the Education of the Mentally Retarded

(in thousands)

(continued)

Notes:

(1) Based on PL 89-313, an amendment to Title I of the Elementary and Secondary Education Act(ESEA) of 1965.

(2) Title VIB of PL 94-142 were special education state grants.

(3) PL 91-230 amended the 1965 ESEA. There are five separate funding sources which have been collapsed into one in this table. The five funding streams are: (1)regional resource centers, (2)early childhood projects, (3)severely handicapped retarded, (4)deaf-blind centers over half of whose clients are mentally retarded, and (5)instructional media programs. (4)Impact aid goes to school districts with at least 3% of their enrollment or 400 students from a federal installation such as an Indian reservation or military base families at a rate of 150% of normal reimbursement if the student is handicapped.

Source: Based on Braddock(1987) who has made estimates of total MR/DD funding that is allocated for the education of just the mentally retarded.

has been a prodigious increase in federal funding for all MR/DD services and activities. In 1963 total federal funding for all MR/DD services and activities was under one billion dollars, twenty-two years later in 1985 it was approaching eight billion dollars. Perhaps a better indicator of our national commitment to MR/DD programs is the growing proportion of our federal budget allowance to all MR/DD activities. In 1950 roughly .01% of the federal budget was for MR/DD activities, but by 1960 that had grown to .1%, to about .35% in 1970, .56% in 1975 and .82% in 1985.

Table 8.1 illustrates the growth of the federal commitment to the education of the mentally retarded from 1966 to 1985. In 1966, $22,931,000 was spent in aid to the states and public schools. By 1976 when new programs had been added and other funding streams increased, the estimated total federal contribution to education of the retarded had increased to $187,868,000--a 719% increase. By 1985 it had more than doubled again to $476,583,000. And the federal contribution to the education of the retarded probably constitutes no more than 10% of the "excess" public costs with the remainder coming from local school districts and the states. Table 8.1 does not include teacher training costs for those serving the mentally retarded but only the main federal programs that assist in the costs of their education.

AN APPROPRIATE EDUCATION IN THE LEAST RESTRICTIVE ENVIRONMENT

Legislative Base

The legislative base which mandates a free, appropriate public education in the least restrictive environment is P.L. 94-142, The Education for All Handicapped Children Act of 1975. Each state must develop a statewide plan that is in compliance with this law which requires a comprehensive system of special education practices that is to be implemented statewide and therefore nationally. By this method Congress established a minimum standard for educating handicapped children throughout the country.

269

The federal categories of who were handicapped children included those who were mentally retarded, deaf and hard of hearing, visually handicapped, speech impaired, orthopedically impaired, seriously emotionally disturbed, those with other health problems, the multi-handicapped and those having specific learning disabilities(Lerner, Dawson & Horvath, 1980).

Section 504 of the Vocational Rehabilitation Act of 1973(P.L. 93-112) is similar to P.L. 94-142 in that it too requires "equal program accessibility" for handicapped persons being served by agencies receiving federal funds.

Key Requirements of P.L. 94-142

The Education for All Handicapped Children Act outlines a comprehensive series of practices and procedures for the education of the handicapped. The following five components are part of those requirements with the first one probably being the most important component.

Development of an Individual Education Program. Each handicapped child is to have developed within thirty days of the date he is determined to be handicapped an Individualized Education Program or IEP. An IEP is a written statement that involves an evaluation of the student's strengths and deficiencies that includes a plan for the most appropriate placement of the student, describes the educational objectives for the child, and specifies the teaching methodology. The school and the state must review each student's IEP periodically but no less than annually. The IEP is a management tool to help insure that the education designed for each handicapped child is appropriate to their special needs and that the services are actually delivered and periodically revised as the child changes.

P.L. 94-142 also specifies who is to be at the IEP planning meeting. The persons involved in this formal IEP planning meeting are: (1)a representative of the public educational agency who is qualified to provide and/or supervise special education other than the child's teacher, (2)the child's teacher, (3)one or both parents, (4)the child, if appropriate, and (5)other individuals at the discretion of the parents or educational agency. According to Lerner, Dawson and Horvath(1980), there are six stages in developing the IEP only the fourth of which is the formal IEP

270

planning meeting. Stage I is the referral when a student is believed by some party, such as a teacher, parents or supervisor, to be handicapped. Stage II involves the appointment of a coordinator to determine who is going to do the evaluation, what tests and observations need to be undertaken and the timing of these. Stage III involves evaluating the child by a multidisciplinary evaluation team as regards the child's health, developmental progress as compared to peers of the same age, and identifying particular strengths and weakness in a number of areas such as reading, writing and listening skills, speaking skills, self-help skills, etc. Stage IV is the planning meeting where the child's needs are reviewed and an individualized educational program developed. Stage V is the implementation of the program where particular adjustments to the program may need to be made. Stage VI involves a review of progress toward meeting the objectives of the IEP and a reformulation of the IEP, if necessary, during the year but no less than annually.

Parent Participation. P.L. 94-142 attempts to involve parents in their child's education. The law requires that steps be taken to notify and involve parents in the development of the IEP. If parents are unwilling or unable to attend, records must be kept to indicate their participation was encouraged and that the parents were kept informed about the results of the planning meeting, annual reviews and that efforts are made to insure that parents understand the proceedings of such meetings(Lerner, Dawson & Horvath, 1980).

The Content of the IEP. The legal minimum standards for what is to be included in a written IEP are (1)a statement on the child's present levels of performance; (2)a statement on both short term educational objectives as well as annual goals; (3)a statement specifying the range of educational services that will be provided to the child and where these will be provided; (4)the beginning date and expected duration of the educational services; and (5)the schedules for evaluating and the criteria to be used on whether the instructional objectives are being met(Lerner, Dawson & Horvath, 1980).

Procedural Safeguards. P.L. 94-142 contains four types of procedural safeguard regulations to protect the rights of handicapped children(Lerner, Dawson & Horvath, 1980). The first of these procedural safeguards are due

271

process safeguards for insuring that the child, parents and schools are each afforded their rights under the law. These due process safeguards include: (1)the right of parents to see all of their child's educational records; (2)the right of parents to be duly notified about any evaluation of their child, any change in the child's designation or placement and the options considered but rejected, the evaluative data used with such communication given in their native language and done in such a way as to be understandable to them. The parents are also to have explained to them the procedural safeguards contained in P.L. 94-142; (3)the parent's consent must be obtained before carrying out either a preplacement evaluation or the initial placement of the child in any special education program; (4)either the school or parents may request an impartial hearing if they disagree about evaluations or placement with such hearing appealable to the state education agency and then to civil law if unresolvable by the state education agency; (5)surrogate parents are to be appointed by the public agency to the handicapped child in cases where parents cannot be located; and (6)parents have a right to request an independent evaluation if they are dissatisfied by the school's evaluation with the provision that the agency must pay for this evaluation if a due process hearing has determined that the agency's evaluation of the child was inappropriate.

The second type of procedural safeguards are protection in evaluation procedures to insure that the child is fairly and fully evaluated before he is placed in a special education program. These safeguards require that (1)tests be administered in the child's native language or mode of communication if at all feasible; (2)tests be validated for the assessment purposes for which they are used; (3)the evaluator is appropriately trained in using the methods he does; (4)multiple assessment techniques be used by a multidisciplinary evaluation team; (5)if a child has impaired manual, speaking or sensory skills, the test results measure the child's true skills and not his impaired abilities only.

The third type of procedural safeguards requires that each public agency develop written procedures to be made available as public documents about the confidentiality of information collected on handicapped students. Each agency must develop confidentiality regulations on who has the right to see and communicate information about handicapped children, their parents, school decisions,

272

and when it is necessary to destroy or obscure personally identifiable information.

The fourth area of procedural safeguards are those involved with placing the child in the least restrictive environment. This provision requires that to the maximum extent appropriate handicapped children are to be integrated into regular classrooms and regular schools. However, complex educational judgments are involved in determining what type(s) of educational placements will be most appropriate for a given child.

P.L. 94-142 does not use the term mainstreaming even though it is used by many educators almost synonymously with an appropriate education in the least restrictive environment. According to the Council for Exceptional Children(1975), mainstreaming involves: (1)determining the educational needs of each child rather than relying on diagnostic labels; (2)creating educational alternatives that will allow general teachers to serve children who have learning or adjustment problems in the same classrooms as other children; (3)uniting the skills of special and general education so that all children have equal educational opportunities, and (4)providing children the most appropriate eduction in light of their needs in the least restrictive setting possible. The Council for Exceptional Children points out that mainstreaming does not: (1)involve returning all exceptional children from special classes to regular classes, (2)permit putting exceptional children into regular classes without the special support services they need, (3)ignore the needs of some handicapped children for specialized programs that may be providable in regular public schools, or (4)mean that educating handicapped students in regular schools and/or classes will be less expensive than teaching them in self-contained special education classes.

Alternative Placements for handicapped students have been developed conceptually and practically. M. C. Reynolds(1962) has developed a hierarchy of services and placements for special need students that offer a contiuum of instructional services at one or more locations. The list of alternative placements given below range from the least restrictive to the most restrictive settings in that order:

1. The Regular Classroom. In this plan a mildly retarded child is fully integrated into a regular classroom

with nonretarded classmates. At the same time his regular teacher may use some special instructional materials, equipment or methods with the child.

2. The Regular Classroom with Consultative Services. The retarded child remains in an integrated class with the same teacher in each class. However, this teacher may get consultation from a specialist to meet the child's special needs.

3. Itinerant Instruction in the Regular Classroom. In this plan a special itinerant teacher may spend some time each day or week using special instructional materials or methods with the handicapped student.

4. Resource Room Instructional Support. This popular and widely used model involves the retarded student leaving his regular classroom for a brief period each day to go to a resource room where he receives special instruction in one or more specific areas such as math, reading, geography or science. A special teacher occupies the resource room but coordinates her instructional areas and activities with those of the regular classroom teacher who retains primary control. A number of advantages are seen as stemming from this fourth plan including: (1)the child spends most of his time in the regular classroom; (2)children can be served in it without being labeled or categorized, (3)more appropriate instructional techniques can be used in content areas where the child is having problems, (4)it can provide preventive services to children who might develop worse problems in the future; (5)it can serve more children than a self-contained special education room and can allow for flexible entrances and exits, (6)the special consultative teacher can provide diagnostic, prescriptive and consultative services to others(Reger, 1973; Westling, 1986). However, some critics of the resource room program suggest it is not adequate to the comprehensive developmental life skill needs of the mildly retarded but is more relevant to the remedial or specific needs of persons with other learning disabilities(Gresham, 1982).

5. Part-time Special Class. This plan places a child in a special class for part, perhaps half, of the day. The teacher in this class is responsible for the student's main academic curriculum. Here the content and goals of the special part-time education class is more oriented to developing lifetime social skills and prevocational training. But for part of the day the child will be integrated with

274

normal children in other classes that are less academic in content such as art, music, physical education, and home economics.

6. Full-time Special Class. In this plan retarded students spend their entire school day in a special class usually with the same teacher at least at the elementary school level. Special education classes are integrated only in the sense of being in the same school. Such classes are more restrictive but may be the most appropriate for some mildly and many moderately retarded children who otherwise would lag behind and perhaps cause problems if they were integrated with other students in regular classes.

7. Special Schools. A more restrictive educational environment is one provided in a special nonresidential school. Such schools primarily serve the moderately and severely retarded and even some profoundly retarded students in recent years. These schools have curriculums designed for the functional and basic developmental needs of their students. The students in such schools are also more likely to include those with multiple handicaps that include physical, emotional and mental problems. The physical layout of such schools may be substantially different than regular schools with greater access to bathrooms, adaptive physical education equipment and a range of classroom sizes to accommodate a variety of instructional settings from individual tutoring to large classes.

8. Residential Institutions. While a lower proportion of all retarded students are now housed at residential institutions than formerly, such institutions still are used to provide for the total life needs of the severely and profoundly retarded or the multiply handicapped with less severe levels of retardation. All persons of school age retain a legal right to a free and appropriate public school education. While some students from such residential campuses may be transported to public or private schools, most such institutions offer habilitation and educational programs on their own grounds. The types of programs offered are those seen as appropriate for the developmental needs of their students. These range from language and speech training, behavior management, motor training, self-help training and self-feeding and toileting, to somewhat more formal educational programs. Some residential institutions may also be the setting for special school pro-

grams for students who live elsewhere but are transported there for educational programming.

This continuum of placement possibilities points to the need for thorough and ongoing diagnostic evaluation of students to place them in the educational setting most appropriate for their academic and social growth. Ideally, students should be placed in the most normal and least restrictive environments as possible. Over time, with any given student, it may be possible to move them to a less restrictive environment. But, depending on ongoing evaluations of student performance, it may be necessary and most educationally appropriate to move them to a more restrictive setting.

Personnel Development. The fifth and last key component of P.L. 94-142 was that each state assess its personnel needs for special education and then design and implement a comprehensive program of educational personnel development. State agencies were to coordinate such planning with local school districts, private schools, colleges and universities, advocacy and other related organizations(Lerner, Dawson & Horvath, 1980).

The federal government has assisted in the cost of training special educational personnel since 1960. After the first four years when about $985,000 was allocated annually for training the teachers of the mentally retarded, approximately $3 million has been allocated annually for the education of persons serving the mentally retarded and about another $6 million annually for teacher training for those serving all other forms of developmental disabilities(Braddock, 1987).

INFANT AND PRESCHOOL INTERVENTION PROGRAMS

Infant stimulation programs cover the years 0 to 2 while preschool programs cover the age period of 2 to 6.

General Objectives of Early Intervention Programs

The education of the retarded should begin early as it does for other children. Three general objectives of such programs are (1)to maximize age-related development skills in the infant and preschool years; (2)to assist the child's family members in understanding the nature of the handicap and the roles they may take in developing skills in the retarded child; and (3)to prepare the child to participate fully in the everyday world which includes both handicapped and nonhandicapped persons(Baroff, 1986). Galloway and Chandler(1980) include in this third goal the subgoal of "stigma reduction/removal." Some retarded children's differences are visible--head sizes and shapes that are different, unusual gaits, an absence of smiling, pica(eating nonedible things), or the use of visible protheses. Such difference may be perceived as stigmata--characteristics that reduce their worth as normal humans. Such differences will influence how people respond to the child and in turn how the child responds to people and the ways in which he develops his own self-concept. The goal of stigma reduction/removal is to work on eliminating or reducing the visible physical or behavioral differences insofar as possible as well as to change public attitudes toward greater acceptance of those who are different.

The developmental tasks of early childhood are to develop competencies in self-help skills(toileting, feeding, and dressing), cognitive skills, functional communication skills, gross and fine motor skills, and social interaction skills. The early identification of children who are retarded enables caretakers to give them special stimulation to develop competencies in all the above listed skill areas. Sensory stimulation and specific skill training has the goal of accelerating development when the child has been assessed as likely to have delayed development or when the delay is already noticeable. Early recognition and treatment of motor problems that interfere with feeding and movement in infancy are important. And the quality of parent-infant interaction may be vitally important in preventing socially induced "iatrogenic" retardation(Baroff, 1986).

Preschool Program Models

Three models have been developed for infant and early childhood stimulation programs: (1)home-based programs, (2)center-based programs, and (3)a combination of these two in home-and-center-based programs. In the home-based program a teacher comes into the home primarily to teach the parents how to assess their child's behaviors and develop instructional objectives and teach skills to the parents so that they may reach these objectives. In the Portage project, developed in Wisconsin to serve preschool children in rural areas where no center-based program existed, teachers visited homes of preschoolers weekly to assist and train parents for early childhood stimulation. In center-based programs, preschool educational specialists do the assessment and establish the stimulation activities to work toward enhancing developmental skills. In the mixed programs that combine center and home-based locations and personnel, children spend some time in a day-care center program. And their parents attend some of these sessions to learn assessment and teaching techniques and behavior modification procedures. The parents are encouraged and expected to continue these activities at home. Home-based programs are particularly suitable and more extensively used for infants while center-based and home-and-center-based programs are more likely to be used during the preschool ages of 2-6(Baroff, 1986; Galloway & Chandler, 1980).

Financial Support of Preschool Programs

The federal government has been supporting preschool intervention programs for over 19 years starting in the late 1960s. Approximately 25 new model programs have been funded each year by Special Education Programs. These programs have been geographically disbursed across the country. While the programs often show benefits for the children while they are in them, the long range results have not been carefully investigated(Fredericks, 1985). Braddock(1987) reports that in the 17 year period from 1969 through 1985, $260,145,000 has been allocated by the federal government for early childhood intervention grants to the states. Of this total, he estimates that $57,318,000 of it was for programs for the mentally retarded at an average rate of $3,371,647 per year.

OUTCOME STUDIES OF EDUCATIONAL INTERVENTION

There are several evaluative questions to be asked as regards educational intervention on behalf of the mentally retarded. The first is whether it works or how well it works. Does it reach its goals? The second and perhaps more relevant question in light of the legal mandate to educate the retarded in the least restrictive environment is whether such education is effective and appropriate? We will concentrate our attention on this second question for the Educable Mentally Retarded(EMR) and Trainable Mentally Retarded(TMR) at the elementary and secondary school level. However, we will first briefly look at evaluative questions as regards preschool education.

Effects of Preschool Programs

The evaluation of preschool programs is most difficult because to do it well involves setting up experimental designs using treatment and control groups of youngsters who are measured to be equal at the outset. Such measurement is most difficult because of the difficulty of assessing children and because the changes that may occur in early childhood may be due to either/or or both/and stimulation and maturation during this time period. Furthermore, while both organic and social environmental sources of retardation have been identified conceptually, at early ages it may not always be possible to positively diagnose the source of retardation so that treatment and control groups can be made comparable.

The limited but existing research "suggests the programs of stimulation to the handicapped infant can accelerate the rate of development"(Baroff, 1986, 290). An accelerated rate of development for gross motor skills appears to be most likely followed by sensorimotor cognitive processes. But accelerating speech development at an early age does not presently appear very feasible. Once rates of development have been accelerated, can they be maintained? Research in the cognitive domain show conflicting reports(Baroff, 1986).

During the preschool years, ages 2-6, intervention stimulation appears to enhance development. Studies by Skeels and Heber, reported on in Chapter 3, strongly suggest that enriched experiences in a caring environment can improve the development of intelligence and adaptive social and motor skills--especially if begun at an early age.

One follow-up study of 13 Down Syndrome children exposed to early intervention, showed enhanced development compared to usual Down Syndrome children. While many of these children remained in the retarded range, their retardation was not as severe as is typical of Down Syndrome children(Hayden & Haring, 1976).

After reviewing the growing literature on the effect of intervention programs on young children, Karnes and Teska(1975, 219) concluded:

> It is possible to move groups of children from one-half to one standard deviation higher on measures of intellectual ability. There is substantial evidence that many children will lose the temporary gain in intellectual ability as measured by standard tests, but will keep achievement and motivational gains for a longer period of time. There is substantial evidence to support the general principle, "the earlier the instructional program is begun, the better."

In a similar vein, after reviewing over forty longitudinal studies of children "at risk" for developmental deficits, Stedman(1977, 2-3) concluded the environment into which a child is born, including the family's method of stimulating social role development, has a significant impact on the child's early development. "Where access to children can be gained in the early years, preferably during the language emergent years(one to two years of age), intervention programs will be more effective than those begun at later ages."

Effects of EMR Mainstreaming Programs

The central question to be answered here is whether the integration of retarded children into the least restrictive education environment is working. The answer need not be a "yes" or "no". It may be sometimes "yes" and sometimes "no" with a variety of shading in between depending on the characteristics of the handicapped pupils, teacher skills and attitudes, the school environment, and the evaluative criteria being used. Simply placing a retarded child with non-handicapped peers would not be expected to create educational miracles or transform the attitudes of normal classmates.

One of the factors that will influence the success of integrating mildly retarded students into regular classrooms is the teacher's knowledge and attitudes. If teachers are optimistic about the ability of all students to learn and accepts where the handicapped child is developmentally and accepts the fact that it is the teacher's responsibility to adjust instructional methodologies to the needs of the child, then some of the conditions are ripe for success(Baroff, 1986). Teachers of EMR students also need to recognize that such students have either slower or qualitatively different learning patterns. They probably learn language and mathematical concepts and problem solving in the same way and sequence as other children but at a slower pace. By age 18 many mildly retarded children will learn the academic skills expected at the sixth grade level. However, their generally shorter attention spans, lesser ability in generalization, lower frustration levels, greater experience of failure as responded to by others, and lower levels of incidental learning, need to be recognized by teachers in developing instructional techniques that will be successful. Kirk and Gallagher(1983, 156-8) suggest that teachers of EMR students need to systematically apply the following fourteen principles in order to facilitate learning:

1. Let the child experience success. Organize materials and use methods that lead the child to the right answer. Provide clues where necessary. Narrow the choices in responding. . . . Never leave the child in failure, but carry him or her along to success.

2. Provide feedback. The child should know where he or she has responded correctly. . . .

3. Reinforce correct responses. Reinforcement should be immediate and clear. It can be either tangible, as in providing tokens or food, or it can be in the form of social approval and the satisfaction of winning the game.

4. Find the optimum level at which the child should work. If the material is too easy, the child is not challenged to apply the best effort; if too difficult, he or she faces failure and frustration.

5. _Proceed in a systematic way._ Lessons should proceed in a step-by-step fashion so that the more basic and necessary knowledge and habits precede more difficult material.

6. _Use minimal change_ from one step to the next to facilitate learning.

7. _Provide for positive transfer of knowledge from one situation to another._ This is facilitated by helping the child generalize from one situation to another. By having the same concept presented in various settings and various relationships, the child can transfer the common elements in each. . . .

8. _Provide sufficient repetition of experiences to develop overlearning._ . . .

9. _Space the repetitions of material over time_ rather than massing the experience in a short duration. . . .

10. _Consistently associate a given stimulus or cue with one and only one response in the early stages of learning._ . . .

11. _Motivate the child toward greater effort by:_ (1)reinforcement and the satisfaction of succeeding, (b)variation in the presentation of material, (c)enthusiasm on the part of the teacher, and (d)optimal length of sessions.

12. _Limit the number of concepts presented in any one period._ . . .

13. _Arrange materials with the proper cues for attention._

14. _Provide success experiences._ Educable mentally retarded children who have faced failure may have developed low frustration tolerance, negative attitudes toward schoolwork, and possibly some compensatory behavior problems that make them socially unpopular. The best way to cope with those problems is to organize a _day_ to _day_ program presenting the child with short range as well as long range tasks in which to succeed. . . .

When mainstreaming was begun there was some resistance to it by teachers and schools who felt unprepared for the task mandated for them by the federal government. But over time teacher education and a range of support services have been developed in most school systems for determining the most appropriate placement of handicapped children. And the number of retarded students receiving some form of public school education nearly doubled in the ten years following the passage of P.L. 94-142.

The effects of mainstreaming will be noted in three areas: academic, social adjustment and social interaction, and self-concept.

Academic. Since the implementation of mainstreaming will vary from school to school and teacher to teacher and involve different forms or degrees of integration, it is nearly impossible to arrive at a universal and objective assessment of the effectiveness of mainstreaming in the United States. The overall conclusion is that integrated classrooms sometimes produce the same results academically as do special classrooms and sometimes they do better. No evidence has been found that they do worse. Some researchers have found that integrating students does improve their performance(Budoff & Gottlieb, 1976; Gottlieb, 1981), while other researchers have found substantial evidence in many instances where integrated EMR students do better than special class EMR students in reading but not in math and spelling(Meyers, MacMillan & Yoshida, 1975). In all instances integrated EMR students perform more poorly than nonEMR students. While integration may sometimes enhance the academic development of EMR students, it does not mean they will perform at the level of their normal peers. Consequently, one must conclude that mainstreaming has limited academic effects and that these effects are highly dependent on the skills and motivation of the teachers that EMR pupils have and not simply an effect of the integrated placement itself.

Social Adjustment and Social Interaction. The goals of integration go beyond those which are academic in nature. Johnson and Meyer(1985, 83) list six social goals of integration and some of the findings to date as regards the reaching of these goals:

"1. To develop positive attitudes toward handicapped individuals which would facilitate the acceptance of those individuals in various community environments and activities."

This goal starts with the questionable assumption that nonhandicapped children have negative attitudes toward handicapped ones. McHale and Simeonsson(1980) found that nonhandicapped children often had positive attitudes prior to and following interactions with their handicapped peers. However, these positive attitudes sometimes mirrored adult oversolicitousness or globally accepting attitudes that did not square with the children's behavior. But Westling's(1986) review of the literature found that generally EMR students were not only less accepted than normal students but they are more rejected when they are integrated into regular classroom settings. It appears that contact alone does not improve acceptance of retarded children in some settings although it may in others where special efforts are undertaken to hold group discussions on the subject and to engage both types of students in peer tutoring and peer interaction programs.

"2. To provide a social context for the handicapped child to develop various skills(e.g., social, communication, play) which are likely to be facilitated by peer interactions."

This goal involves mixing handicapped and nonhandicapped children in activities that will promote the development of social skills. Voeltz and Brennan(1984) found in one study that nonhandicapped-severely handicapped peer dyads were productive of higher levels of involvement, cooperative planning and appropriate activity in comparison to teacher-student instructional dyads.

"3. To provide a social context for the nonhandicapped child which will facilitate the development of additional skills(e.g., social, communication, play) to interact with others who are 'different'."

This goal is best reached by providing instruction to the nonhandicapped person on how to interact with handicapped peers. Research evidence is generally lacking on whether this outcome is reached, but Voeltz(1980) provides some evidence that nonhandicapped children describe their interaction with handicapped children as better preparing them to deal with individual differences.

"4. To allow for the development of friendships between handicapped and nonhandicapped persons."

There appears to be no research investigating whether such friendship formation takes place as a result of school contacts.

"5. To normalize the social status of severely handicapped individuals; that is, to provide opportunities to participate in various heterogeneous living, working and leisure environments which parallel the kinds of opportunities available to nonhandicapped individuals."

There appears to be no research investigating whether school friendships between the handicapped and nonhandicapped carry over into other environments outside the school.

Self-concept. A third indicator of the effects of integration would be on the self-concept of handicapped students. The research findings here are mixed. One report indicates no difference exists between the self-concepts of EMR students attending integrated and segregated classes. But several reports found that integrated students were less self-derogatory and had better self-concepts(Carroll, 1967) or had more positive attitudes about schooling, were more positive about themselves as students and expressed more internal locus of control than did comparison students in a segregated setting(Budoff & Gottlieb, 1976).

What emerges from this discussion is a need for more research on the outcomes of integrated education in specifying the type of integration, student and teacher attitudes and teaching methodologies. At the same time, while some positive outcomes have been found from mainstreaming EMR students, it is not so much the fact of integration but how it is carried out that appears to make the most significant differences.

Educating the Trainable Mentally Retarded

The education of the Trainable Mentally Retarded presents a different problem than that of the Educable Mentally Retarded. The goal with EMR students is self-sufficiency while this is rarely achievable with TMR students. Rather, the goal is to train them up to their abilities for a state of limited dependency. The goal is seen in training them in self-help skills, economic usefulness, social adjustment in their home and neighborhood, and beginning academic skills. Their education may occur in institutions, community facilities or public schools. If they are mainstreamed it means they go to the same buildings but not the same classrooms as the nonretarded. They will be placed in special classrooms with special teachers who recognize that they usually will not go beyond a first grade reading level of recognizing a few words like danger, stop, men, women, their own names and a few phrases. While both the trainable and profoundly mentally retarded have a right to a public education, that education is more likely to be located in special schools with classrooms and equipment that can accommodate their special needs and which require more individualized attention.

Curriculum Content. The goals of an education for TMR students were listed above as four in number. The first of these is to develop self-help skills so that they will not be totally dependent on others. This involves training in dressing and undressing, eating with manners and the appropriate utensils, managing their own toileting functions and sleep routines in order that they can become largely or wholly independent in their personal care needs.

A second goal is to learn social adjustment--defined as being able to be independent in the home and community at least to some degree. This will involve learning a number of particular things from learning to cross streets safely and recognizing green from red lights, to turn taking in games, sharing, obeying directions, recognizing feelings in others and greeting people. Much of this is learned outside of school, but school activities of recreation, play, singing, dramatics, arts and crafts will aid in the social adjustments of the mentally retarded.

The third goal is to develop economic usefulness. This has a home-life component and a component for some type of work outside the home such as in a sheltered industry or sheltered workshop. The education for home usefulness involves training in cleaning, washing and drying dishes and clothes, table setting, yard work, simple repairs and the ability to complete a variety of simple tasks under minimum supervision. The work component is usually ori-

286

ented to learning prevocational skills related to social helpfulness, punctuality, motor skills for task completion, and an ability to follow directions under limited supervision.

Learning beginning academic skills is the fourth goal. This goal will need to be individualized according to variable TMR student abilities. It will involve teaching letter and word recognition that will usually be limited to about a first grade reading level. Writing, if accomplished, is usually limited to learning to write their own names, addresses and telephone numbers. Language development will involve learning to communicate by words and gestures and understanding verbal concepts. Arithmetic will involve learning about comparative sizes, more or less, perhaps counting up to 10, time-related numbers on a clock, ages, money denominations and other basic numerical concepts as they relate to everyday life. Social studies will involve learning about home life, community locations, public transportation and knowing about the days of the week, holidays, months and seasons. Arts and crafts form an important component of activities that develop motor skills, a sense of color and the satisfaction of completing tasks in drawing, coloring, woodworking, cutting and pasting and in making simple crafts. Both music and drama activities that involve group activities can foster story telling, the use of gestures, cooperation, a sense of timing, motor skills and memory skills. Physical hygiene will involve a discussion of types of food, nutrition and cleansing activities for the body, mouth and clothes as well as physical activities that relate to health, posture, and safety. Motor development will be stimulated by a variety of games, recreational activities and play both indoors and out(Kirk & Gallagher, 1983).

The educational strategies for teaching skills to the retarded, especially the more severely retarded, involve the whole range of teaching methodologies used for all children. However, a special or greater emphasis is usually put on the operant conditioning techniques developed by B. F. Skinner and others. The fundamental principle of operant conditioning is that a person's behavior is determined by responses to it. Thus, in behavior shaping or behavior modification, environmental responses are arranged to encourage desired behavior by reinforcing or rewarding it and to discourage undesired behavior by not reinforcing it or punishing it. Since punishment is often looked down upon, undesirable behavior is usually not responded to in the belief that if it goes unrecognized and unrewarded it will be extinguished.

The training of the severely and profoundly retarded, about half of whom will be multiply handicapped, often relies heavily on behavior modification techniques as well as the use of adaptive devices and task simplification. For example, color cues may be used to identify bathrooms, clothing with enlarged head and arms holes to simplify dressing and undressing will initially be used for learning dressing, enlarged and deep spoons are used to reduce spilling, moisture sensing auditory alarm underpants may be used in toilet training, and special "adaptive" equipment for bowling and other games have been developed(Baroff, 1986).

SUMMARY

The history of the education of the mentally retarded in the United States exhibits what might be called "progressive inclusion." This progressive inclusion has increasingly involved several types: physical, social, numerical, vertical and horizontal. Physically, mentally retarded students have been progressively included in regular schools beginning around 1900 and in regular classrooms beginning mainly in the 1960s. This has progressively involved them in social contacts with the nonhandicapped in schools and sometimes in other institutions. The numbers and percentage of them involved in integrated schooling has increased over time. Vertical integration has occurred in the sense that handicapped children in integrated settings have a greater number of contacts with a greater variety of adults in institutional settings. And horizontal integration has occurred with an increase in the number of contacts with their age peers(Johnson & Meyer, 1985).

Historically, residential schools were developed for the mentally retarded beginning around 1850. Over time these expanded and became more custodial institutions for the moderately and severely retarded. Beginning around 1900 segregated special classes were begun and expanded in public schools. Beginning around 1950 these special classes for EMR students began enrolling more students while special schools for TMR students were begun.

288

Beginning in the late 1960s and especially after the 1975 passage of P.L. 94-142 there was much greater integration of EMR students in regular education classes under the concept of an appropriate education in the least restrictive environment. Federal funding for the education of retarded and handicapped children greatly expanded during the last 19 years. Federal funding for educating only the mentally retarded increased over twenty fold from an estimated $23 million in 1966 to nearly $477 million in 1995. There has been also a commensurate increase in funding by the states and local school districts as well for the education of the retarded.

The Education for All Handicapped Children Act of 1975 has transformed the processes involved in educating mentally retarded and other handicapped children. Under the regulations of this law each handicapped child is to have developed and reviewed no less than annually an Individual Education Program(IEP). This written IEP is to include an evaluation of the student, short- and long-term educational objectives, and the instructional methodologies by which these objectives are to be reached. P.L. 94-142 also specifies regulations and procedures to help insure parental involvement, procedural safeguards to protect the rights of all parties involved, appropriate evaluation procedures so that children may be placed in the least restrictive environment, the maintenance of confidentiality in handling records relative to mentally retarded children, and the development of teacher training programs to prepare teachers for working with the developmentally disabled.

The range of alternative education placements for handicapped children is reviewed. Eight types of placements were reviewed which go from the least to most restrictive educational settings as follows: (1)the regular classroom, (2)the regular classroom with consultative services, (3)itinerant instruction in the regular classroom, (4)resource room instructional support, (5)part-time special classes, (6)full-time special classes, (7)special schools, and (8)residential institutions.

Early education intervention programs have been developed in the last several decades to enhance the growth of children at risk for developmental lags. Infant stimulation programs serve those below two years of age while preschool programs serve those aged two to six. Such programs have the objectives of maximizing age-related developmental skills, assisting the child's family to understand and stimulate the child, and preparing the child to enter the normal world. This includes the reduction or removal of the stigma many persons hold about the handicapped.

Three different models of early stimulation programs are home-based programs where parents are the main stimulators to growth, education-centered programs where specialists stimulate growth and a combined plan where specialists and parents both work on early stimulation. The federal government has financially supported the development of model preschool stimulation programs for twenty years.

An evaluation of the effectiveness of early stimulation programs indicates they are the most effective in enhancing motivation and achievement and only somewhat effective in enhancing cognitive processes. Programs that are begun early in life appear more effective than those begun later in the preschool years.

Evaluating the effectiveness of mainstreaming EMR students is a complex task because of the variety and mix of handicapping conditions, teacher skills and attitudes, and educational environments. Teacher skills and attitudes appear to be particularly important in improving the effectiveness of mainstreaming. The effects of mainstreaming in three areas are discussed. Mainstreamed students sometimes do better academically, but not always, than those in special classes. Integration often has mixed results on social adjustment and self-concepts although more benefits than detrimental effects are usually found with integration.

The goals of education for Trainable Mentally Retarded students is to enhance their abilities for economic usefulness and to minimize their dependence on others. TMR education makes extended use of operant conditioning methodologies.

Chapter 9

Vocational Services and Employment for the Retarded

Perhaps the most central status of moving into adulthood is that of becoming a worker. The work role may be that of gainful employment outside the home or domestic chores or, in reality, some of both. But this central work status, particularly gainful employment outside the home, has been one that has been denied to many of the mentally retarded. The denial of work to those capable of it has many deleterious consequences not only to those who arc denied the work but also the deniers--the larger society. In this chapter we want to explore the role of work for the mentally retarded and how this affects and is affected by the larger society of which they are a part. After noting the importance of work in society, we will explore how levels of retardation are related to daily activities, vocational training and different types of employment of the retarded. We will then discuss how different levels of retardation are related to work adjustment. We will also look at federal, state and local training and work programs for the retarded.

THE IMPORTANCE OF WORK

Going to work is one of the significant transition points in the life cycle of people in our society. It signifies that one is an adult who has assumed responsibility for himself and, as a citizen, is making a contribution to society. It marks a move from dependence to independence. The move to employment also involves some significant changes in self-identity and the way time is spent. To be a worker capable of supporting himself is highly valued in our society. It signifies that the person is not only a competent individual but that the goods or services he produces for society are a benefit to it. Thus, in return for his work, he is paid for the value of his work which enhances his self-worth. He becomes a taxpayer rather than just a tax-user. Furthermore, work becomes an important source of friendships for most people and utilizes about 24% of the 168-hour week and about 36% of a person's waking hours each week if a person is working full time. And the pay for work gives a person much more independence in making decisions about his housing, food, clothing, relationships and leisure time activities. Since a large majority of the mentally retarded are only mildly retarded and about 85% of them are employed, they experience the benefits and responsibilities of working as do most other citizens. However, as we move down the scale of retardation, we find an increasing proportion of the mentally retarded not working even though many have the capacity to do so with adequate training. In this chapter we will give particular attention to those who are unemployed and the reasons and consequences of this. Many consequences follow from the fact that many of the retarded are not employed in some way--their self-image is altered, their daily routines are different, their independence is curtailed, and they become dependent persons whose needs require substantial expenditures for their welfare.

LEVELS OF RETARDATION, VOCATIONAL SERVICES AND WORK PATTERNS

Work in the Developmental Model

As the normal child grows he is exposed to values and ideas about the world of work. Early in childhood the child learns that his parents work and that he can expect to work when he grows up. He will be asked many times what he wants to be when he grows up. He will see his parents working and talking about work and gradually he may formulate some ideas about careers. As the child develops he will be exposed to work around the house, perhaps part-time work while in school or work in the summer, and course decisions in school as to whether to enter a

college-preparatory, academic, business or vocational curriculum. These decisions will be shaped by estimates of
one's talents, vocational interests, and peer group and
parental influences. Eventually this person will go through
job interviews and, perhaps testing, before he takes a job.
But the career developmental process does not end with the
first job. There may be additional training with each job
and learning that accompanies each job. Some people go
through multiple career changes that often involve both
formal and informal learning.

The career shaping influences for mentally and
physically handicapped persons need not be substantially
different from those of normal children if they grow up in
the same kind of family and school environments. However, if they grow up in institutional environments or if
they are treated differently in the developmental process,
then they may have fewer and different opportunities to
learn about the world of work. People with marked disabilities sometimes have vocational learning opportunities
circumscribed in early life and this becomes a self-fulfilling
prophecy with regard to the development of knowledge and
skills relevant to work. If they have limited opportunities
to experience training and work then they may not become
as normal as possible. The developmental principle is that
all persons, no matter what the nature or severity of their
handicap, should have the opportunity to grow and learn in
all areas, including work, throughout the life cycle.

The Goals and Components of a Vocational Service System

Like all other persons, the mentally handicapped
should be exposed to different types of careers, training
options and work options. Like others, they need exposure
to what Durand and Neufeld(1980, 287) call a "vocational
service system." They believe that such a system should
have two goals: (1)providing every individual, irrespective
of the severity of his handicap, "a reasonably normal
expectation that he or she will have the opportunity to
make a career choice", and (2)providing growth opportunities in this system so every individual "can exercise the
right of career choice and so participate in meaningful and
self-enhancing work during the normal adult working life
span". Durand and Neufeld(1980) delineate eleven differ-

293

ent service components of a "vocational service system" that need to be tailored to the individual needs of each person in it. The first two components, (1)recruitment and (2)selection, involve exposing individuals to different careers so they can learn about the tasks and training for a variety of jobs and make use of services in deciding upon a job or career. The next six components, (3)prevocational training, (4)vocational exploration, (5)vocational skill training, (6)work adjustment training, (7)personal adjustment training, and (8)vocational evaluation, deal with preparing an individual for work placement that is appropriate for him. The last three components, (9)placement, (10)job stabilization, and (11)retraining, provide services that help the person get and maintain themselves in a suitable job. To be successful such a system needs to be coordinated with other services within a given community such as residential programs, educational programs, counseling programs, vocational training programs, advocacy programs and other support services.

Employment and Training Options for the Retarded

Since all people vary greatly in their levels of competence and interests, a continuum of work and training options is needed. Because of the lower levels of social competence and the greater training requirements for most retarded workers, the continuum of work and training options need to be extended for them. Table 9.1 shows five steps or kinds of employment options that move from substantial worker dependency in Step 1 to substantial worker independency in Step 5.

Table 9.1 clearly indicates that the mentally retarded and other disabled individuals should have open to them a range of employment opportunities that are related to their prior training, work experiences, and demonstrated and/or potential work capabilities. While this is a prescriptive or "ideal" range of services, it does exist in the United States to a certain extent. In the last decade gains have been made in expanding the work opportunities for the retarded, especially those below the mild level of retardation. The normalization goal, using this model, would have the person enter the work force at the highest level possible. It would also involve ongoing assessment in order to move workers from more segregated, controlled and subsi-

Table 9.1

Continuum of Employment Options from Dependent to Independent

```
                                        WORKER IS
                                        LARGELY
                                        DEPENDENT
                              |
                              ↑
                              |
                              |
                              ↓
                              |
                                        WORKER IS
                                        LARGELY
                                        INDEPENDENT
```

Step 1. SHELTERED EMPLOYMENT
         --All handicapped work force
         --Largely subsidized

Step 2. SHELTERED INDUSTRY
         --Largely handicapped work force with
           nonhandicapped worker-models
         --May be partly subsidized

Step 3. SEMI-SHELTERED EMPLOYMENT(GROUP)
         --Nonhandicapped work-force with
           groups of handicapped
         --Regular industry

Step 4. COMPETITIVE WORK WITH SUPPORT
         --Nonhandicapped work force with
           individual handicapped persons
           with support
         --Regular industry

Step 5. INDIVIDUAL COMPETITIVE EMPLOYMENT
         --Regular work hours
         --All workers treated equally
         --Regular industry

Source: Adapted from Durand and Neufeld(1980, 290)
```
```

dized environments to those which are more integrated, less supervised and less subsidized. Thus, with additional training and work experience it may be possible for workers to "graduate" to higher levels of work independence and more normal work environments.

Adult Day Programs

Mentally retarded adults can be divided into two groups as regards work: (1)those who work at one of the five levels of employment listed in Table 9.1, and (2)those who do not work. Many of this latter group go to adult day programs--also called adult activity centers, developmental centers, day treatment programs, and work activity centers. But this somewhat oversimplifies in that some retarded people may go to an adult day program for several days a week and to a sheltered workshop the rest of the week.

Adult day programs are never oriented to production. Rather, their emphasis is primarily on habilitation and prevocational training for those with more severe levels of retardation and/or those with behavioral problems. They provide day care for adults of all ages and are sometimes sought out by the parents of young retarded adults who are no longer involved in some type of education program but are still living at home. Adult activity centers serve primarily adults who live in community residential facilities or in their natural homes. The programs they provide may help prepare adults for entrance to a sheltered workshop.

Bellamy et al(1980) carried out a national survey of adult day programs. Forty-nine responding states reported the existence of approximately 2,000 adult activity centers serving 105,000 individuals. The number of centers and clients served have grown substantially with the deinstitutionalization movement of the 1970s and 1980s. Such activity centers were seen as a first step in the continuum of services for the more severely retarded. Most of the services in such "treatment" programs attempt to develop basic skills in self care, cooking, understanding time, keeping appointments, verbal communication and the like. Some of the time is spent in arts and crafts and recreational programming. Only a minor emphasis in most centers was oriented to the development of work skills and no paid work was included in these programs.

The funding for adult day programs comes primarily from both the state and federal government under two Social Security Acts: Medicaid(Title XIX) and Social Services(Title XX) wherein the states match federal funds on a formula basis. These programs tend to have a welfare approach to services, and in the view of some, put too little emphasis on training for work. Furthermore, funding caps put a limit on the availability of such services(Westling, 1986).

Sheltered Workshops

Sheltered workshops have three major goals. One is the <u>assessment</u> of <u>clients</u> to determine their level of functioning, their skills and deficiencies, and their vocational interests in order for the staff of the facility to develop a training and work program for them. The second is to <u>train clients</u> in those skills necessary to carry out a particular job as well as those general skills needed for many types of employment. These may include how to take a job interview, how to punch a time clock, learning how to follow directions, learning how to get along with fellow employees and supervisors as well as learning particular skills such as refinishing furniture, assembling circuit boards, mowing lawns, or making beds(for work in motels). The third is to offer clients <u>paid</u> <u>employment</u> in a sheltered environment and under close supervision. The pay is usually performance based--that is related to productivity. Thus if a "normal" production worker can wire six circuit boards per hour at $4.00 per hour, then a retarded worker who can wire three circuit boards per hour will be paid half the wage of the normal worker who is producing twice as much per hour. Over time, some persons who have been trained and worked in a sheltered employment setting may be able to move up one or more steps on the employment ladder given in Table 9.1. However, because of the relatively low skill levels of some sheltered workshop clients and because of the scarcity of job openings at their skill levels, many sheltered workshop clients stay at this level of employment for their lifetimes.

Sheltered workshops come in a variety of forms, sizes and sponsorships. Some are operated by state agencies and may exist in many communities. Some are operated by private for profit agencies while others are operated

297

by nonprofit organizations such as ARC. The funding sources include federal and state funds as well as income from work done for outside firms. Some are relatively small and train people for only a few different types of jobs while others are large and provide a wider range of training and work opportunities. Some workshops serve only the mentally retarded while others are specialized in the sense of serving only the cerebral palsied, the psychiatrically disturbed, or the physically disabled. However, many sheltered workshops serve the whole range of those designated as having developmental disabilities.

Sheltered workshops operate as self-contained businesses. They operate at a loss in the sense that revenues from the products they make or the services they provide do not cover all their operating costs. Usually their production only supplies a small portion of their income while the rest comes from federal and state funds designated for habilitation and rehabilitation services. Workshops employ a variety of types of people to carry out their goals of assessment, training and work. Workshop staff usually include a director, assessment specialists, work trainers, production supervisors, counselors, work-procurement specialists, and job placement specialists. The work-procurement specialists try to locate firms or organizations that need specific types of work done from packaging products, to mowing lawns, to putting together components for a valve assembly. The work done by the clients is often done on a subcontract basis--that is pay is on a piecework basis or for the entire job. Most employees in sheltered workshops earn substantially less than minimum wage with the amount of their pay related to their productivity(Westling, 1986).

Sheltered workshops are and probably will remain for some time one of the largest employers of the more severely retarded. Birenbaum and Cohen(1985) report that there currently are 156,457 mentally retarded persons either being trained or employed in 5,866 Labor Department-certified workshop programs in the U.S. While research has shown that new training techniques can help lower functioning mentally retarded persons assemble complex items at acceptable rates of speed, the diffusion of this technology and the community acceptance of retarded workers into more normalizing work environments is occurring slowly. Therefore, while the ultimate goal is to move peo-

298

ple out of sheltered employment into more integrated work environments, this move will probably occur slowly because of a number of barriers to work integration that will be discussed more fully later in this chapter. In fact, as part of the deinstitutionalization movement, the number of retarded persons placed in sheltered workshops tripled between 1969 and 1977(Vitello & Soskin, 1985).

Sheltered Industry

A sheltered industry is one that offers sheltered employment but is cost-benefit and production-oriented. In this type of setting workers can usually expect to make the minimum wage and perhaps better if their productivity warrants it. Most of the workers are handicapped in this type of setting although there may be contact with non-handicapped workers who act as role models. One example of this type of program was the development of a "Reclamation Shop" at the Naval Air Re-Work Facility in Pensacola, Florida. The cost of employing regular mechanics to disassemble aircraft at this facility was too expensive to justify it being done. So, in the past, nuts, bolts and other small parts were thrown out. A local vocational rchabilitation agency set up a training program at the Naval Air Re-work Facility to train mentally retarded employees how to salvage and sort such parts. In addition to the wages paid to the employees, the Reclamation Shop saved the facility between $10,000 and $15,000 per month(President's Committee on Mental Retardation, 1983).

Semi-Sheltered Employment

In this type of employment program, small groups of handicapped work in an industry where most of the employees are not handicapped. There will no longer be a subsidy for the work although special training, supervision and support services may be offered. For example, one program was developed in the state of Oregon that used a mobile crew model, consisting of five retarded persons with one supervisor, who provided custodial and ground maintenance at a number of work sites. One of the two crews averaged $80 income per person per month while the other crew earned approximately $150 per person per month.

Competitive Work With Support

In this model the handicapped worker is placed in a normal work setting alongside nonhandicapped workers. After training is completed, the workers may receive special support services from a case manager to enable workers to stabilize their work habits. For example, the Trillium Employment Service in cooperation with the Washington State Divisions of Developmental Disabilities and Vocational Rehabilitation developed an "electronics industry enclave" model of employing small groups of four to eight persons with severe and moderate mental retardation and related disabilities. The enclave employees work in the midst of nonhandicapped company employees in the assembly of bio-medical electronic equipment for a firm outside of Seattle, Washington. The workers had IQ scores below 45 and ranged in age from 22 to 28. They are trained for the jobs considered appropriate to them. Like other employees, they work four ten-hour days each week. In 1984 their average earnings were over $400 per person per week.

A number of states like Oregon, Washington, Pennsylvania and Virginia have now developed formal state programs to promote the development of such programs under the title of "supported employment." In such programs, the emphasis is upon placing retarded persons and other developmentally disabled or physically handicapped people in normal work settings while giving them the necessary support and training services they need to hold such jobs(Kiernan & Stark, 1986).

Individual Competitive Employment

In this last step the worker is in a totally normal work environment. He may be self-employed or employed by others. But there are no support services offered him. The mildly retarded, who make up about 88% of all the retarded, are the ones who are to be found in individual competitive employment with few exceptions.

300

WORK PATTERNS OF THE MILDLY RETARDED

Most of the research on the work of the mentally retarded covers primarily the mildly retarded or those classified as educable mentally retarded. No research has been carried out that provides a comprehensive picture of the work lives of those below the mild level of retardation. In this section we will look at employment rates, types of employment, income and the work adjustment of the mildly retarded.

Employment Rates

In 1973 Conley(1973) reviewed 27 follow-up studies on the work and income patterns of mildly retarded persons. He concluded that the vocational success of mildly retarded people was far greater than most people realized. He estimated that 87% of the noninstitutionalized males and 33% of the noninstitutionalized females who had been identified as mildly retarded while in school were employed. At the same time, the unemployment rates ran about double the rest of the population of the same age. Westling(1986) reviewed the employment rates found in nine studies conducted on the mildly retarded between 1960 and 1980 using samples ranging in size from 40 to 383. In these nine studies employment ranged from a low of "slightly over half" to 92.1% of those in the civilian labor force(in this instance 68% of the sample was defined as being in the labor force). Based on this information we can only estimate that a large majority of the mildly retarded are employed. But their unemployment rate appears to run at least double that of the rest of the population and may be even higher. We might assume that most of the mildly retarded who are working in competitive work environments live in independent living arrangements or with their natural families.

Type of Employment

Mildly retarded persons have been found to be in a wide number of occupations but tend to predominate in the area of unskilled service work such as dishwashers, busboys, janitors, gas station attendants, gardeners, domestic service, and laborers in a wide variety of settings. Some have been employed as truck drivers, file clerks, bench work assembly line workers in industrial production firms and in construction work. Brolin et al(1975) found that 50% of their sample of 136 persons were in service occupations with most of the remainder in unskilled or semi-skilled work.

Income

In his 1973 study Conley estimated that mildly retarded employed men had an income of 86% of the norm for men and females 87% of the norm for women. Hard data is difficult to come by here, but Westling's(1986) review of several income studies indicate the incomes of mildly retarded workers to be below national averages but above the poverty line in most instances. That the mildly retarded have below average incomes when working is not surprising in view of the kinds of jobs they hold.

Work Adjustment

Not much research has been done on the work adjustment of the mildly retarded in recent years. Bostwick and Foss(1981) asked mentally retarded persons to rank order the problems they had with regard to employment. Simply finding a job was ranked by them as their number one problem followed by getting to work on time, getting along with the boss, remembering appointments, interviewing for a job, and last, working fast enough. However, this research did not indicate the proportion of persons reporting each of these six problems.

Earlier studies of work adjustment of the mildly retarded conducted in the 1960s generally indicated: (1)most retarded workers make a satisfactory work adjustment, (2)that their unemployment increases during economic recessions, (3)that the adjustment is sometimes affected by the adequacy of community services, (4)that most work in a variety of unskilled or semi-skilled jobs in services, construction or production type businesses, (5)that improved levels of education and training can increase their employment likelihood, (6)that the retarded have the capability to increase their work skills with experience and training and move to new jobs or those requiring more responsibility, and (7)that appearance, health, motor coor-

302

dination, cheerfulness, cooperation, initiative and punctuality are all related to employability(Kolstoe, 1961; Goldstein, 1964; Kokaska, 1968).

A Forty-Year Follow-Up Study of the Mildly Retarded

One piece of research evidence on how well the mildly retarded do is a follow-up study of 160 persons forty years after completing school. In the 1920s and 1930s these subjects had been identified as educable mentally retarded by the San Francisco school system. They were normal in most ways but had been put in special, ungraded, education classes because they had serious and chronic academic failure in regular classes. All had been born between 1915 and 1921. Their average IQ in childhood was 68 with a standard deviation of 9.34. Most of the subjects were 17 and 18 when they began work around 1940. Ross, Begab, Dondes, Giampiccolo and Meyer(1985) then compared them in 1980 to siblings and "controls" on a number of measures as reported on in Table 9.2. The "controls" were persons matched to the subjects on age, sex, language spoken at home, and father's occupation and years of education.

The picture that emerges from Table 9.2 and the larger report was that the mildly retarded had adjusted to work and life quite well and much like other people. However, 20% were unemployed compared to 8% of the siblings and 3% of the controls. The subjects earned $1,345 less than the median income in 1970, while their siblings and controls earned $1,345 and $5,700 more respectively. Around 75% of the male subjects and 66% of the female subjects reported high job satisfaction. For the males this was a little lower than for siblings and controls. Fifty percent of the subjects were in semi-skilled work compared to 25.8% of the siblings and 15.2% of the controls. And 14.8% were in slightly skilled jobs in comparison to 3.3% of siblings and 9.1% of the controls. While fewer of them got married, those that did had about the same number of children(2.48) as did their siblings and controls. The mildly retarded persons showed normal parental roles regarding helping children with school, acting as disciplinarians, having family fights and settling them.

303

Table 9.2

Data on Forty-Year Follow-Up Study of 160 Mildly Retarded Adults in Comparison to Siblings and Controls

(in %)

	Retarded Subjects	Siblings	Controls
Males			
Worked full time prior week	67.5	86.1	94.3
Worked full or part time prior week	80.	92.	97.
Females			
Worked full time prior week	22.5	31.3	40.6
Worked full or part time prior week	39.1	46.9	56.1
Mean Income in 1970	$9,781	$11,603	$15,428
Mean Years of Education	8.75	10.98	12.97
Married, Males	61.3	80.6	97.1
Females	61.2	71.9	81.3
Single, Males	27.5	11.1	0.0
Females	23.7	6.3	6.3
Divorced, Males	10.0	8.3	2.9
Females	8.8	9.4	6.0
Homeowners	66.2	72.1	86.6
Never Received Public Assistance	80.5	81.5	97.0

Source: Adapted from Ross et al, 1985.

The mildly retarded adult subjects in this study had homes of a similar size and rental cost to their siblings. Overall, their self-ratings in health were only a little poorer than their siblings, with just 12.5% rating their health as "rather poor" or "very poor." Over 87% of the male subjects had served in the military service--nearly identical to that of siblings and controls. Going to church and the importance of religion to them was very similar to that of their siblings. Over 80% were registered to vote and over 78% of them had voted in the last election--about 5% less than their siblings. A majority of the subjects had savings accounts and checking accounts and had taken out loans from some source. Half of them had made purchases with credit cards. "In each of these measures of financial independence, however, the subjects ranked about 20-40 percent below the controls"(Ross, et al, 1985, 124). This particular study gives evidence that most of the mildly retarded lead lives quite similar to their brothers and sisters.

CAUSES OF UNEMPLOYMENT AMONG THE MORE SEVERELY RETARDED

About 8% of all the retarded have IQs between 25 and 50 while about 4% have IQs below 25. Relatively few of these persons are employed above the sheltered workshop level although with careful training and the provision of support services it may be possible to increase their workforce participation in steps 1 to 4 of the employment options listed in Table 9.1 and which allow for greater independence and integration. The eight factors that we list below can also be used to explain the higher rates of unemployment(and probably underemployment) among both the mildly and especially the more severely retarded. It should be noted that these eight factors should be viewed as a system to interacting forces that often influence one another.

1.   Jobs are too demanding relative to the social competence of the worker.

Vocational success and failure are closely related to matching the skills of a person to the requirements of a job. Many jobs in our technological society are beyond the skills of those with IQs below 50. They are obviously

305

excluded from jobs that require significant abilities to reason and communicate verbally and in writing. But, as Conley(1985, 196) points out:

> Despite the rapidly evolving technology in our society, there are still, and probably will be for the foreseeable future, many jobs than can use persons with limited intellectual capabilities effectively. In fact, because of the division of labor, severely mentally retarded persons are often able to participate in the assembly of advanced technological products as complicated processes are broken down into simple tasks. In competing for these unskilled jobs, a physically healthy person with limited intellectual capacity might be seen as actually having a slight advantage over his or her more highly skilled counterpart who would be bored and frustrated by such a job, who might be considered overqualified, and who would probably not retain the job long if another became available. Thus, limited intellectual ability is not, in itself, a major barrier to employment for mildly mentally retarded persons or for most persons with IQs below 50.

Thus, a critical point in explaining unemployment is the mismatch of job requirements and available skills. To increase the employment of the mentally retarded, particular efforts would have to be made in many localities to find jobs suitable for them and to train them in the particular skills needed for that work.

2. <u>Some retarded persons have emotional, physical, and medical conditions which interfere with effective work performance.</u>

As indicated in Chapter 2, as the severity of retardation increases so does the probability of having other disabilities. Table 9.3 shows the characteristics of over 9,000 residents living in Community Residential Facilities in Pennsylvania in 1982-83. The estimates in this sample are based on data from 104 responding CRF programs out of 190 programs at over 1500 sites in Pennsylvania. The extrapolated data show 80.5% of the residents of such CRFs are moderately to profoundly retarded, 20.3% are nonambulatory, 13% are medically fragile or have degenerative diseases, over 61% are on medications, 14.6% have seizures, 33.8% are nonverbal, 23.1% have behavioral problems, 7.2% are mentally ill, while 5.3% and 5.8% are respectively legally blind and deaf. Some of the clients have multiple problems which would seriously interfere with work even if training and work support services were available. While some more severely retarded persons can be trained for certain types of work, they often have a range of problems that are formidable in matching their skills to the conditions of employment which require good health and some social competence. Thus, the behavioral and medical problems of an unknown percentage of the more severely retarded clearly act as barriers to any type of work.

3. The attitudes and experiences of retarded people may act as barriers to employment.

Conley(1985, 197) observes, "Largely because of inexperience, many mentally retarded persons are frightened by the prospect of gainful employment, they may doubt if they can get along with their fellow workers, or they may question their own ability to work." Having lived in a protective environment most of their lives and having experienced rebuffs from the "outside world" on many occasions, they may be highly reluctant to try new experiences that may result in failure. These attitudes may have been shaped by parents, board and care home providers, or other caretakers who doubt they can hold on to a steady job. Thus, once conditioned for dependency and failure, some retarded people will find it difficult to reverse these conditions without strong support from others.

4. The attitudes of coworkers may act as barriers to employment.

If the mentally retarded are placed in more integrated and competitive work settings, the negative attitudes of coworkers may militate against steady employment. Teasing, harassment, neglect and indifference may make

307

Table 9.3

Selected Characteristics in Percent of Estimated Number of Clients in 190 Private
Pennsylvania Facilities in 1982-83 By Type of Provider

Type of Provider

Characteristics*	CLA	PLF	ICF/MR	Total
	(127)	(34)	(29)	(190)
Non-ambulatory	5.6	28.9	39.1	20.3
Legally blind	2.8	5.8	10.2	5.3
Deaf	2.9	11.8	3.2	5.8
Medically fragile or with				
degenerative disease	6.3	19.9	17.2	13.0
On medication	59.6	61.0	65.8	61.4
Seizures	9.2	18.5	20.2	14.6
Non-verbal	18.3	39.0	59.1	33.8
Behavioral problems	26.5	17.7	23.0	23.1
Mentally ill	11.8	3.2	3.3	7.2
Level of retardation:				
Profound	7.2	30.2	45.8	22.9
Severe	20.9	28.8	29.6	25.4
Moderate	43.6	25.3	18.0	32.2
Mild/Other**	28.3	15.7	6.6	19.5
Totals (N)	4,216	2,859	1,995	9,070

Table 9.3

Selected Characteristics in Percent of Estimated Number of Clients in 190 Private Pennsylvania Facilities in 1982-83 By Type of Provider

(continued)

*Clients may have multiple characteristics so that percentages cannot be added.

**The "mild/other" category includes only 4% other such as borderline retardation or mentally ill only.

Source: Adapted from Poister Associates, 1984.

their work more difficult and less enjoyable. Research indicates it often takes several years for normal coworkers to accept having retarded people work beside them(Rubin & Roessler, 1983).

5.   The attitudes and policies of employers may act as barriers to employment.

        While discrimination against the disabled is often illegal it persists. The Rehabilitation Act of 1973 contains several sections which prohibits discrimination against the disabled. Section 501 of this act mandates that federal departments, agencies and instrumentalities(e.g., U.S. Postal Service) have an "affirmative action program plan for the hiring, placement, and advancement of handicapped individuals." Thus, the federal government is to act as a model for other employers in this area. Section 503 of the act prohibits discrimination in employment on the basis of physical or mental handicaps and requires affirmative action programs on the part of all employers or their subcontractors who receive annual federal contracts exceeding $2500. About two million employers are covered under this section. Section 504 of this act prohibits discrimination of all types(services, accessibility, and employment) against the disabled by any agency receiving federal financial assistance such as hospitals, schools, colleges, nursing homes, and welfare offices(Rubin & Roessler, 1983). In spite of such legislation, some employers still engage in discrimination against the developmentally disabled whether they are covered under the legislation or not.
        The President's Committee on Mental Retardation(1983) cites seven myths about "problems" employers often recite in refusing to employ mentally retarded workers. The committee rebuffs these "stereotypes" as major obstacles to employment and counter them with illustrative data and facts about employing the mentally retarded. These seven myths follow with information included that is used to undermine their validity.

        MYTH 1: Training mentally retarded workers will be too time-consuming and/or expensive to justify it.
        Very often state and federally funded rehabilitation agencies will train workers for a particular job site at no expense to the employer. Furthermore, the federal gov-

310

ernment has an incentive program for employers, which, if they meet the eligibility requirements, may take a $3,000 tax credit for each new targeted employee's first year of wages and up to $1,500 for the second year of wages. Some federally subsidized programs encourage employers to hire retarded workers by offering them financial incentives to do so. For example, using Department of Labor funds, the Association for Retarded Citizen's On-The-Job Training program reimburses employers for 50% of the entry wage during the first 160 hours of work and 25% of the wage during the next 160 hours.

If we look at the larger economic picture of the whole society, rather than just the financial benefits to employers, we can understand why the President's Committee on Mental Retardation(1983, 4) call mentally retarded workers an "economic discovery":

> Each mentally retarded worker represents an average savings of $29,200 per year in support payments if habilitated in a public institution. Additionally, he contributed $530 tax dollars yearly to the general revenues. Instead of depending upon parental and public support, the mentally retarded workers lightens the economic burdens of both. Of equal importance, to invest in vocational training is wise. Once employed, a mentally retarded person will repay $1.00 for every $1.00 spent to train him in only about 4 years. Thereafter the repayment benefit will be greater than habilitation cost. Lifetime earnings will improve by $10.40 for every dollar spent on his vocational rehabilitation.

MYTH 2: Productivity will be lower with retarded workers.

While no comprehensive surveys are available on this stereotype, the President's Committee on Mental Retardation(1983, 7) quotes Greg Randall of Randall Plating in Butler, Wisconsin who says, "Our business has grown steadily since we first began hiring mentally handicapped persons 10 years ago. The quality of our product has improved and we have substantially fewer rejects."

311

Randall goes on, "Not only that, we haven't had a 'loss of time' injury in years. Frequent injuries had been a tremendous problem in the past." At the beginning of his employment of retarded workers, Randall found there were some complaints about the handicapped workers from their nonhandicapped coworkers. Upon investigation, the true source of the discontent was that the handicapped workers were outproducing the other workers!

MYTH 3: The use of retarded workers will result in accidents and higher insurance rates.

The President's Committee found this commonly held belief to be untrue. They found retarded workers to be careful and reliable workers whose employment did not increase their insurance costs.

MYTH 4: Work absenteeism will be higher among the retarded.

A number of employers report that absenteeism in the service trades such as restaurant work is high among normal workers. But some of the Atlantic City casinos report that their retarded workers, after an eight week training program, have less work absenteeism than regular employees. They attribute this to the fact that regular employees feel they can get other jobs immediately when they get bored with kitchen service work, but that the retarded workers get more satisfaction and perform more conscientiously on the job.

MYTH 5: Turnover rates will be higher among retarded workers.

Most employers dislike high employee turnover because it involves more training costs and is often associated with poor work and absenteeism. The turnover rate among mentally retarded people is less than that of the general population. The Marriott Food Services at the Smithsonian Institution has been employing retarded workers for over 14 years. It found that the average turnover rate was 7.1 years with a daily work attendance of 98%.

MYTH 6: Supervision costs will be excessive for retarded workers.

Certainly a legitimate concern of employers is whether mentally retarded workers will require substantially more supervision time than other employees and thus be more expensive in the long run. The reply here is dependent upon whether the employees are adequately trained in the first place, and whether they, in fact, need more supervision. In the supported work program being developed around the country now, the supervision comes from an outside program that is not a direct cost to the employer. For example, Woodward and Lothrop Department Stores have hired over 100 retarded workers for its housekeeping and food services departments through the District of Columbia Association of Retarded Citizens(DC-ARC). The placement coordinators of the DC-ARC program help retarded people with applications and interviews at the outset and give them on-site supervision as long as they need it and then are on-call to provide assistance when it is needed. At a small cost these citizens have become productive members of society.

MYTH 7: The modification necessary to the work environment will be too expensive.
This factor affects primarily the physically handicapped or the multiply handicapped that includes a physical disability. No general conclusion can be reached about its validity except to say that a case by case determination must be made to see whether the costs outweigh the long range benefits of making modifications to the work site facility. It has often been found that the costs are not as great as originally expected(Stroman, 1982).

6. The training that mentally retarded people receive may not be adequate.

The education and training programs that have been developed for the retarded in the past have often been inadequate to prepare them for specific jobs. Some schools are seen as having make-work curriculums that provide training that is irrelevant to the needs of the more severely retarded. Some adult day treatment programs are seen as dealing with trivialities that develop few prevocational or vocational skills(Halpern, Sackett, Binner & Mohr, 1980). And as we shall see later in this chapter, some sheltered workshops have disincentives for either providing good training or moving workers to less supervised work settings. Since adequate and appropriate education and training are necessary for many jobs, improvements need to be made in many of the training programs for the more severely retarded(President's Committee on Mental Retardation, 1983).

7.   National and local economic employment rates may be a barrier to employment of the retarded.

When the national unemployment rate goes into double digits, the employment of the retarded often nosedives. Even in good economic times there is often a shortage of jobs for all those who want them. But when unemployment reaches 8% or 10% or even higher, the number of available unskilled jobs is greatly reduced and employers usually have less difficulty in recruiting able-bodied persons to fill them.

8.   There are financial disincentives for some mentally retarded workers to work since they could lose guaranteed income supports and health benefits if they earn too much money.

There are over 150 federal programs which provide services or cash income to handicapped persons. These 150 programs fall into 5 general types of programs: (1)income-maintenance--cash support given to the retarded mainly through SSI(Supplemental Security Income), SSDI(Social Security Disability Insurance), the Social Security Childhood Beneficiary Program, and the Food Stamp Program; (2)health care services provided mainly through Medicaid and Medicare; (3)residential care funded mainly through Medicaid; (4)social services provided mainly by Title XX funds, mental health and developmental disabilities legislation; and (5)rehabilitation and reemployment services. As indicated in the previous chapter, many of these 5 types of services or cash supports are matched or supplemented in some way by the states(Conley, 1985).

Where do the financial disincentives arise that may make it more financially beneficial for the retarded to not work than to work? When the mentally retarded are diagnosed as disabled, they are then eligible for (1)cash support mainly through SSI and the Food Stamp Program or less likely through one of the other income maintenance programs unless they have been working for some time, and (2)health services either through Medicaid or Medicare. They also may be eligible for residential, social and rehabilitation services at no cost to them. But the federal and state governments do not want to encourage either not working or of people collecting benefits when they could work or when in fact they are working and earning income. Thus, the government has (1)standards to determine when people are disabled so they won't abuse the system, and (2)income-from-work-standards so that when people make a certain amount of income from work they are cut off from receiving cash benefits or have those benefits reduced at a rate of $1 for every $2 they earn after an $85 incentive is given to work. And once they get to a certain earnings level they also lose medical services under Medicaid or Medicare. But the critical problem is that the amount of income they make from working may not match the dollar value of SSI and Medicaid combined, or SSDI and Medicare combined if one includes the cost of going to work and taxes levied on income. Consequently, they may be better off financially if they earn a little money in a sheltered workshop and still get their SSI benefits and all their health care free than if they earn enough money not to be eligible for either SSI and Medicaid services. Furthermore, no exact dollar amount can be put on the value of Medicaid(or Medicare) since no one knows in advance the dollar value of the medical service he will use in the next year(Conley, 1985).

WEEKDAY ACTIVITY AND WORK PATTERNS AMONG THE MORE SEVERELY RETARDED

How many of those who are moderately to profoundly retarded work? We do not know, but the evidence we have suggests that very few work in relatively competitive work environments. It is probably fair to say that none of the profoundly retarded work. Dittmar, Smith, Bell, Jones and Manzanares(1983) did a survey of 785 residents in seven western states who lived in board and care homes. They found that only 5.1% were employed in competitive jobs, 25% were not working at all, and most of the remaining persons were employed in sheltered workshops or involved in day treatment programs. Table 9.4 gives

315

Table 9.4

Percentage of Estimated Number of Clients Involved in Education, Job or Work Training, or Work in 190 Private Pennsylvania Facilities in 1982-83 by Type of Provider

	Type of Provider			
Type of Program or Work*	CLA (127)	PLF (34)	ICF/MR (29)	Total (190)
Public Education	14	39	26	25
Other Education	4	12	15	9
Work Training	24	29	15	20
Job Training	8	5	5	6
Workshop	38	12	12	24
Competitive Employment	4	1	0	2
Adult Day Care	16	10	28	17
Occupational Therapy	5	21	52	20
Total Estimated Clients	4,216	2,859	1,995	9,070
Percent ages 21-64	83	45	68	68

*Clients may be involved in more than one service or job at a time, thus percentages cannot be added.
Source: Adapted from Poister Associates, 1984.

some evidence that residents in three types of group facilities that house primarily those at moderate retardation levels or below are rarely employed in competitive employment. If we analyze Tables 9.3 and 9.4 together, we find that CLAs(Community Living Arrangements, or group homes), where 83% of the residents are between the ages of 21 and 64, have 4% of their residents engaged in competitive employment, 38% working in sheltered workshops, 32% either in work training or job training(which may occur at sheltered workshops), 16% in adult day care programs, and 18% in some form of education program. However, in Private Licensed Facilities and ICFs/MR which serve proportionally more younger residents and more severely retarded persons, we find only 12% going to sheltered workshops and less than 1% engaged in competitive employment. The picture which emerges from this data is that only a small percentage of the more severely retarded are working above a sheltered workshop level, that only about a fourth are involved in workshop activities with the remaining percentage(about 74%) either not working in any setting or involved in some type of weekday activity that involves education or day treatment programs.

A review of the work patterns of the mentally retarded once again presents evidence that the mentally retarded are a very heterogeneous group. Around 85% of the mildly mentally retarded work. They work in a variety of jobs, mostly unskilled, and earn less than do most people. But as we move from moderate retardation to profound retardation, we find only a minority employed and primarily in sheltered employment settings. The weekday activities of the more severely retarded tend to be located at day treatment programs or some type of training programs or at their place of residence.

SHELTERED WORKSHOPS: ASSETS AND PROBLEMS

The Rehabilitation Act of 1973(P.L. 93-122) increased the level of funding for rehabilitation in comparison to earlier rehabilitation legislation. It kept the federal government's share of rehabilitation programs at 80% while the states were to match the costs of operating such programs with 20%. This legislation and subsequent amendments emphasized: (1)serving the severely disabled, (2)promoting consumer involvement, (3)program evaluation, (4)research, and (5)advancing the civil rights of the disabled(Rubin & Roessler, 1983). Prior to the passage of this act, vocational services had been principally directed to the mildly disabled and primarily those with physical disabilities. This selective emphasis involved a process called "creaming"--that is, rehabilitating those with the least severe disabilities so that the vocational program could show a high success rate of placement. But the 1973 act reversed this emphasis by saying that vocational rehabilitation should give priority attention to the more severely disabled who, it had been found in research, could learn vocational skills and be placed in positions of gainful employment(Laski, 1980).

Sheltered workshops are funded by federal and state funds as well as by income from subcontracted work or products they make for sale. Sheltered workshops grew rapidly during the 1970s when the number of clients grew fourfold in them between 1971 and 1979 when 105,000 placements were reached(Vitello & Soskin, 1985). Sheltered workshops provide a number of benefits to their clients and to society. (1)For one thing, they provide assessment and training to thousands of new people annually as well as to many who remain in the system. (2)They provide meaningful training and work to thousands of disabled persons who otherwise would not have their time occupied in productive or meaningful ways. Some clients "graduate" from workshops to more independent and higher paying forms of work. (3)They yield some income to many of the clients in them from the work they do. This allows these clients to improve their standard of living and gain satisfaction from the products or services they have produced. (4)The income they generate in the workshop and the incomes to those who move out of the workshop to higher levels of work, helps to reduce the total cost of welfare outlay to disabled persons. Thus, sheltered workshops provide important benefits to their clients and the larger society.

At the same time, workshops have been criticized on many grounds as regards how they go about achieving their complex goals. Pomerantz and Marholin(1980) cite the following interrelated problems they see in how workshops operate:

318

(1)Sheltered workshops usually offer only perma-nent employment to the clients who are there. Only about 10 to 13% of the persons trained there ever move up the employment ladder. This is partly due to a lack of staff people to locate higher rung jobs and place clients in them. It is also due to a lack of training programs in such work-shops for higher level employment and assumptions that the dependent characteristics of these clients make training most difficult and eventual job placement unlikely.

(2)Many workshops do not use available instruc-tional technology to prepare moderately and severely retarded persons for outside employment. This is because they are primarily production centers with staff who are uninformed about new training technologies and who do not have adequate time to investigate, develop and promote placement in higher level industry jobs.

(3)Much of the work done in workshops is highly supervised manual work that is neither habilitative nor like normal types of work found higher up the job placement ladder. Thus, work experience in such workshops often does not prepare many people working there for more competitive employment for it is dissimilar from the work they would do in the outside world.

(4)The subcontract work that many workshops rely on is often scarce and episodic in nature. Many workshops have extensive downtime which may be dealt with by shortened workdays, keeping clients busy with makework, or not keeping them busy at all. Such activities do not develop good work habits or production-oriented attitudes.

(5)The structure and operating procedures in some sheltered workshops often work at cross purposes. Pro-duction staff are more oriented to meeting contractual deadlines. They consider the training, evaluation, and habilitation tasks of higher paid professionals in the work-shop as working at cross purposes with production goals. Production staff, feeling underpaid and unappreciated, have higher turnover rates and this tends to undermine the development of sound training programs with continuity over time.

(6)Sheltered workshops are usually underfunded which means they are often working with antiquated equipment or none at all in order to spread the limited work around. But, by not using state-of-the-art and/or automated

319

equipment where it would be appropriate, they are developing skills irrelevant to transition to non-sheltered work settings that are using modern equipment.

(7)Many workshops do not specialize. They work on a variety of jobs about which production personnel have little expertise. Consequently, they do not follow sound business practices and need to be heavily subsidized because of deficiencies in equipment, bidding practices, training programs and a lack of specialization.

(8)One of the characteristics of sheltered employment is to segregate together persons with a variety of different and sometimes multiple handicaps. One of the problems inherent in this is that such workers rarely see a normal person in production except for a supervisor who may spend a small time each day with them. Consequently, they have no or few models of production-oriented workers to follow. This is also sometimes true of segregated prevocational or vocational programs in educational settings. Thus, mainstreaming in vocational training and work is behind the mainstreaming accomplishments in some areas for the retarded.

(9)Sheltered workshops are funded from multiple sources. This complicates their evaluation, control and reform because different funding agencies or subcontractors have different expectations of what they ought to be doing. Until national standards are developed for sheltered employment and workshop goals more clearly specified and prioritized, differential funding cannot be used to reward and further encourage the development of programs that are successful at training and then moving workers to less sheltered forms of employment. Most workshops are reimbursed on a per-client day basis. They receive more money for a larger client load rather than being rewarded for moving workers into more competitive work which requires less public subsidy. While normalization and cost benefit values would emphasize exterior placement of more severely handicapped trainees, current funding, based on client load, reverses such incentives.

(10)The same type of economic incentives also undermine placement of the best workers in higher level placements outside workshops. Insofar as the best workers are those who are the most productive in the workshop, and training their replacements takes time, floor production

320

supervisors are reluctant to see their best workers placed outside the workshop for this inhibits higher production.

(11)The economic contingencies operating on client-workers in sheltered workshops also tend to undermine both productivity and movement out of workshops to better paying jobs. Most workers in workshops are subsidized for their living expenses under the Supplemental Security Income program. The first $85 in earnings from work they get to keep. Over that ceiling of $85, their benefits are reduced $1.00 for every $2.00 they earn(in a sense this is a 50% tax rate). Furthermore, if they reach a certain income level, their right to Medicaid benefits and SSI payments are eliminated. This means the loss of funds they would often need to make the transition to work. This potential loss of important economic benefits presents a considerable deterrent to clients, parents, and program administrators who are aware that once these benefits are lost they are not easy to regain and who are aware too that secure and steady work on the "outside" is highly uncertain even in good economic times.

To alter the disincentives not to work and to alter funding formulas that support sheltered workshop operations is not an easy task. However, both policy alterations may be necessary to improve the performance of workshops.

SUMMARY

Historically, many of our efforts for the mentally retarded have been to help them during the childhood years. But retarded persons grow up. If they are to develop more normal lives as adults, they need to be engaged in daytime activities that are as productive as their potential allows. The barriers to integrating the retarded into significant work roles are many and formidable, particularly for those below the level of mild retardation. While the level of unemployment(no gainful work activity that allows economic independence) is about 15% for the mildly retarded, it may be around 90% or probably higher for those who are moderately and severely retarded. The barriers to employment include: deficiencies in the intellectual, physical and social skills of the retarded for many types of work; relatively high levels of unemployment for many unskilled workers; the negative attitudes of many employers, coworkers, parents, trainers and the disabled themselves about their employability; the difficulties associated with training and placing more severely retarded workers in jobs which match their skill levels; and, the existence of a number of myths which negatively stereotype the risks associated with employing the mentally disabled. Consequently, more severely retarded workers spend much of their weekday time in training, education and day treatment programs, some of which are poorly suited to their vocational needs, or in sheltered workshops where incentives often exist to keep them there rather than moving them out into more normalizing work environments. Alterations in various social policies and stereotypes affecting the employment of the mentally retarded would allow more of them to be productive workers in more integrated work environments.

Bibliography

Abuelo, D.N. (1983). Genetic Disorders. In J. Matson & J. Mulick(Eds.). *Handbook of Mental Retardation.* New York: Pergammon Press, 105-120.

Ainsworth, M.D. & B.A. Wittig. (1969). Attachment and Exploratory Behavior of One-Year Olds in a Strange Situation. In B.M. Foss(Ed). *Determinants of Infant Behavior.* Vol. 4. New York: Wiley.

Amary, I.B. (1980). *The Rights of the Mentally Retarded-Developmentally Disabled to Treatment and Education.* Springfield: Charles C. Thomas.

American Heritage Dictionary of the English Language. (1976). Boston: Houghton Mifflin.

American Psychiatric Association. (1980). *Diagnostic and Statistical Manual of Mental Disorders.* (3rd Ed.). Washington: American Psychiatric Association.

Bank-Mikkelsen, N.E. (1980). Denmark. In R. Flynn & K. Nitsch(Eds). *Normalization, Social Integration and Community Services.* Baltimore: University Park Press, 51-70.

Baroff, G.S. (1986). *Mental Retardation: Nature, Cause and Management.* Washington: Hemisphere Publishing Co.

Bass, M.S. (1973). Marriage and Parenthood. In M.S. Bass(Ed.). *Sexual Rights and Responsibilities of the Mentally Retarded.* Santa Barbara: Channel Lithographs.

Baumeister, A.A. & J.R. Muma. (1975). On Defining Mental Retardation. *Journal of Special Education,* 9, 293-306.

Begab, M.J. (1981). Issues in the Prevention of Psychosocial Retardation. In M.J. Begab, H.C. Haywood & H.L. Garber(Eds.). *Psychosocial Influences in Retarded Performance.*(Vol. 1). Baltimore: University Park Press, 3-27.

Bell, N.J., C. Schoenrock, & G. Bensberg. (1981). Change Over Time in the Community: Findings of a Longitudinal Study. In R. Bruininks, E. Meyers, B. Sigford & K.C. Lakin(Eds.). *Deinstitutionalization and Community Adjustment of Mentally Retarded People*. Washington: American Association of Mental Deficiency, 195-216.

Bellamy, G.T., M.R. Sheehan, R.H. Horner, & S.M. Bales. (1980). Community Programs for Severely Handicapped Adults: An Analysis. *Journal of the Association for the Severely Handicapped*, 5(4), 307-324.

Bercovici, S.M. (1983). *Barriers to Normalization: The Restrictive Management of Retarded Persons*. Baltimore: University Park Press.

Berg, J.M. (1965). Aetiological Aspects of Mental Subnormality: Pathological Factors. In A.M. Clarke & A.D.B. Clarke(Eds.). *Mental Deficiency*(Rev. Ed). New York: Free Press, 138-165.

Berkson, G. (1983). Developmental Teaching Enhancement of Intelligence. In F.J. Menolascino, R. Neman & J.A. Stark(Eds.). *Curative Aspects of Mental Retardation*. Baltimore: Paul H. Brookes.

Berlin, C.M. (1978). Biology and Retardation. In J.T. Neisworth & R.M. Smith(Eds.). *Retardation: Issues and Intervention*. New York: McGraw-Hill, 117-137.

Bijou, S.W. (1981). The Prevention of Retarded Development in Disadvantaged Children. In B.J. Begab, H.C. Haywood & H.L. Garber(Eds.). *Psychosocial Influences in Retarded Performance*. Vol. 1. Baltimore: University Park Press, 29-46.

Bijou, S.W. (1983). The Prevention of Mild and Moderate Retarded Development. In F.J. Menolascino, R. Neman & J.A. Stark(Eds.). *Curative Aspects of Mental Retardation*. Baltimore: Paul Brookes, 223-241.

Binet, A. & T. Simon. (1907). *Mentally Defective Children*. London: E. Arnold.

Birenbaum, A. & H.J. Cohen. (1985). *Community Services for the Mentally Retarded*. Totawa: Roman & Allanheld.

Bostwick, D.H. & G. Foss. (1981). Obtaining Consumer Input: Two Strategies for Identifying and Ranking the Problems of Mentally Retarded Young Adults. *Education and Training of the Mentally Retarded,* 16, 207-12.

Bouchard, T.J. & N.L. Segal. (1985). Environment and IQ. In B.J. Wolman(Ed.). *Handbook of Intelligence.* New York: Wiley, 391-464.

Braddock, D. (1986a). From Roosevelt to Reagan: Federal Spending for Mental Retardation and Developmental Disabilities. *American Journal of Mental Deficiency,* 90, 5, 479-489.

Braddock, D. (1986b). *Deinstitutionalization in the Eighties: Trends in Georgia, the South and the United States.* Chicago: University of Illinois: Institute for the Study of Developmental Disabilities; Public Policy Monograph #25.

Braddock, D. (1986c). *Financing Mental Retardation Programs in the United States: A Review of Recent Trends.* Chicago: University of Illinois: Institute for the Study of Developmental Disabilities; Public Policy Monograph #27.

Braddock, D. (1987). *Federal Policy Toward Mental Retardation and Developmental Disabilities.* Baltimore: Paul H. Brookes.

Brakel, S.J. (1985). Family Laws. In S. Brakel, J. Parry & B.A. Weiner(Eds.). *The Mentally Disabled and the Law*(3rd ed.). Chicago: American Bar Foundation, 507-58.

Breen, P. & G. Richman. (1979). Evolution of the Developmental Disabilities Concept. In R. Wiegerink & J.W. Petosi(Eds.). *Developmental Disabilities: The DD Movement.* Baltimore: Paul H. Brookes, 3-6.

Breen, P. & G. Richman. (1979b). The Developmental Disabilities Council and Its Membership. In R. Wiegerink and J.S. Petosi(Eds.). *Developmental Disabilities: The DD Movement.* Baltimore: Paul H. Brookes, 27-33.

Briar, S. (1968). The Social Worker's Responsibility for the Civil Rights of Clients. *New Perspectives,* 1, Spring, 90.

Brolin, D., R. Durand, K. Kramer, & P. Muller. (1975). Post-School Adjustment of Educable Retarded Students. *Education and Training of the Mentally Retarded,* 10, 144-49.

Bronfenbrenner, U. (1972). The Roots of Alienation. In U. Bronfenbrenner(Ed.). *Influences on Human Development*. Hinsdale: Dryden.

Bruininks, R.H., M.L. Thurlow, S.K. Thurman, & J.S. Fiorello. Deinstitutionalization and Community Services. In J. Worlis(Ed.). *Mental Retardation and Developmental Disabilities*, Vol. XI. New York: Brunner & Mazel, 55-101.

Budoff, M. & J. Gottlieb. (1976). Special Class Students Mainstreamed: A Study of Aptitude(learning potential) X Treatment Interaction. *American Journal of Mental Deficiency*, 81, 1-11.

Burkart, J., R.A. Fox, & A. Rotatori. (1985). Obesity of Mentally Retarded Individuals: Prevalence, Characteristics and Intervention. *American Journal of Mental Deficiency*, 90, 303-312.

Carr, J. (1984). Family Processes and Parental Involvement. In J. Dobbing(Ed). *Scientific Studies in Mental Retardation*. London: MacMillan Press Ltd., 443-455.

Carroll, A.W. (1967). The Effects of Segregated and Partially Integrated School Programs on Self-Concept and Academic Achievement of Educable Mentally Retarded. *Exceptional Children,* 34, 93-99.

Cartwright, G.P. & C.C. Cartwright. (1978). Definitions and Classification Approaches. In J.T. Neisworth and R.M. Smith(Eds.). *Retardation: Issues, Assessment and Intervention*. New York: McGraw-Hill.

Cattell, R.B. (1971). *Abilities: Their Structure, Growth and Action*. Boston: Houghton Mifflin.

Caviness, V.S. Jr. & R.S. Williams. (1983). Normal and Pathological Development of the Cerebral Cortex. In F.J. Menolascino et al(Eds.). *Curative Aspects of Mental Retardation*. Baltimore: Paul H. Brookes, 43-45.

Clarke, D. (1982). *Mentally Handicapped People*. London: Bailliere Tindall.

Cockerham, W.C. (1981). *Sociology of Mental Disorders*. Englewood Cliffs: Prentice Hall.

Committee on Classification of Feeble-Minded. (1910). *Journal of Psycho-Asthenics*, 28, 61-67.

Community Residences Information Services Program. (1986). *There Goes the Neighborhood . . .* Community Residences Information Services Program. (Mimeo).

Conley, R. (1973). *The Economics of Mental Retardation.* Baltimore: Johns Hopkins Univ. Press.

Conley, R.W. (1985). Impact of Federal Programs on Employment of Mentally Retarded Persons. In K.C. Lakin & R.H. Bruininks(Eds.). *Strategies for Achieving Community Integration of Developmentally Disabled Citizens.* Baltimore: Paul H. Brookes, 193-218.

Conroy, J.W. & K.E. Derr. (1971). *Survey and Analysis of the Habilitation and Rehabilitation Status of the Mentally Retarded and Associated Handicapping Conditions.* Washington: Department of Health, Education and Welfare.

Coon, D. (1985). *Essentials of Psychology*(3rd Ed.). St. Paul: West Publishing Co.

Copeland, W.C. & I.A. Iversen. (1985). Developing Financial Incentives for Placement in the Least Restrictive Alternative. In K.C. Lakin & R.H. Bruininks(Eds.). *Strategies for Achieving Community Integration of Developmentally Disabled Citizens.* Baltimore: Paul H. Brookes, 291-312.

Council for Exceptional Children. (1975). What is Mainstreaming? *Exceptional Children,* 42, 174.

Cronbach, L.J. (1984). *Essentials of Psychological Testing*(4th Ed.). New York: Harper and Row.

Davidson, B. & D.A. Dosser Jr. (1983). A Support System for Families with Developmentally Disabled Infants. In L. Wikler & M. Keenan(Eds.). *Developmental Disabilities.* Washington: National Association of Social Workers and American Association of Mental Deficiency, 115-120.

Dingman, H.F. & G. Tarjan. (1960). Mental Retardation and the Normal Distribution Curve. *American Journal of Mental Deficiency,* 64, 991-994.

Dittmar, N.D., G.P. Smith, J.C. Bell, C.B.C. Jones, & D.L. Manzanares. (1982). *Board and Care for Elderly and Mentally Disabled Population, Vol. I: A Survey of Seven States.* Denver: University of Denver Research Institute.

Dudley, J.R. (1983). *Living with Stigma.* Springfield: Charles C. Thomas.

Edgar, E.B. (1978). Learning Disabilities. In R.M. Goldenson(Ed.). *Disability and Rehabilitation Handbook*. New York: McGraw-Hill, 433-442.

Ellis, N.R., D. Balla, O. Estes, J. Hollis, R. Isaacson, R. Orlando, B.E. Palls, S.A. Warren, & P.S. Segal. (1978). *Wayatt v. Hardin, C.A. 3195-N*. U.S. District Court, Middle District of Alabama, Oct. 18, 1978(Memorandum of Balla, et al).

Erikson, K.T. (1966). *Wayward Puritans*. New York: John Wiley.

Evans, B. & B. Waites. (1981). *IQ and Mental Testing*. London: MacMillian Ltd.

Federico, R.C. (1980). *The Social Welfare Institution*(3rd Ed.). Lexington: D.C. Heath & Co.

Fernald, W. (1903). Mentally Defective Children in the Public Schools. *Journal of Psycho-Asthenics, 8*, 25-35.

Fernald, W. (1912). The Burden of Feeble-Mindedness. *Journal of Psycho-Asthenics*, 17, 87-111.

Flynn, R.J. & K.E. Nitsch. (1980). Normalization. In R.J. Flynn & K.E. Nitsch(Eds.). *Normalization, Social Integration and Community Services*. Baltimore: University Park Press.

Fortier, L.W. & R.L. Wanless. (1984). Family Crisis Following the Diagnosis of a Handicapped Child. *Family Relations,* 33, 13-24.

Fredericks, H.D. (1985). Research Needs: Educational, Community Based, Social and Policy. In M.P. Brady and P.L. Genter(Eds.). *Integrating Moderately and Severely Handicapped Learners*. Springfield: Charles C. Thomas, 267-281.

Galloway, C. & P. Chandler. (1980). The Marriage of Special and Generic Early Education Services. In R.J. Flynn and K.E. Nitsch(Eds.). *Normalization, Social Integration and Community Services*. Baltimore: University Park Press, 187-213.

Gilhool, T. (1980). Some Necessary Conditions for a Community Services System. In P. Roos, B.M. McCann & M.R. Addison(Eds.). *Shaping the Future*. Baltimore: University Park Press, 1-11.

Goldstein, H. (1964). Social and Occupational Adjustment. In H.A. Stevens & R. Heber(Eds.). *Mental Retardation: A Review of Research*. Chicago: University of Chicago Press.

Gollay, E., R. Freedman, M. Wyngaarden, & N.R. Kurtz. (1978). *Coming Back: The Experiences of Deinstitutionalized Mentally Retarded People.* Cambridge, Ma.: Abt Books.

Goodman, L. (1970). Continuing Treatment of Parents with Congenitally Defective Infants. In M. Schreiber(Ed.). *Social Work and Mental Retardation.* New York: The John Day Co., 370-385.

Gottlieb, J. (1981). Mainstreaming: Fulfilling the Promise? *American Journal of Mental Deficiency,* 86, 115-126.

Graham, J.R. & R.S. Lilly. (1984). *Psychological Testing.* Englewood Cliffs: Prentice Hall.

Gresham, F.M. (1982). Misguided Mainstreaming: The Case for Social Skills Training with Handicapped Children. *Exceptional Children,* 48, 422-433.

Grossman, H.J. (1983). *Classification in Mental Retardation.* Washington: American Association of Mental Deficiency.

Gruber, K.(Ed.). (1987). *Encyclopedia of Associations*(21st Ed.). Detroit: Gale Research Co.

Grunewald, K. (1972). The Guiding Environment: The Dynamic of Residential Living. In D.M. Boswell and J.N. Wingrove(Eds.). *The Handicapped Person in the Community.* London: Tavistock.

Grunewald, K. (1974). The Practical Experiences of Settling the Mentally Handicapped in the Community-- the Swedish Model. In H.C. Gunzburg(Ed.). *Experiments in the Rehabilitation of the Mentally Handicapped.* London: Butterworths.

Guilford, J.P. (1967). *The Nature of Human Intelligence.* New York: McGraw-Hill.

Guillemin, J. & L. Holmstrom. (1986). *Mixed Blessings: Intensive Care for Newborns.* New York: Oxford University Press.

Guskin, S.L. & H.H. Spicker. (1968). Educational Research in Mental Retardation. In N.R. Ellis(Ed.). *Handbook of Mental Deficiency: Psychological Theory and Practice*(Vol. 3). New York: Academic Press.

Halpern, A.S., D.W. Close, & D.J. Nelson. (1986). *On My Own: The Impact of Semi-Independent Living Programs for Adults with Mental Retardation.* Baltimore: Paul H. Brooks.

Hauber, F.A., R.H. Bruininks, B.K. Hill, H.C. Lakin, R.C. Scheerenberger, & C.C. White. (1984). National Census of Residential Facilities: A 1982 Profile of Facilities and Residents. *American Journal of Mental Deficiency,* 89, 3, 236-245.

Hayden, A.H. & N.G. Haring. (1976). The Acceleration and Maintenance of Developmental Gains in Down's School-Age Children. Paper presented at the Fourth International Congress of the International Association for the Study of Mental Deficiency.

Haywood, H.C. & T.H. Wachs. (1981). Intelligence, Cognition, and Individual Differences. In H. Haywood & M. Begab(Eds.). *Psychosocial Influences in Retarded Performance*(Vol. 1). Baltimore: University Park Press, 95-126.

Hebb, D.O. (1949). *The Organization of Behavior.* New York: Wiley.

Heber, R. & H. Garber. (1975). The Milwaukee Project: A Study of the Use of Family Intervention to Prevent Cultural-Familial Mental Retardation. In B.Z. Friedland, G.M. Sterrit & G.E. Kirk(Eds.). *Exceptional Infant*(Vol. 3): *Assessment and Intervention.* New York: Brunner/Mazel.

Helsel, E.D. (1971). Residential Service. In J. Wortis(Ed.). *Mental Retardation and Developmental Disabilities*(Vol. III). New York: Brunner/Mazel.

Horejsi, C.R. (1983). Social and Psychological Factors in Family Care. In R. Perlman(Ed.). *Family Home Care.* New York: Haworth Press, 56-71.

Horner, R., S. Stoner, & D. Ferguson. (1988). *An Activity-Based Analysis of Deinstitutionalization: The Effects of Community Re-Entry in the Lives of Residents Leaving Oregon's Fairview Training Center.* Salem, Or.: Developmental Disabilities Program Office, Mental Health Division, Department of Human Resources.

Howse, J.L. (1980). Piecing Together Existing Financial Resources. In P. Roos, B.M. McCann and M.R. Addison(Eds.). *Shaping the Future.* Baltimore: University Park Press.

Hutt, M. & R. Gibby. (1976). *The Mentally Retarded Child: Development, Education and Treatment*(3rd Ed.). Boston: Allyn & Bacon.

Jensen, A.R. (1981). Raising the IQ: The Ramey and Haskins Study. *Intelligence*, 5, 29-40.

Kanner, L. (1953). Parent's Feelings about Retarded Children. *American Journal of Mental Deficiency, 37*, 375-83.

Kanner, L. (1964). *A History of the Care and Study of the Mentally Retarded.* Springfield: Charles C. Thomas.

Kaplan, R.M. & D.P. Saccuzzo. (1982). *Psychological Testing: Principles, Applications and Issues.* Monterey: Brooks/Cole.

Kazdin, J. (1978). Assessment of Retardation. In J.T. Neisworth & R. Smith(Eds.). *Retardation: Issues, Assessment and Intervention.* New York: McGraw-Hill, 269-95.

Keenan, M.F. & D.R. Parker. (1983). Deinstitutionalization: A Policy Analysis. In L. Wikler & M.F. Keenan(Eds.). *Developmental Disabilities: No Longer a Private Tragedy.* Silver Spring: National Association of Social Workers, 224-233.

Kennedy, W.A. (1973). *Intelligence and Economics: A Confounded Relationship.* Morristown, N.J.: General Learning Press.

Kindred, M. (1984). The Legal Rights of Mentally Retarded Persons in Twentieth Century America. In L. Kopelman & J.C. Moskop(Eds.). *Ethics and Mental Retardation.* Boston: D. Reidel Publishing Co., 185-208.

Kirk, S.A. & J.J. Gallagher. (198379). *Educating Exceptional Children*(4th Ed.). New York: Houghton Mifflin.

Knox, T. (1979). Vermont's Project Awareness. In R. Wiegerink & J.W. Petosi(Eds.). *Developmental Disabilities: The DD Movement.* Baltimore: Paul H. Brookes, 97-103.

Kokaska, C.J. (1968). The Occupational Status of the Educable Mentally Retarded: A Review of Follow-up Studies. *Journal of Special Education, 2*, 369-377.

Kolstoe, O.P. (1961). An Examination of Some Characteristics which Discriminate between Employed and

Not Employed Mentally Retarded Adults. *American Journal of Mental Deficiency*, 66, 472-82.

Kolstoe, O.P. (1976). *Teaching Educable Mentally Retarded Children*(2nd Ed.). New York: Hold, Rinehart & Winston.

Kugel, R. (1976). Professionals and Parents. In R. Kugel & A. Shearer(Eds.). *Changing Patterns in Residential Services for the Mentally Retarded*. Washington: President's Committee on Mental Retardation, 341-43.

Landers, A. (1970). Publishers Hall Syndication in M. Schreiber(Ed.). *Social Work and Mental Retardation*. New York: John Day Co., 38-39.

Lakin, K.C. & R. Bruininks. Social Integration of Developmentally Disabled Persons. In K.C. Lakin & R. Bruininks(Eds.). *Strategies for Achieving Community Integration of Developmentally Disabled Citizens*. Baltimore: Paul H. Brookes.

Laski, F. (1980). The Right to Live in the Community: The Legal Foundation. In P. Roos, B.M. McCann & M.R. Addison(Eds.). *Shaping the Future*. Baltimore: University Park Press, 151-162.

Lei, T., L. Nihira, N. Sheehy, & C.E. Meyers. (1981). A Study of Small Family Care for Mentally Retarded People. In R.H. Bruininks, C.E. Meyers, B. Sigford & K.C. Lakin(Eds.). *Deinstitutionalization and Community Adjustment of Mentally Retarded People*. Washington: American Association of Mental Deficiency, 265-281.

Lensink, B.R. (1980). Establishing Programs and Services in an Accountable System. In P. Roos, B.M. McCann and M. Addison(Eds.). *Shaping the Future*. Baltimore: University Park Press, 49-66.

Lerner, J., D. Dawson & L. Horvath. (1980). *Cases in Learning and Behavior Problems*. Boston: Houghton Mifflin.

Lott, I.T. (1983). Perinatal Factors in Mental Retardation. In J.L. Matson and J.A. Mulick(Eds.). *Handbook of Mental Retardation*. New York: Pergammon Press, 97-103.

Mayeda, T. & P. Sutter. (1981). Deinstitutionalization: Phase II. In R.H. Bruininks, C.E. Meyers, B. Sigford & K.C. Lakin(Eds.). *Deinstitutionalization and Community Adjustment of Mentally Retarded*

People. Washington: American Association of Mental Deficiency, 375-81.

Mayer, D.O. (1979). Legal Advocacy for Developmentally Disabled People. In R. Wiegerink and J.W. Petosi(Eds.). *Developmental Disabilities: The DD Movement.* Baltimore: Paul H. Brookes, 67-75.

McHale, S. & R.J. Simeonsson. (1980). Effects of Interaction on Nonhandicapped Children's Attitudes Toward Autistic Children. *American Journal of Mental Deficiency,* 85, 18-24.

Meazzini, P. (1984). Mainstreaming Handicapped Students. In J. Dobbing(Ed.). *Scientific Studies in Mental Retardation.* London: MacMillan, 527-539.

Meir, J.H. (1976). *Developmental and Learning Disabilities.* Baltimore: University Park Press.

Menolascino, F.J. (1983). Bridging the Gap Between Mental Retardation and Mental Illness. In F.J. Menolascino and B.M. McCann(Eds.). *Mental Health and Mental Retardation: Briding the Gap.* Baltimore: University Park Press, 3-64.

Menolascino, F.J. (1983b). Introduction; Conclusion. In F.J. Menolascino, R. Newman & J.A. Stark(Eds.). *Curative Aspects of Mental Retardation.* Baltimore: Paul H. Brookes.

Mercer, J.R. (1973). *Labelling the Mentally Retarded.* Berkeley: University of California Press.

Mercer, J.R. (1976). The Meaning of Mental Retardation. In R. Koch and J. Dobson(Eds.). *The Mentally Retarded Child and His Family*(2nd ed.). New York: Brunner/Mazel.

Mercer, J.R. & J. Lewis. (1978). *SOMPA: Student Assessment Manual.* New York: Psychological Corporation.

Meyers, C.E., D.L. MacMillan & R.K. Yoshida. (1975). Correlation of Success in Transition of MR to Regular Class. (Final Report, Grant No. OEG-0-73-5263) Pomona, Ca.: U.S. Department of Health, Education and Welfare.

Miller, J.O. (1970). Cultural Deprivation and its Modification: 'Effects of Intervention'. In H.C. Haywood(Ed.). *Social-Cultural Aspects of Mental Retardation.* New York: Appleton-Century Crofts.

Milunsky, A. (1983). Genetic Aspects of Mental Retardation: From Prevention to Cure. In F.J. Menolascino, R. Newman & J.A. Stark(Eds.). *Curative Aspects of Mental Retardation.* Baltimore: Paul H. Brookes, 15-26.

Mink, I., C.E. Meyers & K. Nihira. (1984). Taxonomy of Family Life Styles: II. Homes with Slow-Learning Children. *American Journal of Mental Deficiency,* 89, 111-123.

Moroney, R.M. (1979). Allocation of Resources for Family Care. In L. Wikler and M.P. Keenan(Eds.). *Developmental Disabilities.* Washington: National Association of Social Workers & American Association of Mental Deficiency, 208-218.

Moroney, R.M. (1986). *Shared Responsibilities: Families and Social Policy.* New York: Aldine Publishing Co.

National Association for Retarded Citizens. (1976). Information Sheet.

National Association of Superintendents of Public Residential Facilities for the Mentally Retarded. (1974). *Contemporary Issues in Residential Programming.* Washington: President's Committee on Mental Retardation.

Neisworth, J. & R. Smith. (1978). Environment and Retardation. In J. Neisworth & R. Smith(Eds.). *Retardation: Issues, Assessment and Intervention.* New York: McGraw-Hill, 139-166.

Neufeld, G.R. (1979). The Advocacy Role and Functions of Developmental Disabilities Councils. In R. Wiegerink and J.W. Petosi(Eds.). *Developmental Disabilities: The DD Movement.* Baltimore: Paul H. Brookes, 45-60.

Nichols, R.C. (1981). Origins, Nature, and Determinants of Intellectual Development. In M.J. Begab, H.C. Haywood & H.C. Garber(Eds.). *Psychosocial Influences in Retarded Performance*(Vol. 1). Baltimore: University Park Press, 127-154.

Nirje, B. (1980). The Normalization Principle. In R. Flynn & K. Nitsch. *Normalization, Social Integration and Community Services.* Baltimore: University Park Press, 31-50.

Oakland, T. & R. Parmelee. (1985). Mental Measurement of Minority-Group Children. In B. Wolman(Ed.).

Handbook of Intelligence. New York: John Wiley and Sons, 699-736.

Olshansky, S. (1970). Chronic Sorrow: A Response to Having a Mentally Deficient Child. In M. Screiber(Ed.). *Social Work and Mental Retardation.* New York: John Day Co., 228-231.

Pancsofar, E. (1986). *A User's Guide to Community Entry for the Severely Handicapped.* Albany: State University of New York Press.

Parry, J. (1985). Incompetency, Guardianship, and Restoration. In S.J. Brakel, J. Parry & B.A. Weiner(Eds.). *The Mentally Disabled and the Law*(3rd Ed.). Chicago: American Bar Foundation, 369-434.

Patterson, G. (1980). Basic Principles and Philosophies for Developing Residential Services in the Community. In P. Roos, B. McCann & M.R. Addison(Eds.). *Shaping the Future.* Baltimore: University Park Press, 137-149.

Perlman, R. (1983). Use of the Tax System in Home Care: A Brief Note. In R. Perlman(Ed.). *Family Home Care.* New York: Haworth Press, 280-83.

Perlman, R. & J.Z. Giele. (1983). An Unstable Triad: Dependents' Demands, Family Resources, Community Supports. In R. Perlman(Ed.). *Family Home Care.* New York: Haworth press, 12-44.

Peterson, R.M. (1980). Neurological Factors in Causation. In R. Koch & J. Dobson(Eds.). *The Mentally Retarded Child and His Family*(2nd Ed.). New York: Brunner/Mazel, 144-154.

Piaget, J. (1966). *Psychology of Intelligence.* Totawa, N.J.: Littlefield, Adams.

Poister Associates, T. (1984). *A Profile of Private Residential Services for Mentally Retarded Persons in the Commonwealth of Pennsylvania.* Harrisburg: Pennsylvania Association of Residences for the Retarded.

Poister Associates, T. (1985). *A Cost-Function Analysis of Private Residential Facilities for Mentally Retarded Persons in the Commonwealth of Pennsylvania.* Harrisburg: Pennsylvania Association of Residences for the Retarded.

Pomerantz, D.J. (1980). Vocational Habilitation: A Time for Change. In R.J. Flynn and K.E. Nitsch(Eds.).

Normalization, Social Integration and Community
Services. Baltimore: University Park Press, 259-282.

President's Committee on Mental Retardation. (1975).
Mental Retardation: The Known and Unknown.
Washington: U.S. Government Printing Office.

President's Committee on Mental Retardation. (1978).
*Mental Retardation: The Leading Edge, Service
Programs that Work.* Washington: U.S.
Government Printing Office.

President's Committee on Mental Retardation. (1980).
Mental Retardation and the Law. Boston: Center
for Law and Health Sciences, Boston University
School of Law.

President's Committee on Mental Retardation. (1980).
*Mental Retardation: Prevention Strategies that
Work.* Washington: U.S. Government Printing
Office.

President's Committee on Mental Retardation. (1983).
*The Mentally Retarded Worker: An Economic Dis
covery.* Washington: Department of Health and
Human Services.

President's Committee on Mental Retardation. (1986). *A
Historical Review: 1966-1985.* Washington:
Department of Health and Human Services.

President's Panel on Mental Retardation. (1962). *A Proposed Program for National Action to Combat
Mental Retardation.* Washington: Superintendent
of Documents.

Proctor, N.K. (1983). New Directions for Work with Parents of Retarded Children. In L. Wikler & M.
Keenan(Eds.). *Developmental Disabilities.* Washington: National Association of Social Workers and
American Association of Mental Deficiency, 121-
126.

Pueschel, S.M. & H.C. Thuline. (1983). Chromosome
Disorders. In J. Matson & J. Mulick(Eds.). *Handbook of Mental Retardation.* New York: Pergammon Press, 121-141.

Ramey, C.T. & N.W. Finkelstein. (1981). Psychosocial
Mental Retardation: A Biological and Social Coa-
lescence. In M.J. Begab, H.C. Haywood & H.L.
Garber(Eds.). *Psychosocial Influences in Retarded*

Performance(Vol. I). Baltimore: University Park Press, 65-92.

Raynes, N., M. Pratt & S. Roses. (1979). *Organizational Structure and the Care of the Mentally Retarded.* New York: Praeger Publishers.

Reger, R. (1973). What is a Resource Room Program? *Journal of Learning Disabilities,* 6, 609-14.

Reynolds, M.C. (1962). A Framework for Considering Some Issues in Special Education. *Exceptional Children,* 28, 367-70.

Risherman, B. & J. Cocozza. (1984). Stress in Families of the Developmentally Disabled: A Literature Review of Factors Affecting the Decision to Seek Out-of-Home Placements. *Family Relations,* 33, 95-103.

Rosen, L. (1955). Selected Aspects in the Development of the Mother's Understanding of Her Mentally Retarded Child. *American Journal of Mental Deficiency,* 59, 522-528.

Ross, R.T., M.J. Begab, E.H. Dondes, J.S. Giampiccolo & C.E. Meyer. (1985). *Lives of the Mentally Retarded: A Forty-Year Follow Up Study.* Stanford: Stanford University Press.

Rothman, D.J. & S. Rothman. (1984). *The Willowbrook Wars.* New York: Harper and Row.

Rubin, S.E. & R.T. Roessler. (1983). *Foundations of the Vocational Rehabilitation Process*(2nd Ed.). Baltimore: University Park Press.

Salvia, J. (1978). Perspectives on the Nature of Mental Retardation. In J. Neisworth & R.M. Smith(Eds.). *Retardation: Issues, Assessment and Intervention.* New York: McGraw-Hill, 25-48.

Scarr-Salapatek, S. (1975). Genetics and the Development of Intelligence. In F.D. Horowitz(Ed.). *Review of Child Development Research*(Vol. 4). Chicago: University of Chicago Press.

Schaefer, E.W. (1981). Development of Adaptive Behavior: Conceptual Models and Family Correlates. In M.J. Begab, H.C. Haywood & H.L. Garber(Eds.). *Psychosocial Influences in Retarded Performance.* Baltimore: University Park Press, 155-178.

Schalock, R.L. & M.D. Lilley. (1986). Placement from Community-Based Mental Retardation Programs: How Well Do Clients Do after 8 to 10 Years?

337

American Journal of Mental Deficiency, 90, 669-676.

Scheerenberger, R.C. (1983). *A History of Mental Retardation.* Baltimore: Paul H. Brookes.

Scheerenberger, R.C. (1983). *Public Residential Facilities for the Mentally Retarded 1982.* National Association of Superintendents of Public Residential Facilities of the Mentally Retarded.

Schild, S. (1970). Counseling with Parents of Retarded Children Living at Home. In M. Schreiber(Ed.). *Social Work and Mental Retardation.* New York: The John Day Co., 350-363.

Scotch, R.K. (1984). *From Good Will to Civil Rights: Transforming Federal Disability Policy.* Philadelphia: Temple University Press.

Shearer, A. (1976). The News Media. In R. Shearer & A. Shearer(Eds.). *Changing Patterns in Residential Services for the Mentally Retarded*(Rev. Ed.). Washington: President's Committee on Mental Retardation.

Skeels, H.H. (1966). Adult Status of Children with Contrasting Life Experiences. *Monographs of the Society for Research in Child Development,* 31, 3.

Smith, D.W. & A.A. Wilson. (1973). *The Child with Down's Syndrome(Mongolism).* Philadelphia: Saunders.

Stark, J.A. (1983). *The Search for Cures of Mental Retardation.* In F.J. Menolascino, R. Newman & J.A. Stark(Eds.). *Curative Aspects of Mental Retardation.* Baltimore: Paul H. Brookes, 1-8.

Stark, J.A., J.J. McGee & F. J. Menolascino. (1984). *International Handbook of Community Services for the Mentally Retarded.* Hillsdale: Lawerence Erblaum Associates, Publishers.

Sternberg, R.J. (1981). The Nature of Intelligence. *New York University Education Quarterly,* 12, 10-17.

Sternberg, R.J. (1985). Cognitive Approaches to Intelligence. In B.B. Wolman(Ed.). *Handbook of Intelligence.* New York: John Wiley, 59-118.

Stroman, D.F. (1982). *The Awakening Minorities: The Physically Handicapped.* Washington: University Press of America.

Terman, L.M. (1916). *The Measurement of Intelligence.* Boston: Houghton Mifflin.

Thurstone, L.L. & T.G. Thurstone. (1941). *Factorial Studies of Intelligence*. Chicago: University of Chicago Press.

Tizard, J. (1965). Introduction. In A. Clarke & A.D.B. Clarke(Eds.). *Mental Deficiency: The Changing Outlook*. New York: The Free Press.

Tompkins, A.R. (1986). *Report to Congress on Policies for Improving Services for Mentally Retarded and Other Developmentally Disabled Persons Served Under Title XX of the Social Security Act*. Washington: Department of Health and Human Services.

Trevino, F. (1983). Siblings of Handicapped Children: Identifying Those at Risk. In L. Wikler & M. Keenan(Eds.). *Developmental Disabilities*. Washington: National Association of Social Workers & American Association of Mental Deficiency, 133-138.

Turnbull, H.R. & M.J. Wheat. (1983). Legal Responses to Classification. In M. Matson & J.A. Mulick(Eds.). *Handbook of Mental Retardation*. New York: Pergammon Press, 157-169.

Tyor, P.L. & L.V. Bell. (1984). *Caring for the Retarded in America*. Westport: Greenwood Press.

U.S. Department of Education. (1980). *Second Annual Report to Congress on the Implementation of Public Law 94-142: The Education for All Handicapped Children Act*.

Vadasy, P. et al. (1984). Siblings of Handicapped Children: A Developmental Perspective on Family Interactions. *Family Relations*, 33, 155-167.

Vitello, S.J. & R.M. Soskin. (1985). *Mental Retardation: Its Social and Legal Context*. Englewood Cliffs: Prentice-Hall.

Voeltz, L.M. (1980). Special Friends in Hawaii. *Education Unlimited*, 2, 10-11.

Voeltz, L.M. & J. Brennan. (1984). Analysis of Interactions between Nonhandicapped and Severely Handicapped Persons Using Multiple Measures. In J.M. Berg(Ed.). *Perspective and Progress in Mental Retardation*(Vol. 1): *Social, Program and Educational Aspects*. Baltimore: University Park Press.

Ward, R.A. (1984). *The Aging Experience*(2nd Ed.). New York: Harper and Row.

Wechsler, D. (1958). *The Measurement and Appraisal of Adult Intelligence*(4th Ed.). Baltimore: Williams & Wilkins.

Weiner, F. (1973). *Help for the Handicapped Child.* New York: McGraw-Hill.

Westling, D.L. (1986). *Introduction to Mental Retardation.* Englewood Cliffs: Prentice-Hall.

Wiegerink, R. (1979). Preface. In R. Wiegerink & J.W. Petosi(Eds.). *Developmental Disabilities: The DD Movement.* Baltimore: Paul H. Brookes.

Wikler, L. (1983). Chronic Stresses on Families of Mentally Retarded Children. In L. Wikler & M.P. Keenan(Eds.). *Developmental Disabilities.* Washington: National Association of Social Workers and the American Association of Mental Deficiency, 102-110.

Willer, B. & J. Intagliata. (1984). *Promises and Realities for Mentally Retarded Citizens.* Baltimore: University Park Press.

Williams, P. & B. Shoultz. (1982). *We Can Speak for Ourselves.* Bloomington: Indiana University Press.

Wolfensberger, W. (1976). The Origin and Nature of Our Institutional Models. In R. Kugel & A. Shearer(Eds.). *Changing Patterns in Residential Services for the Mentally Retarded*(Rev. Ed.). Washington: President's Committee on Mental Retardation, 35-82.

Wolfensberger, W. (1980). A Brief Overview of the Principle of Normalization. In R. Flynn & K. Nitsch(Eds.). *Normalization, Social Integration, and Community Services.* Baltimore: University Park Press, 7-30.

Zastrow, C. (1981). *The Practice of Social Work.* Homewood: Dorsey Press.

Zastrow, C. (1982). *Introduction to Social Welfare Institutions.* Homewood: Dorsey Press.

Zimmerman, S.L. (1984). The Mental Retardation Family Subsidy Program: Its Effects on Families with a Mentally Handicapped Child. *Family Relations*, 33, 105-118.

Index

AAMD definition of mental retardation, 17-19, 22-26, 34, 41-42, 114, 265

Abuelo, D.N., 58-64, 71, 91

Acceptance response, 141-142

Activist role, 184

Adaptive skills, 7, 246

Adoptive home, 150, 152-153, 216-217, 257

Adult activity centers, 297

Adult day programs, 253, 297-298

Advocacy
  dimensions of, 182, 184
  external, 183, 186
  for the retarded, 121, 126, 163, 179-182, 184
  movement, 121, 126, 163, 179-182, 184, 196-198, 203, 206, 257

Advocate role, 184
  external, 183, 186
  internal, 183, 185

Age appropriate structures, 234

Ainsworth, M.D. & Wittig, B.A., 74

Alpert Syndrome, 60

Amary, I.B., 180

American Psychiatric Association, 18, 24-25, 46, 47, 49, 77-78

Association for Retarded Citizens (ARC), 121, 130, 182, 183, 185-87, 190, 197-199, 203, 264, 299, 314

Autism, 23, 26, 37, 45, 46, 48, 50, 119

Autosomal abnormalities, 57

Bank-Mikkelsen, N.E., 126-127

Baroff, G.S., 9, 14-15, 22, 24, 46, 55-59, 61-63, 67-68, 70-71, 75, 93, 95, 158, 277-279, 281, 288

Basic mental capacities, 9

Environmental model, 80
Environmental toxins, 71, 73
Epilepsy, 26, 37-38, 44-46, 48, 50, 60, 66, 71
Erikson, K.T., 28
Eugenics movement, 110
Evans, B. & Waites, B., 25

Federico, R.C., 183
Feeble-minded, 35-37, 102-103, 108-111, 114
Fernald, W., 108-109
Fluid intelligence, 10
Flynn, R.J. & Nitsch, K.E., 189
Fortier, L.W. & Wanless, R.L., 138
Foster home, 153, 168, 172, 217-218, 228, 230, 249, 257
Functional integration, 129

Galactosemia, 63
Galloway, C. & Chandler, P., 277-278
Genetic abnormalities, 54, 59
Genetic model, 80
Genetic-Environmental interaction model, 80
Genotype, 81, 83, 85
Gilhool, T., 205
Goal of deinstitutionalization, 201-203
Goldstein, H., 303
Gollay, E. et al., 239-242
Goodman, L., 142
Gottlieb, J., 283
Graham, J.R. & Lilly, R.S., 10
Gresham, F.M., 274
Grossman, H. J., 18-23, 25-26, 34, 45-47, 56
Group home, 151, 167-169, 208-210, 213, 216, 220, 228, 230
Group residence, 213-214, 218, 220, 224, 228
Gruber, K., 182-183, 187, 196
Grunewald, K., 165-167
Guilford, J.P., 10
Guillemin, J. & Holmstrom, L., 69
Guskin, S.L. & Spicker, H.H., 264

Halpern, A.S. et al., 247-251
Hauber, F.A. et al., 130, 214, 217, 220, 222, 224, 227-228

Kugel, R., 138

Landers, A., 145-146
Lakin, K.C. & Bruininks, R., 220
Laski, F., 318
Least restrictive environment, 120, 122, 131, 180, 182, 204, 208, 252-253, 258
Legal rights, 127, 179-180, 199, 275
Lei, T. et al., 251
Lensink, B.R., 186
Lerner, J. et al., 270-271, 276
Lesch-Nyhan Syndrome, 64-65
Lott, I.T., 69
Low grade mental defective, 36

Mainstreaming, 118, 120, 126, 164, 169, 172, 182, 202, 260, 263, 265, 273, 280, 283, 285, 290
Maintaining environments, 242
Mayeda, T. & Sutter, P., 251
Mayer, D.O., 189-190
McHale, S. & Simeonsson, R.J., 284
Medicaid, 210-213, 220, 223, 252-255
Medicaid waiver program, 156, 217, 253-255
Medical model, 210, 215
Meir, J.H., 47-48
Menolascino, F.J., 47, 89, 91
Mental age, 13-14, 20-22, 36-37
Mental illness, 2, 46, 50, 119, 123
Mental retardation,
  clinical perspective of, 27-30-31, 33
  definitions of, 17-26
  medical perspective of, 27
  terms for, 35-37
Mental Retardation Facilities and Community Mental Health Centers Construction Act, 124, 210, 263
Mentally deficient, 35-36, 145
Mercer, J.R., 29-34
Mercer, J.R. & Lewis, Jr., 27, 34
Meyers, C.E. et al., 283
Miller, J.O., 75
Milunsky, A., 65-68
Milwaukee Project, 86, 94

Mink, I. et al., 153
Models of family care, 134
Models of perception, 98
Moron, 35, 37, 49, 114
Moroney, R.M., 148, 217
Mortification, 244
Mortification practices, 243
MR/DD costs, 213, 252-253, 255, 269
Myotonic Distrophy, 61

National Association for Retarded Citizens, 121, 133, 204, 207
National Association for Superintendents of Public Residential
        Facilities for the Mentally Retarded, 129
Neisworth, J. & Smith, R., 74-75, 79, 81, 95
Neufeld, G.R., 182-183, 190
Nichols, R.C., 83-85
Nirje, B., 126-129, 206
Normalization, 101, 126-129, 131, 149, 163-164, 166, 168-172, 176,
        181, 198, 202, 207, 213, 232, 242-245, 250
Normalization principle, 127-128, 157, 168, 203, 206, 209, 257
Nuerofibromatosis, 61
Nursing home, 202, 214, 216, 221, 225, 228-229, 257, 311

Oakland, T. & Parmelee, R., 25
Olshansky, S., 142
Organizational integration, 129
Overprotection, 144, 237

Parry, J., 148
Patterson, G., 204, 207-208
Pennsylvania Association for Retarded Citizens, 121, 204, 264
People first, 193-197
People First International, 196
Perinatal hazards, 69
Perlman, R., 217
Perlman, R. & Giele, J.Z., 134
Personal care home, 214, 219, 225, 228, 230, 257
Personal integration, 129
Peterson, R.M., 48
Phenotype, 83
Physical integration, 128

Sternberg, R.J., 8, 11
Stigma, 3, 34, 38, 141, 143, 146, 148-149, 152, 243, 265, 277
Stroman, D.F., 43, 120, 122, 124, 131, 313
Supervised independent living arrangements, 219, 257
Supplemental Security Income (SSI), 152, 211, 252, 254, 315, 322
Supported employment, 301

Tay-Sachs, 63-65
Teratogenic effects, 68
Tertiary prevention, 88
Thurstone, L.L. & Thurstone, T.G., 10
Tizard, J., 36, 230
Tompkins, A.R., 225-226
Trainable Mentally Retarded (TMR), 153, 155, 260, 262-263, 279,
    286-288, 290
Transactional model, 80
Trevino, F., 145-146
Tuberous Sclerosis, 60, 65
Turnbull, H.R. & Wheat, M.J., 25
Turner Syndrome, 58, 119
Tyor, P.L. & Bell, L.V., 35-36, 98, 102, 104-106, 110-113, 116-117,
    120

Vadasy, P. et al., 146
Vitello, S.J. & Soskin, R.M., 25-26, 38, 40-41, 72, 89, 91, 95, 131,
    139, 150, 155-158, 204-205, 208, 216-218, 221, 223, 299, 318
Vocational Rehabilitation Act, 211, 270
Vocational service system, 293-294
Vocational services, 171-172, 174-175, 180, 182, 292
Voeltz, L.M., 284
Voeltz, L.M. & Brennan, J., 284

Ward, R.A., 202
Wechsler, 9, 15
Wechsler intelligence scale, 13-16, 24-25, 32
Westling, D.L., 83-84, 91, 146, 149, 222, 228, 262-263, 274, 284, 298,
    301-302
Wiegerink, R., 122, 131, 189
Wikler, L., 144
Willer, B. & Intagliata, J., 150-151, 187, 218, 220, 251
Williams, P. & Shoultz, B., 191-198

Autobiographical Sketch of the Author

Dr. Duane F. Stroman is a Professor of Sociology at Juniata College, Huntingdon, Pennsylvania. He has taught there since 1963. He teaches courses in both the sociology and social work curriculums including one entitled "Mental and Physical Handicaps."

The author graduated from Ohio Wesleyan University in 1956 with a B.A. in philosophy, from Boston University School of Theology in 1959 with an S.T.B., and from Boston University in 1966 with a Ph.D. in sociology and social ethics. His doctoral dissertation was on the policies of the American Medical Association. He has done postdoctoral work at both Harvard University and The Pennsylvania State University.

In addition to publishing a number of monographs and book reviews, he has published *The Medical Establishment and Social Responsibility*(Kennikat Press, 1976), *The Quick Knife: Unnecessary Surgery U.S.A.*(Kennikat Press, 1979), and *The Awakening Minorities: The Physically Handicapped*(University Press of America, 1982).

Professor Stroman has been active in many community affairs. Currently he is also President of Raystown Development Services Inc., which provides residential services to persons with mental retardation; Raystown Community Resources Inc., which provides job training, placement and employment to persons with developmental disabilities; and Mr. Janitor, which employs persons with handicaps.